If you have managed to read the earlier parts of this series, you will understand my motivation and you will be familiar with conclusions concerning the veracity and relevance of the OT to the issue of whether you believe or follow the teaching of Jesus.

This book tries to identify what men have fabricated concerning Jesus life and Christian beliefs to reveal the true core – which, in my view, has only been undermined by such embellishment.

Hebrews 8:13 states "By calling this Covenant 'new', Jesus has made the first one obsolete; and what is obsolete and aging will soon disappear." The Ten Commandments and the 613 Mitzvot were seemingly abolished; replaced by Galatians 5:6 "The only thing that counts is faith expressing itself through love", and Galatians 5:14 "The entire law is summed up in a single command: 'Love your neighbour as yourself'".

I dedicate this booklet to Peggy Joan, my Mother, whom I dimly remember telling me when I was very young that Jesus uncle, Joseph of Arimathæa, migrated to live in Britain a few years after the crucifixion.

All you need is love,
Love is all you need
(J. Lennon, 1967)

The Truth Will Set You Free
SECOND EDITION

Part Three

Jesus, the Nazarene

Puzzling aspects of the biblical coverage of Jesus and his disciples

GLYN THOMAS

Truth Publications
truthmakesyoufree@icloud.com

Copyright © 2022 by Glyn Thomas

All rights reserved, including the right to reproduce this work in any form whatsoever, without permission in writing from the publisher except for brief passages in reviews or in citations and references.

Printed by Ingram Spark and affiliates – Lightning Source UK Ltd, Milton Keynes, United Kingdom (see inside back for this copy). Second Edition, published July 2022.

Paperback ISBN: 9789887448969
Ebook ISBN: 9789887448976

Typeset, layout and cover design by Greg Thomas
Bullet Design, London, United Kingdom
www.gregthomas.design | www.bulletdesign.com

Contents

1 Introduction
2 Who wrote the Gospels and why?
3 Summary profiles of the canonised Gospels
4 Early life of Jesus – major differences Matthew v Luke
5 Misleading early life statements in Matthew and Luke
6 Theological academic teaching
7 The meaning of Messiah
8 Qumran scrolls reveal contemporary thinking 2000 years ago
9 Jesus 'the Nazarene'
10 Jesus views on Judaism
11 Did Jesus associate with the Zealots?
12 The Church founded by Jesus followers
13 The Sign
14 The Transfiguration
15 The Apostolic Mission to Britain
16 Evidence of the split between Nazarene and Pauline theology
17 Constantine's profound impact on Christianity
18 Concepts of 'God's Son' and 'Only Son'
19 John chapter 8 – Jesus own words debunk claims he is God
20 Comma Johanneum and Matthew 28:19
21 Prophesies in the Old Testament considered fulfilled by Jesus
22 Conclusions on the two questions left from Part One
23 Puzzling aspects of Jesus strategy
24 Conclusions

Appendix: Key family members of the ancient 'gods'
Index
Biblical references
Bibliography
Books in this series

1

Introduction

1.1 A dear friend said to me that religion is what man constructs in order to try to control God. My modest knowledge of two religions, Christianity and Judaism, certainly supports this view.

1.2 I sincerely hope that those who find themselves in possession of this book find it helpful in gaining a fresh and meaningful understanding of Creation and humanity's role therein. My research has led me to dimly perceive a grand unified theory for this paramount knowledge.

1.3 Firstly, by discovering proof that our universe and its physical laws were developed by an intelligence – itself proof of the existence of a Creator, which for want of a better title, is surely an entity worthy of the name God. This is covered by chapters 2 and 3 of Part One – yes, the sections that put off a lot of readers. If you have skipped over these chapters, I really do recommend persevering, maybe seek help from friends – you will be amazed once it becomes clear!!

1.4 Secondly, by studying the texts of the New Testament and, where fragments remain, other gospels that the Roman Church almost succeeded in entirely obliterating, I feel the original content of Jesus message may be revealed. There appears to be a mass of dogma that has been 'constructed by man' (to use the phrase in the opening paragraph) – so what can be peeled away?

1.5 Delightfully, Jesus message is amazingly simple – that we should love God and love one another. Jesus asked us to believe he was carrying out his Father's command and to follow the lifestyle example he set. The command to love one another may be expressed as treating others as one would like to be treated oneself. It is easy to see this as the route to an extremely happy and harmonious life. If you treat everyone well, there are many who will respond in kind. Dogma assumes Jesus refers to God as 'Father' but this assumption warrants close examination. Jesus command to love God logically flows from recognition that God's designs ultimately led to our existence. It is extremely comforting to think our ultimate Creator seeks a relationship with us and we assume this is exemplified by the benevolent father – obedient son relationship Jesus illustrated for us.

1.6 During my study, I have puzzled as to why Jesus did not write his own gospel. The evidence suggests he was certainly literate and very lucid – and why risk leaving such a vital task to others? The gospels even record that Jesus said to his disciples on more than one occasion that they did not understand his message. There are references to Jesus entering into correspondence and we are told he wrote messages in the dust. It seems very odd that if his mission was to give a message to humanity, he did not get around to writing it down. Alternatively, for conspiracy theorists – is it possible that Jesus did write something but the Roman church found it so explosive that it was deemed heretical along with many other texts ruthlessly hunted down and destroyed. After all, in his introduction, Luke refers to numerous eyewitness accounts he had used in drafting his gospel – where are these? Virtually none have survived but many of the "lost" gospels, that we only know of from 3rd party literary references, appear to have been written by original apostles.

1.7 My apologies to traditionalists if any offense is caused by the radical ideas set out herein. I only ask that you ponder for moment the joy felt by Paul when he realized he was set free from the false rigidities of the 613 mitzvot. Such is my joy at discovering the truth and hence the title of this series.

1.8 As examined in this book, there is evidence that Jesus rejected every tenet of Judaism except where it paralleled his two commands. For example, Jesus says there is no food that God commands not be eaten (maybe not even the fruit of a tree that grew near Basra?) and circumcision was not a command of God. In Part One, I set out my conclusions indicating that Yahweh was definitely not God, now in Part Three we shall see evidence

INTRODUCTION

that points to Jesus expressing the same view.

1.9 Man has constructed a sturdy framework of false dogma around Jesus – which surprisingly contradicts numerous direct quotes by Jesus as set out in the few surviving gospels. Jesus never claimed to be God and his original followers never believed he was God, but this came to be man's view a few centuries later. Jesus repeatedly stated he was sent by his father, empowered by his father and was carrying out his father's commands – it seems that man decided that both Jesus and his father are God. For political reasons, man then invented the awkward concept of the Trinity. Given the progressive elevation over time of Jesus mother, Mary, by the Catholic Church – it is possible that the Roman church may eventually move to see the Trinity superseded by a Quaternity or Tetrad.

1.10 Jesus clearly stated more than once that God was Spirit – and yet Man has decided that there is both God and there is a holy Spirit. Man has decided that Jesus was fathered by a spirit based upon two surviving gospels, written by persons who never met Jesus, that also make various other unfounded, unsupportable and contradictory claims.

1.11 Jesus plainly stated that no one has ever seen God and that no one has visited "heaven" except Himself. Despite the obvious meaning when saying this in front of many people, i.e. that Jesus is clearly stating that he himself is not God – man has still persisted in asserting that Jesus is God. Man persists with fabrications such as the Trinity and continues to revere old scriptural texts from Judaism which state many patriarchs saw God and visited heaven. With such blatant contradictions, it is difficult to maintain that both the Old Testament scripts and the quotes attributed to Jesus can be the Word of God?

1.12 I truly hope you are engaged by this little book and I very much welcome your observations – particularly better arguments for and against the numerous conclusions. Please email your thoughts to me at truthmakesyoufree@icloud.com. Also, you may wish to check the website www.truthpublications.co.uk for more about this series and for downloadable maps, charts, a listing of books ruled heretical by Rome and my attempt to draft a radical update of the Nicaean Creed – which the more you study the more deficient it seems.

May the Spirit awaken you.

2

Who wrote the Gospels and why?

2.1 I, like many Christians I know, was originally taught to believe the Gospels were all written by Jesus hand-picked disciples who had travelled with him during his three year ministry. This gave me comfort that these gospels were reliable and provided accurate portrayals of Jesus teaching and life. However, the truth is quite different.

2.2 The only surviving Gospel written even partly by a first-hand disciple is that of John. The synoptic gospels appear to have used a common source document – usually referred to as the Logia or 'Q' (from 'quelle', meaning source) document, whose authorship is unknown. This tradition is attributed to Clement of Alexandria (150-215) in the Catholic Encyclopaedia, with Clement naming Johannis Marcus writing the eponymous gospel in Rome in AD66, describing the author as the colleague of Paul referred to in Acts 12:25 and 15:37. The Gospel of Matthew appears to be a substantially developed and 'enhanced' text which may have originated as a gospel written in Aramaic which was translated and added to during the 2nd, 3rd and 4th centuries. Luke and Mark were written by authors who had never met Jesus and relied upon second hand sources. The impression is allowed that church Councils selecting books to include in Canon chose between titles, in fact the minutes show a selection of versions of each book had to be considered.

2.3 According to Acts 4:13, Peter and John were almost illiterate ("unlearned and ignorant men") whilst other disciples, where identified, are as fishermen and a tax collector. There are hints that others had occupations

PART THREE: JESUS, THE NAZARENE

which also render them unlikely authors – more on them later. However, the gospels attributed to the disciples are written in truly exquisite Greek. The Gospel of Luke in particular is universally praised for the beautiful Greek prose. It seems highly unlikely these books could have been written by Galilean Jews. Some theological academics attribute Matthew and John to the disciples of that name, but Luke is believed to have been a companion of Paul, and, Mark an assistant of Peter. However, dig a little deeper and even this is far from evidence based. It transpires that the only source of the idea that Luke was a companion of Paul rests upon writing by Papias (cAD60 to AD130), a Bishop of Asia Minor (at that time a small province of what is now the western coast of Turkey). However, nothing written by Papias now survives – only quotes from his writing by two other Church fathers – neither of which is very compelling. Eusebius, in AD324 refers to Papias saying Luke was a companion of Paul but Eusebius also makes many statements asserting that Papias was wrong on many other points. At a much earlier date, AD180, Irenaeus quoted Papias as saying that "Matthew had written down the 'sayings of Jesus' in Hebrew" – which, whilst potentially very important, does not really support Matthew the disciple having been the author of the eponymous Gospel in Greek. (See 'Fragments of Papias' in *The Apostolic Fathers* by Justin Martyr and Irenaeus and *Against Heresies* by Irenaeus.)

2.4 Even the Gospel of John includes a statement pointing to another author – in John 21:20 it states that the writer got the story "***from*** the disciple whom Jesus loved".

2.5 The views of the Catholic Church are set out in two documents: Vatican II's *'Dei Verbum'* of 1965 (§19) and the Pontifical Biblical Commission's *'Instruction on the Historical Truth of the Gospels'* issued 1993 (§6-9). These papers state the Gospels contain material that originated in three distinct first-century time periods: the first period dating from Jesus Ministry recording his words and deeds; the second period from the post resurrection period of Apostolic teaching, including <u>beliefs about Jesus that arose after the resurrection</u>, especially that he was 'divine' and the 'Son of God' (giving John 9:22 as an example) [yes, please read that again!!]; and a third period during which the Gospels were actually written, with texts about Jesus that are shaped by the situations, concerns, and insights of the Gospel writers themselves [example: the blind man's parents fear "the Jews" – as if Jews are a separate group, John 9:22]. Thus, the official Catholic view is that the Gospels were gradually assembled, over decades, before achieving their current form between, say, AD70 and AD90. And that beliefs that Jesus was 'divine' and the 'Son of God' only arose after his resurrection. This seems to strongly support the view that Jesus never claimed even to be divine (let alone God himself) nor that he was a descendant of God.

2.6 Clearly, the purpose of the writers of the Gospels (those that have survived and also those that were ruthlessly destroyed) was in their title – to bring the Good News (the definition of the word 'gospel'). When written, there were two key audiences – Jews who needed convincing Jesus was a promised Messiah and Gentiles who needed to be convinced that Jesus mission was to redeem them as well as the Jews. But the expectations and the messages needed to be quite different. The Jews looked specifically for an eligible King Messiah, to restore the throne of David and lead them militarily – it was national salvation and restoration of righteous government – not personal redemption, because as Chosen People they knew they were already saved. The concept of Messiah is not referred to in the Torah but had grown from the utterances of the Prophets. For Jews, such a messiah would be a righteous man but certainly not divine. During the period these Gospels were written, Christians everywhere were aware of bouts of fierce persecution and martyrdom – therefore hope and reassurance was welcome.

2.7 It seems to me that the synoptic gospels probably did evolve over time. Given the sensational impact Jesus teaching had and the large audiences he attracted, it is reasonable to presume that eyewitnesses, including some of the disciples, tried to make a record of what Jesus had said. Therefore, the quote attributed to Papias, of "Matthew had written down the 'sayings of Jesus' in Hebrew" sounds very plausible. Similarly, the existence of the 'Logia' or 'Q', the presumed source document used by all of the synoptic authors is the most credible explanation for the huge number of common elements in the synoptic gospels.

2.8 The key argument about dating of the Gospels revolves around the absence of references to the destruction of the Temple in AD70. Surely all the gospels would have mentioned such a key event. Well maybe not, if the gospels had already existed in an early form then adding late news actually detracts from the power of Jesus prophesy of the event. There is also clear indications of post AD70 additions caused by the destruction of the Temple and all its genealogical records. During Jesus life, his descent from the House of David was never doubted, the adoring crowds accepted him as a rightful Messiah because his genealogy would have been public knowledge – accessible from the Temple records.

2.9 According to the papers published by the Theology Department of the Boston College, "although some scholars disagree, the vast majority of researchers believe that Mark was the earliest written of the gospels that survived Nicaea, being compiled sometime around AD70".

2.10 The consensus view is that Matthew and Luke were composed, independently of one another, sometime in the 80s or 90s. Both used a written form of the Gospel of Mark as source material for their own narratives. In addition, because both Matthew and Luke contain a large amount of material in common that is not found in Mark, most researchers hold that both authors also had a collection of Jesus' sayings that they incorporated into their works – a source known as "Q" which may date to the 40s or 50s.

2.11 The Gospel of John emerges from an independent literary tradition that is not directly connected to the Synoptic tradition. This explains the major differences between John and the Synoptics. The Johannine narrative is indebted to oral and possibly written traditions that were transmitted from earlier decades. Analysis of early manuscripts raises various issues around the authenticity of what we have today as the Gospel of John. Many bible versions indicate the story of the woman caught in adultery (John 7:53-8:11) is a late addition but the story is exactly what one would expect of Jesus. More seriously, when examined carefully (see Part Four chapter 14), the long passage telling of the resurrection of Lazarus, John 11:1-44, is clearly revealed as plagiarism – blatant copying of a popular pagan myth.

2.12 But the most devastating issue are questions concerning the authenticity of the last two chapters – 20 & 21. These chapters provide the most detailed account of the resurrection. Without these chapters, John's gospel ends with Jesus being laid in the tomb. The Roman church is subtle in how it admits these chapters are 'unreliable' – official Catholic bible commentaries on John finish at the end of chapter 19. A reigning pope, Benedict XVI, in his book *Jesus of Nazareth*, quoting verses of chapter 21, states these are in the 'appendix' to the gospel. So originally, John, along with other very popular early texts such as the Didache and the Gospel of Thomas made no reference at all to the resurrection of Jesus. When one then looks at the second most extensive record of the resurrection – Mark 16, it is disconcerting to find modern bible versions admit verses 9 to 20 do not appear in the earliest and best manuscripts either. This is rather uncomfortable for the church which makes Jesus resurrection the central pillar of the faith.

2.13 Joseph Ratzinger, publishing when Pope Benedict XVI, and thereby in effect making his book *ex cathedra*, makes further revealing statements concerning the authenticity of John's gospel. On p225 of *Jesus of Nazareth*, Ratzinger states nevertheless, the complexity of the Gospel's redaction raises further questions. So, the Vatican is disclosing not only that chunks of John's gospel are not original but the redactions (editing and rewriting) are so extensive as to be *'complex'*!!

2.14 On p242 Ratzinger states *"in John chapter 7, which according to a convincing hypothesis of modern exegesis, in all likelihood originally followed directly after chapter 5, we find Jesus attending the Feast of Tabernacles."* The casual aside infers that either chapter 6 (Jesus feeding the 5000 and then walking on water) was not in the original text or chapters were in a different sequence. Note: we have already identified the story of Jesus healing blind man at Pool of Bethesda, at the beginning of chapter 5, is also suspect as it appears to describe a building which has been found to incorporate a dedication stating it was erected in the year 135, during the reign of Emperor Hadrian.

2.15 If you have found the above few paragraphs unsettling, it may come as even more of a surprise to find a pope publicly stating that it is unlikely John was the author of the eponymous gospel. Benedict XVI writes that the Gospel of John was largely the eyewitness account of the disciple that Jesus loved written up by his literary executor, Presbyter John – which also helps explain the prevalence of its use of "we" rather than "I". Benedict XVI points to evidence that the Apostle John founded a college in Ephesus, and another John, known as Presbyter John (to distinguish him from the Apostle), acted as John's literary trustee. Papias, bishop of Hierapolis, died c120, published a 5-volume work in which he records having met Presbyter John but not the Apostle John. Papias is quoted by Eusebius in *Historia Ecclesiastica III* p.39. The 2nd and 3rd Letters of John specifically describe the author as Presbyter John. Thus it seems that only the first epistle attributed to John was actually written by the Apostle.

2.16   John writes from a more spiritual perspective, with some (e.g. Jakob Lorber, a visionary who wrote *Das große Evangelium Johannis* 'the Great Gospel of John') believing that Jesus instructed John to record his gospel during Jesus ministry. If so, then the opening words of John take on even greater significance. It would mean Jesus specifically instructed John to inform us that Jesus was the Logos, an intermediary created by the Creator to convey God's thoughts to humanity in the form of words. (For more analysis on the *Logos* – see Chapter 16 of Part One)

2.17   However, the gospel stories of Jesus birth and early life in Luke and Matthew appear wholly manufactured. The journey to Bethlehem for a Roman census, the Virgin Birth, the 'sign' of the star hovering over Bethlehem, the Massacre of the innocents and the Flight to Egypt – all seem conceived to fulfil supposed prophesies and echo the Mosaic tradition whilst replacing a real sign that identified Jesus as messianic at birth. This last point is covered later in this booklet.

2.18   The Gospel writers took different positions, as described below, but shared common objectives. According to Boston College the key objectives were:

- To enable Christianity to become a legal religion in the Roman Empire, which contributed to the de-emphasis of Roman responsibility for the crucifixion and to highlight Jewish responsibility;

- To explain how to be Jewish after the destruction of the Temple in AD70;

- To explain why the Temple was destroyed;

- To show how Jesus resurrection was consistent with Jewish scripture;

- To validate bringing the Gospel to non-Jewish Gentiles;

2.19   It is incredibly sad to have lost almost all of the early Christian texts that were circulating during the first century. Part Four will look at some of the key messages that were suppressed and also evidence from the oldest manuscripts of the many subtle edits made to the surviving gospels to ensure consistency with later dogma. One only has to look at Enoch and Jubilees to appreciate the likely importance of what has been destroyed. Indeed, the Book of Jubilees provides the key to understanding the whole

Old Testament saga from Abraham onwards.

3

Summary profiles of the canonised synoptic Gospels

3.1   I set out summarised profiles of Mark, Matthew and Luke to identify their target audiences and the differences in how they positioned Jesus.

Profile: The Gospel of Mark

3.2   By tradition, John Mark is held to be the author. There was a John Mark noted as the son of a widow named Mary (Acts 12:12-17) in whose home the disciples met. John Mark was also the cousin of Barnabas (Colossians 4:10). This tradition is attributed to Clement of Alexandria (150-215) in the Catholic Encyclopaedia, with Clement naming Johannis Marcus writing the eponymous gospel in Rome in AD66, describing the author as the colleague of Paul referred to in Acts 12:25 and 15:37. Mark accompanied Paul and Barnabas on their missionary journeys until Paul appeared to fall out with Mark for reasons that were not explained and cut short Mark's mission (Acts 13:13). Later Paul and Mark became reconciled and Paul writes to the Colossians (4:10) that Mark was useful for his ministry.

3.3   Mark starts with Jesus baptism by John. Mark is fast-paced, using the term "immediately" often and focuses on the humanity of Jesus, often referring to his emotions. Mark is believed to be addressed to Roman audiences, as it explains Jewish customs and uses Latin terms – including census (12:14), centurion (15:39, 44, 45), denarius (12:15). The man who carried Jesus's cross is identified as Simon of Cyrene, the father of Alexander and Rufus – who were known to the believers in Rome. Mark refers many times to Simon Peter, it is said that Mark was an assistant to Peter. But if so, and if written in the AD70's, then it is odd that Mark makes no reference to Peter's martyrdom.

Profile: The Gospel of Matthew

3.4 This Gospel is widely held to have been written in the mid-80s. The traditional point of origin is Antioch in Syria, although some favour nearby Damascus or Galilee. It was plainly written by a Jewish scribe who is very familiar with Jewish scripture. The author may see himself as the "scribe trained for the kingdom of Heaven... who brings out of his treasure what is new and what is old." (13:52)

3.5 Matthew is written for a predominantly Jewish community of believers in Jesus, whilst there are Gentile members they are expected to obey Torah norms (22:11-14), possibly including circumcision. Matthew is competing with other Jewish leaders for influence in Judaism amidst the power-vacuum left by the destruction of the Temple in AD70. Matthew considers himself to be more authentically Jewish than other Jewish groups, because he follows those parts of the Torah that he posits as authoritatively taught by Jesus. Other post-AD70 Jews interpret the Torah according to different norms, particularly the Pharisees, whose traditions greatly contributed to the birth of rabbinic Judaism. Matthew appears to be in competition with the Pharisees for the heart and soul of Judaism – which explains the Pharisees intensely negative portrayal in Matthew's Gospel. The core of Matthew's debate is who interprets the Torah correctly.

3.6 Therefore, the Matthean Jesus "comes not to abolish the Law, but to fulfil it" (5:17). Those who advocate the negation of the least of the Torah's rules are least in God's Kingdom (5:19). This may be aimed at Christians like Mark, whose Gentile context led him to show Jesus nullifying kosher laws (Mark 7:19). It is only in Matthew that claims can be made that Jesus supported all the laws of the Torah – in all the other surviving texts, Jesus speaks out against every tenet of Judaism which does not equate to loving one's fellow man or loving God.

3.7 Matthew's Gospel is organized for instructional purposes. It contains five sermons of Jesus. In the "Sermon on the Mount", Jesus presents his definitive teaching. The sermon contains six "hypertheses" in which Jesus declares "you have heard it said of old... but I say to you... " in which Jesus takes a principle found in the Torah and intensifies the instruction.

3.8 Jesus is seen by Matthew as the embodiment of Jewish history, and one may conclude that Matthew thinks of Jesus as sort of a Living Torah whose teachings must be followed. The Matthean church is to put the Torah of Jesus into practice, with a particular emphasis on reconciliation and forgiveness (5:23-24; 18:23), using extreme measures only as a last resort (18:15-17). The Gospel fittingly concludes with a final emphasis on Jesus as Teacher: "Go, therefore, and make disciples of all nations . . . teaching them to observe all that I have commanded you." (28:9-10)

3.9 The main Christological idea in Matthew is that Jesus is the definitive teacher of the Torah because he himself personifies it. His instructions on love and forgiveness must be put into practice in the Church. Authentic discipleship is thus defined by ***doing*** what Jesus commands.

Profile: The Gospel of Luke

3.10 Written about the same time as Matthew's, it seems that neither writer was aware of the other's work. The text is believed to have originated around the Aegean Sea or in Asia Minor.

3.11 Luke has two related interests. To non-Christians in the Roman Empire, he positions the teaching as philosophically enlightened, politically harmless, socially benevolent and philanthropic. He presents Christianity as a religion for Jews and Gentiles, worthy of legal recognition by the Roman Empire. Luke diminishes the embarrassing fact that the church's founder had been executed for sedition by a Roman prefect by reporting Pilate had declared Jesus innocent three times (23:4, 14, 22). Furthermore, in Luke, the centurion at the foot of the cross (unlike in Mark and Matthew) exclaims, "Surely, this man was innocent." (23:47). Almost every Roman character in Luke and Acts is portrayed favourably.

3.12 To members of the church, Luke has a second goal. It seems Luke feels the proclamation to Jews is failing whilst being accepted by increasing numbers of Gentiles – leading some to wonder if God is being faithful to the promises of blessings made to the people of Israel. If blessing through Jesus was now shifting onto Gentiles, what did that say about divine promises to Jews? Perhaps the new sect was a heretical deviation from Judaism as some were complaining? Luke's reply is to stress that the church began, as God so willed, among pious, law-abiding Jews and that Jewish-Christians form the irreplaceable Jewish heart of an increasingly Gentile church. Through them comes "a light for revelation to the Gentiles and glory to the people Israel." (2:32)

3.13 Luke's portrait of Jesus relates to three purposes: Jesus is the bringer of authentic peace, of spiritual and physical wholeness, and of healing and reconciliation. At the Lucan Jesus' birth, angelic messengers proclaim, "Good news of great joy for all the people: to you is born this day . . . a Saviour!... Peace on earth among those whom God favours!" (2:10-11, 14). These words echo monument inscriptions which praised Augustus Caesar as "god" and "saviour," the bringer of the Roman Peace, whose birth "marks the beginning of good news, through him, for the world." Luke is hereby claiming that Jesus completes more fully the work of Augustus. He is the one who brings true peace in the world. Similarly, the Lucan John the Baptist is described as one who will "guide our feet into the way of peace." (2:14)

3.14 In Luke's Gospel, Jesus is surrounded by an aura of healing and reconciliation that affects all who come into contact with him. This Lucan trait can be seen in several unique passages in his passion narrative. It is only in Luke that Jesus heals the servant's ear that was severed during the scuffle at Jesus' arrest (22:51). Only in Luke do Herod Antipas and Pontius Pilate become unlikely fast friends after being in Jesus' presence (23:12). Jesus prays for forgiveness for his crucifiers only in Luke's Gospel (23:34). And only in Luke does one of those crucified with Jesus express faith in him (23:39-43).

3.15 The main perspective in Luke is that Jesus is the one who brings shalom, that is, peace, healing, reconciliation, forgiveness, and wholeness. He brings God's promises of blessings for the world through Israel to fulfilment. Authentic discipleship is defined by promoting the well-being of all, especially the marginalized, and by fostering peace and unity.

SUMMARY PROFILES OF THE CANONISED SYNOPTIC GOSPELS

4

Early life of Jesus – major differences between Matthew and Luke

4.1 Distinguishing the different and distinctive voices of Matthew and Luke is made more difficult by the blending of their two accounts in the story of Christmas. The traditional blending obscures the contradictions, unique aspects are submerged in a combined story – often seen in Christmas crèches – in which, for example, Matthean magi find Jesus in the Lucan manger. The major differences include:

4.2 **Different locations:** In Luke's narrative, Mary and Joseph are Galileans who travel to Bethlehem because of a Roman census. The new-born Jesus is placed in a manger. They return home to Nazareth afterwards, seemingly stopping at the Temple in Jerusalem on their way. In Matthew, Joseph and Mary are introduced as natives of Bethlehem, where they reside in a house. After fleeing to Egypt to escape the murderous designs of Herod the Great, they return following Herod's death and then strangely decide to relocate to live in Galilee.

4.3 **Different visitors:** Luke repeatedly compares Jesus with John the Baptist, who is not mentioned at all in Matthew's infancy account. In Matthew's narrative, Jesus' birth is acknowledged by foreign savants – maybe Sabeans or Persian magi whilst in Luke it is a couple of local shepherds who first learn the news.

4.4 **Differing political climate:** In Matthew's narrative, upon learning of a potential claimant to his throne, King Herod orders the killing of all young infants in Bethlehem. Luke has the new born child publicly proclaimed in the Jerusalem temple by Simeon and Anna. Luke portrays Jesus' family observantly going to Jerusalem before returning to Galilee, but in Matthew they avoid the city and flee to Egypt.

4.5 **Different parental focus:** In Matthew's narrative the spotlight shines on Joseph. It is he who receives divine guidance in a series of dreams. In Luke's account it is Mary who is portrayed as the one who hears and keeps God's word. The genealogies incorporated share few commonalities.

4.6 These differences point to late glosses woven into the texts to add more examples of prophesies fulfilled and parallels to the Mosaic traditions – the blessed baby in mortal danger, fleeing to/from Egypt, etc.

4.7 Compare the circumstances, where known, of these Gospel authors with Paul. We know that Paul, a highly trained theologian and very articulate, largely avoided time in Jerusalem with James and other leaders of the original church. The Book of Acts records the growing division between Paul and the Jerusalem Church, formed by the Nazarenes, as Jesus followers were known and identified themselves. The Nazarenes saw themselves as devout Jews who had correctly identified a true Messiah. Paul, however, facing the challenge of converting Gentiles from a variety of other religions, focused on the person of Jesus and sought to drop adherence to the Mosaic Law. Paul gradually developed a theology which positioned the Law as something specifically for Jews who had been given priority but had failed the test set by God. This grew into a schism which, after the repeated destructions of Jerusalem and multiple massacres of Jews by Roman armies caused the original Nazarene church to be scattered, whilst Paul's successful church planting across western Turkey, Greece and in Rome enabled successors to his tradition to assume leadership after Paul's death.

EARLY LIFE OF JESUS – MAJOR DIFFERENCES BETWEEN MATTHEW AND LUKE

5

Misleading early life statements contained within Matthew and Luke

5.1 The early years of Jesus life told in Matthew and Luke include many embellishments of dubious veracity and many that are simply not historically credible – e.g. the virgin birth, the journey to Bethlehem, the flight to Egypt, the massacre of the Innocents and Jesus genealogy.

The Virgin Birth

5.2 The Virgin Birth seems a blatant copying of a widely used explanation for the origin of pagan gods. There is no need for a virgin birth for Jesus and some difficulty in explaining what it means. Whose seed did the Holy Spirit implant? It seems implausible to think our Creator God has semen, Jesus repeatedly tells us God is Spirit. If Jesus came from alien semen, one could hardly describe him as fully man, surely his divine side came from indwelling of Spirit? To be fully human, Jesus had to have the full quota of both X and Y chromosomes – therefore two human parents. In 2012, even Pope Benedict XVI wrote that the spiritual birth "is always a virgin birth, because it is not related in any sense (except symbolically) to physical birth" in the final work in his trilogy *Jesus of Nazareth: The Infancy Narratives*.

5.3 The Catholic Church's pursuit of establishing a sinless origin led to Mary being progressively purified. The Council of Chalcedon (AD451) declared her Divine Motherhood, the "Theotokos", who had been kept sinless from birth by the grace of God. The Council of the Lateran (AD649) declared Mary's perpetual virginity whilst in 1854 a Papal Edict

PART THREE: JESUS, THE NAZARENE

(Ineffabilis Deus) declared that Mary herself was born from a virgin and finally in 1950 Pope Pius XII declared in his *Encyclical Munificentissimus Deus* that Mary had not died but ascended bodily to heaven.

5.4 Jesus divine side more likely descended at his baptism, or following his crucifixion – the Nazarene Church does not mention anything about a virgin birth and neither does Mark, John or Paul. The absence of any reference by John is highly significant – after all, following the crucifixion, John spent many years looking after Jesus mother. Try to picture Mary and John sharing simple food at supper, no doubt mulling over their amazing life experiences, John would doubtless recount to Mary the times he had spent following Jesus during his three year ministry. However, can it be that Mary never mentions Jesus miraculous birth – the most staggering event in her life? Surely, at some point during these years Mary would have reminisced about visits she received from angels, her worries about Joseph's reaction, etc? Quite how long John looked after Mary we are not sure – but such a direct request from Jesus, and the circumstances in which it was requested – would surely have been honoured. According to ancient Jewish custom, Hyppolitus of Thebes claims that Mary lived for 11 years after the death of her son Jesus. Another early record claims Mary travelled to England and died at Avalon (Glastonbury) in AD49.

5.5 We also know Paul spent years in Jerusalem with James and other members of Jesus' family. Surely, if it was believed at that time – such a miraculous birth would have been referred to in Paul's epistles?

5.6 It would appear that the authors who wrote Matthew and Luke, whom there is no indication ever met either Jesus or his Mother, imported the concept of a virgin birth to be 'competitive' with the origin of other contemporary gods.

5.7 A study of ancient literature discloses the fact that myths of virgin births were part of many – if not all – of the surrounding pagan religions in the place where, and at the time when, Christianity arose.

5.8 About **two thousand years before** the Christian era, Mut-em-ua, the virgin Queen of Egypt, was said to have given birth to the Pharaoh Amenophis III, who built the temple of Luxor, on the walls of which were represented:

(i) The **Annunciation**: the god Taht announcing to the virgin Queen that she is about to become a mother.

(ii) The **Immaculate Conception**: the god Kneph (described as a holy spirit) mystically impregnating the virgin by holding a cross, the symbol of life, to her mouth.

(iii) The **Birth** of the man-god.

(iv) The **Adoration** of the newly born infant by gods and men, including three kings who are offering him gifts. In this sculpture the cross again appears as a symbol.

5.9 In another Egyptian temple, one dedicated to Hathor, at Denderah, one of the chambers was called 'The Hall of the Child in his Cradle'; and in a painting which was once on the walls of that temple, and is now in Paris, we can see represented the Holy Virgin Mother with her Divine Child in her arms. The temple and the painting are undoubtedly pre-Christian. The origin of this representation is quite staggering – Hathor was the Egyptian name for Ninharsag, sister of Enki and Enlil (using their Sumerian names). The Sumerian chronicles credit Ninharsag with creating the first hybrid human, Adamu, which she carried to term herself – hence the temple painting is portraying the 'god mother' giving birth to the first human.

5.10 Therefore, we find that long before the Christian era there were already pictured – in many places of worship – virgin mothers and their divine children, and that such pictures included scenes of an Annunciation, an Incarnation, a Birth and an Adoration, just as the Gospels written late in the first century AD describe them, and that these events were in some way connected with the God Taht, who was identified by Gnostics with the Logos.

5.11 And, besides these myths about Mut-em-ua and Hathor, many other origins of a virgin birth story can be traced in Egypt. Another Egyptian god, Ra (aka Marduk), was said in Egyptian tradition to have been born of a virgin mother, Net, and to have had no earthly father (because his father was the god, Enki).

5.12 Horus was said to be the parthenogenetic child of the Virgin Mother, Isis. In the catacombs of Rome, black statues of this Egyptian divine

Mother and Infant still survive from the early Christian worship of the Virgin and Child to which they were converted. In these, the Virgin Mary is represented as a black negress, and often with the face veiled in the tradition of Isis. When Christianity absorbed the pagan myths and rites it also adopted the pagan statues, and renamed them as saints, or even as apostles.

5.13 Statues of the goddess Isis with the child Horus in her arms were common in Egypt, and were exported to all neighboring and to many remote countries, where they are still to be found with new names attached to them – Christian (Roman Catholicism) in Europe, Buddhist in Turkestan, Taoist in China and Japan. Figures of the virgin Isis do duty as representations of Mary, of Hariti, of Kuan-Yin, of Kwannon, and of other virgin mothers of gods.

5.14 And these were not the only pre-Christian statuettes and engravings of divine mothers and children. Such figures were stamped on very ancient Athenian coins. Among the oldest relics of Carthage, Cyprus, and Assyria are found figures of a divine mother and her babe-god. Such figures were known under a great variety of names to the followers of various sects; the mothers as Venus, Juno, Mother-Earth, etc., and the children as Hercules, Dionysus, Jove, etc. In India similar figures are not uncommon, many of them representing Devaki with the babe Krishna at her breast.

5.15 Nevertheless, some popular Christian writers try to claim Jesus was <u>uniquely</u> born of a virgin – which they then claim is therefore proof that Jesus is God – e.g. Josh McDowell.

The journey to Bethlehem for a Roman Census

5.16 Luke needs the story of the Census because he believes Mary and Joseph lived in Nazareth and has to explain how Jesus was born in Bethlehem. Matthew has the opposite problem, from living in a house in Bethlehem – he has to explain why when coming from Egypt, instead of returning to Bethlehem, they move to Nazareth – which he does by weaving in a fake 'to fulfil the prophesy that the Messiah would live in Nazareth' idea that cannot be found anywhere in the OT.

5.17 There are formidable historical difficulties with every aspect of the census that Luke describes:

(i) there is no record of any pan Empire census being held under Augustus;

(ii) a Roman census did not require registration at the place of some former ancestor – tax was payable where you lived;

(iii) women did not register;

(iv) the purpose of a census was to register adult males fit for military service – and were conducted within the Empire. Judea was a protectorate in 4BC and did not become a province until AD6. Tax collection was farmed out to locals with good knowledge and contacts, who had to bid against each other for the right to squeeze the local pips – a crude but quite effective method;

(v) whilst Herod died in 4BC, Quirinius was not appointed until AD6. Josephus's reference to Quirinius in *Antiquities of the Jews* informs us that the "taxings conducted by Quirinius while governing Syria were made in the 37th year of Caesar's victory over Anthony at Actium" the victory occurred in 31BC, therefore the census was AD6 – when Jesus would have been 10 years old.

5.18 The Romans were excellent administrators – organising an empire wide census which required everyone to travel to the ancestral home would create total chaos, clog the roads and moreover serve no obvious purpose.

5.19 Further, a journey by donkey from Nazareth area to Bethlehem, c170km, would have taken many days. Who, supposedly knowing his heavily pregnant wife is carrying the 'Son of God', would subject Mary to such a needless journey – which would also have taken Mary far away from her close community of female friends expecting to support her during her confinement? No female gospel writer would have made such an obvious mistake.

5.20 My dear friend Alberto also pointed out that according to the Proto-Evangelium of James *(aka The Infancy Gospel of James)* which is quoted by Origen and Clement of Alexandria (and therefore dating to before 150), John the Baptist was born in Ein Karem. This is now a suburb of Jerusalem and lies 11km north of Bethlehem – i.e. between Nazareth and Bethlehem. Mary knew the exact location of John's parents' house as she spent a few months there when she was pregnant with Jesus.

PART THREE: JESUS, THE NAZARENE

5.21   This further undermines the credibility of Luke. If Mary had already stayed with sister in Jerusalem whilst pregnant and then returned to Nazareth, why travel back to Bethlehem (almost going past her sister) only to end up in a stable to give birth with no female family around her. Even if there was a census (which as stated above there is no evidence of nor makes any sense for Joseph to attend), why take your heavily pregnant wife who was not required and why tempt the wrath of God by forcing your wife to sit on a donkey for 150 kms – when it had been divinely revealed to you that she was carrying the Son of God? Matthew avoids all this nonsense by having Joseph and Mary living in Bethlehem.

5.22   Luke may have weaved in the story of the census because Jews knew these could be catastrophic – David was punished for holding a census by Yahweh sending a plague (why is never explained?); whilst the more recent census under Quirinius started the terrorist campaign by the Zealots which had culminated in the destruction of the Temple.

5.23   I suggest another intriguing possibility arises from the late authorship of both Matthew and Luke, generally agreed as gospels written sometime after AD70. If written earlier, neither would have embroidered their gospels with clearly fake genealogies (see below) when accurate and accessible records would have been available in the Temple. Is it possible that Jesus was born much nearer to Nazareth, in Beth Lehem Zoria *(aka Zebulun)* an ancient village known nowadays as Bethlehem of Galilee. This Bethlehem is only 10 kilometres north east of Nazareth – and not only do we know that it existed contemporaneously with Jesus birth – but that the town dates back at least to the time of the Judges.

The star over Bethlehem

5.24   The idea of a star or comet remaining stationary in geosynchronous orbit above Bethlehem long enough to guide shepherds and magi is clearly nonsense but there may have been a quite different sign – which has been largely written out of the record. We examine this possibility in a later chapter.

The flight to Egypt

5.25   This seems to have been designed to echo the Mosaic tale linking a special babe at risk and associating him with Egypt and justified by the Massacre of the Innocents. But as a reaction to Herod's threats it makes no sense at all – escaping Herod's and Rome's jurisdiction would have been accomplished by travelling 25km eastwards to the Jordan valley – Egypt lay 10 times further away, 250km including a long journey through the Negev desert and inhospitable Sinai – surely a nightmare with an infant not much more than 1 year old. Moreover, Egypt was also a province within the Roman empire, and as Paul did when pursuing Christians in Damascus – Herod could have secured a Roman arrest warrant and pursued Joseph to Egypt.

Massacre of the Innocents

5.26   Historical evidence suggests that if this Massacre took place it would have been just before Herod's death in 4BC, when Jesus would have been almost 2 years old – fixing his birth in 6BC.

5.27   Many doubt the veracity of the massacre story partly because of the scale of massacre claimed and the absence of any historical reference to such an event. However, analysis of the evidence available indicates such action would have been very typical of Herod. Whilst horrific, it may have been on such a small scale as not to have been noticed outside Bethlehem.

5.28   Matthew's story of the Massacre by Herod is often dismissed because of other events chronicled as part of Jesus early life which seem implausible and it is positioned as another fulfilment of a vague prophesy (Jeremiah 31:15).

5.29   Dr. Isaiah Gafni, a leading authority on the Second Temple period at the Hebrew University teaches that Herod was diagnosed (by experts in 2007) as a paranoid schizophrenic with Paranoid Personality Disorder. A recurring pattern has been detected in the life of Herod. He would hear a rumour that somebody was going to kill him and take over his throne, but Herod would kill that person first. Then he would become depressed but soon afterwards would launch a building spree. He would hear another rumour and would kill that person, starting the cycle again, which repeated a number of times in which numerous people were killed, including one of his ten wives as well as three of his sons!

5.30   Whilst there is no historical record of the Massacre of the Innocents, there are extensive records of many ruthless murders by Herod to keep his throne secure.

PART THREE: JESUS, THE NAZARENE

5.31   Herod was crowned "King of the Jews" by the Roman Senate in 40BC in Rome but he was a king without a kingdom. However, with the help of a Roman Legion, he was able to capture Jerusalem. The first order of business was to eliminate his Hasmonean predecessors. Mattathias Antigonus was executed with the help of Mark Antony and Herod killed 45 leading men of Antigonus' household in 37BC. In 35BC, he eliminated his brother-in-law, Aristobulus, who was at the time an 18 year old High Priest because he feared the Romans would favour Aristobulus as ruler of Judea instead of him. In 29BC he killed his beloved Hasmonean wife Miriamme, followed by Alexandra, her mother, a year later. Herod also had three of his sons killed. The first two, Alexander and Aristobulus, the sons of Mariamme, were strangled in Sebaste (Samaria) in 7BC. The last, Antipater, only five days before Herod's own death.

5.32   Herod the Great became extremely paranoid during the last four years of his life (8-4 BC). On one occasion, in 7BC, he had 300 military leaders executed. On another, he had a number of Pharisees executed in the same year after it was revealed that they predicted to Pheroras' wife (Pheroras was Herod's youngest brother and tetrarch of Perea) "that by God's decree Herod's throne would be taken from him, both from himself and his descendants, and the royal power would fall to her and Pheroras and to any children they might have". With prophecies like these circulating within his kingdom, is it hardly surprising that Herod acted to try to eliminate Jesus when the wise men revealed a new "king of the Jews" had been born.

5.33   Church records massively exaggerate the likely scale of the massacre: The *Martyrdom of Matthew* states that 3,000 were slaughtered. The Byzantine liturgy places the number at 14,000 and the Syrian tradition says 64,000 innocent children were killed. Yet Professor William F. Albright, the dean of American archaeology in the Holy Land, estimates that the population of Bethlehem at the time of Jesus' birth to be about 300 people (Albright and Mann 1971:19). The number of male children, two years old or younger, would be about six or seven (Maier 1998:178). This would hardly be a newsworthy event in light of what else was going on at the time.

5.34   It is believed that Jesus was born in late September 6BC. Biblical references point to Jesus birth occurring in late September – based on the conception and birth of John the Baptist. According to Luke 1:24-36,

Elizabeth (John's mother) was in her sixth month of pregnancy when Jesus was conceived. So, we can determine the time of year Jesus was born if we know when John was born. John's father, Zacharias, was a priest serving in the Jerusalem temple during the course of Abijah (Luke 1:5). Historical calculations indicate this service would have taken place from 13th to 19th corresponded to June that year (*The Companion Bible*, 1974, Appendix 179, p200). It was during this time of temple service that Zacharias was told that he and his wife Elizabeth would have a child (Luke 1:8-13). After Zacharias completed his service and travelled home, Elizabeth conceived (Luke 1:23-24). Assuming John's conception took place near the end of June, adding nine months brings us to the end of March as the most likely time for John's birth. Adding another six months (the difference in ages between John and Jesus) brings us to the end of September as the likely time of Jesus' birth.

The year 6BC is derived from Quirinius still being Governor of Syria whilst Herod continued to rule Judea long enough to order the massacre of innocents in Bethlehem that were 2 years old or younger.

5.35　When Mary performed the ritual of purification for her firstborn in the Temple she offered two turtledoves, the offering of the poor (Luke 2:22-24). If the Magi had already arrived with their gold, frankincense and myrrh, Mary would have been obligated to offer a lamb. According to Matthew, Herod inquired of the wise men when the star first appeared and calculated the age of the young child based on the testimony of the wise men as to when the star first appeared. He ordered the killing of all male children in Bethlehem who were two years old and younger.

5.36　The slaughter of the innocents is unattested in secular records, but the historical plausibility of this event happening is consistent with the character and actions of Herod. Besides killing his enemies, he had no qualms in killing family members and friends as well. Herod would not have given a second thought about killing a handful of babies in a small, obscure village.

Examination of the genealogies of Luke and Matthew

5.37　The inclusion of these two contradictory genealogies in Luke and Matthew is solid proof that authorship of these Gospels occurred after the destruction of the Temple in AD70 – which destroyed the official Jewish genealogical records. Desperate to 'prove' Jesus fulfilled prophesy through descent from David, the genealogies were assembled from whatever the authors could find or remember – and analysis shows both Luke and Matthew include much outright fabrication.

5.38 The standard explanation for the significant differences between the genealogies in the two Gospels is that Matthew is providing Joseph's family line whilst Luke is providing the line of Mary. The superficial reader might accept this explanation at face value but anyone taking a closer look quickly concludes that the veracity of each genealogy is rather dubious. If one accepts this explanation at face value it creates a major problem:- according to prophesy the Messiah shall be from line of the House of David and rule over Israel but this would not fit if Jesus physical father was the Holy Spirit. Alternatively, Jeremiah 22:30 prophesied that "No future king would follow from the issue of Jehoiachin" who was carted off by Nebuchadnezzar – in prophetic terms, Joseph cannot be the father either.

5.39 Paul, trained by the leading rabbinical authorities of his time, would have instantly identified the genealogies as fake – and he repeatedly warned his key staff about them – see 1 Timothy 1:4 and Titus 3:9.

5.40 Analysis of both genealogies identifies various problems. The lists are identical between Abraham and David, but differ radically from that point. Traditional Christian scholars (starting with the historian Eusebius) have put forward various theories that seek to explain why the lineages are so different, such as the idea that Matthew's account follows the lineage of Joseph, while Luke's follows the lineage of Mary. Modern biblical scholars such as Marcus J. Borg and John Dominic Crossan see both genealogies as inventions, conforming to Jewish literary convention.

5.41 Matthew's genealogy is considerably more complex than Luke's. It is overtly schematic, organized into three tesseradecads (sets of fourteen), each of a distinct character:

- The first is rich in annotations, including four mothers and mentioning the brothers of Judah and the brother Zerah of Perez.

- The second spans the Davidic royal line, but omits several generations, ending with "Jeconiah and his brothers at the time of the exile to Babylon."

- The last, which appears to span only thirteen generations, connects Joseph to Zerubbabel through a series of otherwise unknown names, remarkably few for such a long period – resulting in an average gap between generations of an improbable 47 years.

5.42 The total of 42 generations is achieved only by omitting several names – for example three consecutive kings of Judah are omitted: Ahaziah, Jehoash, and Amaziah are missed out of the second span. These three kings are seen as especially wicked, from the cursed line of Ahab through his daughter Athaliah to the third and fourth generation – so the author probably felt justified in omitting them in creating a second set of fourteen. The choice of three sets of fourteen seems deliberate. Various explanations have been suggested: fourteen is twice seven, symbolizing perfection and covenant, and is also the gematria (numerical value) of the name *David*.

5.43 Robert H. Gundry suggests the series of unknown names in Matthew connecting Joseph's grandfather to Zerubbabel as an outright fabrication, produced by collecting and then modifying various names from the first book of Chronicles. Sivertsen sees Luke's as artificially pieced together out of oral traditions. The pre-exilic series *Levi, Simeon, Judah, Joseph* consists of the names of tribal patriarchs, far more common after the exile than before, while the name *Mattathias* and its variants begin at least three suspiciously similar segments. Kuhn likewise suggests that the two series *Jesus–Mattathias* (77–63) and *Jesus–Mattatha* (49–37) are duplicates.

5.44 Modern scholarship tends to see the genealogies of Jesus as theological constructs rather than factual history: family pedigrees would not usually have been available for non-priestly families, and the contradictions between the two lists are seen as clear evidence that these were not based on genealogical records. Additionally, the use of the term 'Son of God', as in Luke 1:35, is evidence that the genealogy does not come from the earliest Gospel traditions.

6

Theological academic teaching

6.1   Before we look further at some other detailed points on which evidence-based analysis challenges parts of the Gospel story as it is conventionally maintained, it is worth considering how this analysis arises and how it is has historically been dealt with.

6.2   The points I have raised in this book, and in Part One, are derived from two types of sources – from researching analysis published by other writers (where I always seek to identify and disclose the original source – so that interested readers may either check or try to delve deeper) or my own deductions and proposals based upon a synthesis of the available information.

6.3   One recurring aspect which has puzzled me in my research is that many of the most headline grabbing issues have a very long pedigree and strong supporting evidence and yet are treated as earth shattering news each time a fresh analysis is put forward. The process seems starkly different to other academic disciplines where the conventional view becomes redefined, established, modified and developed by successive discoveries.

6.4   A recurring theme I have read from many authors is that when they discuss with theological academics, points that are at stark variance with the Biblical text, which the authors regard as potentially controversial, the reaction is always relaxed, being told that they are not putting forward anything not already widely understood within the religious establishment.

6.5 Leading theological academics apparently freely admit widespread awareness and the inclusion in seminary curricula of arguments that the story of Jesus birth (including Mary conceiving as a virgin) is not an historical fact. It is widely acknowledged that the virgin birth was made up decades after Jesus crucifixion; that the idea of the Trinity was similarly developed centuries later supported by a couple of late tweaks to individual Gospels; and, that Christians should not place any faith in so called prophesies of Jesus in the Old Testament.

6.6 Priests and pastors graduating from seminaries must be regarded as considerably above average intelligence – most, if not all, are university graduates and have gained some familiarity with Greek, Aramaic and Hebrew. How does one reconcile such clear intellect with deliberate suppression of the vast evidence undermining the accuracy of canonised Biblical texts? It seems to me that the only explanation is overpowering professional need to stand together and maintain the fiction that the Bible is accurate – fearing that admitting key parts of the established dogma have no foundation in truth would shatter public belief in Christianity and make them unemployable. If so, in the words of John Lennon, *"How do they sleep"*?

6.7 As described in Part One, the past twenty years has witnessed humanity accumulate overwhelming hard evidential proof of the existence of a Creator God – which is truly sensational information!! There also exists a mass of evidence, touched upon in both Part One and this booklet, which enables us to identify the leading Israelite gods – El Elyon (the Lord Most High, in Hebrew) and Yahweh (possibly initially his son, Nannar, and around a millennium later his grandson, Shamash) – who then fit snuggly into the long established genealogy of "pagan" gods of the early pre-Christian civilisations between 4000BC and Jesus time. Yes, the Israelites belief in Yahweh was no different from the Greeks belief in Zeus – and clearly neither had played any role whatsoever in the creation of our universe, nor will play any role in our salvation.

6.8 Discovery of the evidence of a Creator God enables Christians to firmly divorce their religious beliefs from the Old Testament. In chapter 10 we examine the evidence, *in the Gospels*, that points to Jesus denying the authenticity of key parts of the Torah and dismissing almost every tenet of Judaism. There are serious doubts about parts of the New Testament, some of which are touched on in the rest of this booklet, and I for one would prefer to focus on the teaching of Jesus and the beliefs of the original Nazarene Church before Rome started fantasising and went on to develop several elements of dogma which are clearly man-made. There are references to writings and notes recording Jesus sayings, which, given Jesus impact, one can assume that contemporaries recorded and hopefully many did make it more or less accurately into the extant Gospels. Certainly, the parables attributed to Jesus seem to be of a style and genre suggestive of a single author and the widely postulated existence of a source document (referred to as "Q") underlying the common elements of the three synoptic Gospels.

6.9 My conclusion is that the "established" church (in its numerous denominations) has got itself firmly stuck to a Bible containing a melange of oral traditions derived from older, possibly factual, accounts mixed with tribal myths and legends. To this melange has been added heavily glossed promotional material – by various authors trying to promote Jesus to different audiences, edited with post facto rationalisation of theological dogma made up centuries after Jesus life. Having reached this point, the Christian establishment cannot recant its wholehearted commitment to the Biblical record – and we see a classic human response by Evangelicals, to dig in deeper by cleaving to disturbing claims of biblical "inerrancy" – please see chapter 18 in Part Two for a discussion of this strange phenomenon.

6.10 I was deeply encouraged to hear Pope Francis declare that "God is not a magician" when challenging assertions that God literally spoke physical matter into existence. Even more encouraging is Pope Francis attitude to translation errors – including his announcement in late 2017 that the statement in the Lord's Prayer "and lead us not into temptation" is clearly a mistranslation because why would a loving Father lead his children *into* temptation? This made me think of writing to His Holiness, inviting him to follow up on Pope Benedict XVI's admission that the Comma Johannan was "invented in Rome" and ordain the correction of the text of Matthew 28:19 – more in chapter 20 below.

6.11 Turning to something potentially more controversial, have you ever wondered about worship? Yes, if we believe in a Creator God, then acknowledgment and fulsome thanks are well in order. If we believe, the Creator, or some portion thereof, assumed an incarnate human form to come amongst us to teach and guide us to live more fulfilling lives – then we should be extremely thankful and acknowledge the grace granted.

6.12 However, whilst priests understandably urge regular worship and scripture speaks of constant non-stop praise and worship when describing heaven – a moment's thought shows this might be a human idea rather than a godly idea. We would be aghast if a human creator – of a child, a hybrid plant or Dolly the cloned sheep – sought to be worshipped by what they had created. We would surely characterise such needs as sycophantic and a condition needing psychological help. Surely, our worship of God might be more appreciated if we were to create beautiful landscapes in which we live and grow food, if we try to minimise un-recycled waste and remove toxicity from manufacturing processes to try to preserve the natural beauty of the planet. One might question, what is humanity for? – surely not just to provide worship to God? Do we consider ourselves as pets for God? Or maybe that Earth is God's version of Simcity?

THEOLOGICAL ACADEMIC TEACHING

7

The meaning of Messiah

7.1   Academic research by both generalist historians and by biblical archaeologists has enabled us to gain a detailed understanding of life in Palestine 2000 years ago. The Gospels, like most of the Bible, are sketchy documents – which no responsible scholar would for a moment consider absolutely reliable as historical testimony. Hence speculation is required to interpret statements recorded therein – but whilst historical research speculates on the basis of historical fact, theology and clerical teachings speculate almost entirely based on the text of the scriptures themselves. In Church tradition, when confronted by various biblical ambiguities and contradictions, Church Fathers speculated about its meaning, attempting to interpret it. Once accepted, their speculation, i.e. their interpretation, would be enshrined as dogma. Over the centuries, dogma became regarded as established fact. On the contrary, dogma represents speculation and interpretation congealed into a tradition – and this tradition is constantly mistaken for fact.

7.2   A good example of this process is Pilate's affixing an inscription to Jesus cross bearing the title "King of the Jews". Gospel accounts give odd references to this point. In John 6:15 there is a curious statement that, *Jesus, who could see why they were about to come and take him by force and make him king, escaped back to the hills by himself.* We generally conclude that this reflects Jesus not harbouring any political ambitions on Earth – but that does not appear to be what his contemporaries believed. Again, in John 19:21 *the Jewish Chief Priests said to Pilate, you should not write 'king of the Jews', but Pilate answered 'This man said I am king of the Jews'.* There is no elucidation or explanation of whether this title was warranted or not, nor of what Pilate sought to achieve by marking this title. Maybe Pilate, who would have hated the Jewish priests, was just trying to annoy them. At some point in the history of the church, it was speculated that this title was used by Pilate mockingly – any alternative raises awkward questions. Today, all Christians assume Pilate used this title in derision. But this is not established fact at all – there is nothing to suggest that the title was not used in all seriousness. Was it not perfectly legitimate and acknowledged by many of Jesus followers? In Matthew's account of Jesus birth, the three Magi ask 'where is the infant King of the Jews?' Where they being derisive? Surely not, so if they were referring to a legitimate title why should not Pilate also have been?

7.3 A minor point, which again illustrates just how myths get created. Every nativity scene shows three Magi visiting Jesus – but Matthew only tells of three gifts brought by wise men – men plural, not three men.

7.4 In Jewish culture 2000 years ago, people considered themselves God's chosen and their king was regarded as something more than other kings, more than the Emperor of Rome – their rightful king was a manifestation of God's will, of God's divine plan. Herod was a usurper, an immigrant from a family of Nabatean traders endorsed by Rome as king. Messiah was a term meaning 'the anointed one' and applied to every legitimate king of Israel descended from the House of David; the concept of 'anointed' was also reflected in High Priests being referred to as 'the Priest Messiah'. Needless to say, there was nothing divine about such figures. To assert that any man, including any Messiah, was God or even the son of God would have been, for Jesus and his contemporaries, blasphemous in the extreme. For Jesus and his contemporaries, the idea of a divine Messiah would have been utterly unthinkable.

7.5 The character of the Messiah is defined by a contemporary historian as "a charismatically endowed descendant of David whom the Jews believed would be raised up by God to break the yoke of the heathen and to reign over a restored kingdom of Israel to which all Jews of the Exile would return". Christian tradition focuses on Jesus claim to Messiahship without understanding what it meant, because for centuries this was simply not understood. To accept Jesus as a Messiah whilst denying his regal and political role is simply to ignore the facts and to ignore the historical context of what the title Messiah meant. Christians have been taught to believe the Messiah was a non-political figure who posed no challenge to temporal authority, who had no secular or political aspirations but only beckoned his followers to a kingdom not of this world. Biblical scholarship over the past two centuries has acknowledged Judaism in Jesus time acknowledged no distinction between religion and politics.

7.6 Both Matthew and Luke explicitly state Jesus was of royal blood, a literal and legitimate descendant of David. This represented an important qualification for being a Messiah. The validity of the royal claim is backed by the references to the Magi bearing gifts; Luke 23 where Jesus is accused of claiming to be Christ, the King; (i.e. the King Messiah); in Matthew 21:9 on entering Jerusalem, Jesus is greeted by a multitude shouting 'Hosanna, to the son of David'; in John 1:49 Jesus is bluntly told by Nathanael: 'You are the king of Israel'. Then, of course, there is the plaque ordered by Pilate with the description 'King of the Jews'. As noted above, Christian tradition interprets this as derision – but it makes no sense as derision unless in fact Jesus was King of the Jews. If one is a bully, what does one accomplish calling a poor prophet a king, if indeed Jesus was the rightful king, then one would indeed assert one's power by humbling him.

7.7 There is further evidence of Jesus royal status in the gospel narrative of Herod's massacre of the innocents. Although a highly dubious record, it may reflect real anxiety on Herod's part about the birth of a legitimate descendant of the House of David. Certainly, Herod cannot have been concerned by rumours of a mystical or religious figure – a prophet or teacher of the kind in which the Judah abounded at that time.

7.8 The gospels record various incidents where at the crucial time, Jesus acts like a king and does so quite deliberately. One of the best examples is Jesus triumphal entry into Jerusalem riding on an ass. This seems calculated to attract maximum attention amongst onlookers by quite flamboyantly fulfilling OT prophesy. Indeed, Matthew 21:4 makes it explicit that the procession was intended to fulfil the prophesy in Zechariah 9:9 'your king comes to you, humble and riding on a donkey'. Given Jesus word perfect knowledge of scripture, he can hardly have fulfilled the prophesy unwittingly or through sheer coincidence. The intention was clearly to identify himself in the eyes of the population as a King Messiah, a rightful king, an anointed one.

PART THREE: JESUS, THE NAZARENE

7.9 Mark 14, Matthew 26 and John 12 record that Jesus had been anointed the day prior to his triumphant entry into Jerusalem – they recognized claiming to be a messiah required anointment. Mark and Matthew record that Mary Magdalene anointed Jesus (although John says she washed his feet) with a jar of spikenard, supposedly valued by Judas at 300 denarii (about a year's income for a labourer). However, spikenard is an extract from the aromatic root of a plant found in the Himalayas, not the official mixture of olive oil and specified herbs to be used in the Mosaic anointment ritual. In Mark 14:8, Jesus himself recognises this anointing is not related to being recognised as a messiah but preparation for his burial.

7.10 Even before this, there had been public recognition as Israel's King Messiah. John the Baptist's ritual at the Jordan, had given Jesus a 'seal of approval' by an accepted and established prophet – just as Saul (held to have been Israel's first king) received a seal of approval from the prophet Samuel. With John closely related to Jesus, his seal of approval would have carried the additional authority of a royal warrant. Immediately after his baptism, Jesus undergoes significant change, quickly moving to publicly address large crowds and exhibiting leadership behaviour expected of a rightful king.

7.11 According to John, the Jews were anticipating a Messiah who would perform many signs (John 7:31); rule their nation forever (John 12:34) and to come from Bethlehem (John 12:34) – and who would be a political leader that would defeat the Romans and re-establish rule by the House of David.

7.12 Do we have a record of Jesus saying he was that King Messiah? John 4:25-26 describes the woman at the well in Samaria saying that when the expected King Messiah comes, he will explain everything, Jesus is recorded as replying that *'I who speak to you am he'*. But one must ask how this private conversation got recorded for posterity? It seems unlikely that Jesus filed a contact report with his team – so how reliable are these verses?

7.13 During the trial before his crucifixion, Jesus implies that He is the Messiah: Matthew 26:62-64 relates the High Priest saying to Jesus *'I charge you under oath by the living God: Tell us if you are the Christ, the Son of God.' 'Yes, it is as you say,'* Jesus replied. *'But I say to all of you: In the future you will see the Son of Man sitting at the right hand of the Mighty One and coming on the clouds of heav-*

en.' But, again, this text is clearly unreliable – no High Priest would ever say "are you the Christ, (the Messiah), the Son of God" – as no Messiah was thought of as divine just that they were eligible descendants of David or Aaron. Therefore, one can immediately identify the quote *"Son of God"* as textual corruption in Matthew. The most likely original text was a record of Jesus not only confirming that he was a messiah but that he was a Son of Man – a very specific message of importance to us.

7.14 Jesus also discussed topic of messiah with Peter in Matthew 16:16-18: Simon Peter answered, *'You are the Christ, the Son of the living God.'* Jesus replied, *'Blessed are you, Simon son of Jonah, for this was not revealed to you by man, but by my Father in heaven.'* But, again the same textual changes look to have been added, Peter would never have called a messiah the 'Son of God'.

7.15 If Jesus saw himself as a messiah, why didn't Jesus openly proclaim his status as a messiah more clearly? The people were expecting a political messiah, a King Messiah, but Jesus described himself as a Son of Man – which carried a very different meaning (see Part Four).

7.16 New Testament scholarship points to the gospels depoliticising and transferring responsibility for the crucifixion from the Roman administration to the Jews. From a common sense perspective, it makes little sense that only a few days after his triumphal entry into Jerusalem to wild acclaim from the Jewish people, that there is a complete about turn and they clamour to have him killed in the place of a common criminal, who is then freed. It is conceivable that the crowd with whom Jesus was popularly acclaimed as the King Messiah, was largely kept away from the crucifixion which was perhaps attended only by Temple officials, administrators and guards.

7.17 If, as many deduce, the gospels were written after the revolt of AD66 and the destruction of Jerusalem in AD70, they date from a period of cataclysmic turmoil when the country was ravaged by war, the most sacred shrine destroyed, all records scattered and people's memories of events were blurred or modified by recent upheavals. The Roman destruction of the Temple included the burning of the dynastic family records from which Jesus royal ancestry would have been known. The much criticised genealogies contained in Luke and Matthew probably represent subsequent attempts to remember the genealogy – which perhaps accounts for the differences and manifest errors and guesses contained in both. The fake genealogies clearly indicate either later authorship or early additions to original Gospel manuscripts. It is also noteworthy that Paul wrote warning his followers against placing any store on genealogies – either because he knew they were fake or perhaps because he already sought to downplay Jesus earthly royalty to focus on the spiritual.

7.18 The revolt of AD66 was not a sudden event, Palestine had been smouldering since the time of Jesus birth. In AD6, Judah was annexed and incorporated into the Roman Empire as a province with Caesarea as its capital. Almost immediately, nationalist resistance erupted, led by one Judas of Galilee. This Judas was quickly killed but leadership of his Zealots (also known as Lestai, meaning outlaws; and Sicarii, i.e. daggermen) seems to have been hereditary, with leadership passing to his sons and grandsons until the capture of Masada in AD73. The Zealots were not a religious sect but a military group. Rome was the enemy, no Jew should pay tribute, no Jew should acknowledge the Roman Emperor as his master – there was no master but God. They believed the religious and patriotic duty of every Jew was to fight for the reinstatement of a rightful king ruling over Israel. For this objective, all means were sanctioned, however ruthless – today they would be regarded as terrorists. The Zealots, and other militant factions, remained active – raiding Roman supply caravans, attacking isolated contingents of troops and harassing garrisons.

7.19 Under Judaism, two central problems arise in considering Christian claims that Jesus was a messiah, let alone that Jesus was 'The' messiah. Firstly, there are no surviving dynastic records to prove Jesus was a descendant of either David (even setting aside any claimed involvement of a Holy Spirit) or Aaron, and secondly, even Christian records provide no evidence that Jesus was contemporaneously proved to be eligible to be a messiah or that he was properly anointed by the High Priest or even by a prophet. Jesus was born almost 600 years after the last king of Judah, Zedekiah, had been deposed by Nebuchadnezzar – a 600 year gap points to a contested lineage even if any records existed. The genealogies provided by Luke and Matthew are easily shown to be fake.

7.20 The Hebrew word מָשִׁיחַ (moshiach) translated in English as "messiah" or when translated from Greek as "christ" means "anointed one." The noun מָשִׁיחַ (moshiach) appears 39 times in Hebrew scripture. However, Christian bibles of the OT only use the word "messiah" in Daniel 9:25 or sometimes Psalm 2:2 – the other 30+ instances of the word are NOT translated as "messiah" – misleading Christians into thinking there is only one messiah when in reality every properly anointed Jewish high priest and king was a messiah. To be a messiah requires both ancestral eligibility and anointing with a very specific oil. This anointing oil is called שֶׁמֶן מִשְׁחַת קֹדֶשׁ (shemen mish'hat kodesh) the Oil of Anointment and its formula is set out in great detail in Exodus 30:22-33 – comprising myrrh, cinnamon, cane, cassia and olive oil. Neither Matthew 3:16 nor Hebrews 1:9 refer to any anointing with oil. Neither is spikenard, see 7.9 above, even a specified ingredient.

8

Qumran – the scrolls reveal contemporary thinking 2000 years ago

8.1 Two of the main documents recovered from the 'Dead Sea Scrolls' at Qumran have important implications for Christian understanding – these are referred to as the Community Rule and the Damascus Document. The Qumran community of Essenes is believed to have been established around 157BC and existed until destroyed by the Romans, soon after the Temple, in AD70. Thus, their beliefs certainly affected contemporary thinking during the time of Jesus.

8.2 The Community Rule manuscript, confirms that whilst most believed that, after death, a person's soul existed in a shadow world, Shoel, an underworld where even God is forgotten, the man who is admitted and faithfully keeps the Covenant joins the 'Sons of Heaven'. Mainstream Hebrew references contain pleas for Yahweh to bless them during their life, "for in death there is no remembrance of God, in Sheol who can praise God?" – Psalm 6:5, Psalm 78:10-12; Isaiah 38:18. The hope was to be blessed with a long and prosperous life, a peaceful death in the midst of one's family and a place in the family tomb.

8.3 In the post exilic period, dissatisfaction of religious thinkers with a divine justice that allowed the wicked to flourish on earth whilst the just suffered, led to the adoption from Persian Zoroastrianism of the idea of an 'end times' revival of the dead – a reunion of the soul with the dead body.

8.4 Later, the experience of martyrdom under Antiochus Epiphanes led to resurrection being thought of as the true reward for individuals who freely gave their lives for God. This idea was incorporated into the books of Daniel and Maccabees. Antiochus Epiphanes was a Hellenistic Greek king of the Seleucid Empire from 175 BC until his death in 164 BC. He was a ruthless and often capricious ruler. Formally, he was Antiochus IV, but he took upon himself the title "Epiphanes," meaning "illustrious one" or "god manifest." However, his bizarre and blasphemous behaviour earned him another nickname among the Jews: "Epimanes", which means "mad one". He was a vicious enemy of the Jewish people, outlawing Judaism and desecrating the Temple.

8.5 Incidentally, it is now widely believed, for example by the US Conference of Catholic Bishops, that the Book of Daniel was written during the reign of Antiochus IV to strengthen and comfort the Jewish people during their ordeal with tales of moral wisdom. So much for its pretensions of prophesy relating to events in Babylon 400 years before it was written and the adoption of Daniel by the Council of Nicaea as a script conveying the words of God. NB Previously, in Part One, I have referred to the fundamental error that invalidates the story about Daniel in the lions' den.

8.6 During the period of Antiochus IV, a different notion of immortality also emerged – that the righteous souls live forever in God's presence – as described in the Book of Wisdom. The Book of Wisdom, written in Greek in Alexandria during the 2nd century BC, aimed to convince young Jews of the superiority of Jewish beliefs over Greek materialism using Greek philosophy and rhetoric. The historian Josephus tells us that the Essenes adopted this second Hellenistic view of immortality – that the flesh is a prison from which the indestructible soul of the just is released into limitless bliss. The Community Rule, discussing the rewards of the just and the wicked, assures the just that their reward is eternal joy in everlasting life whilst sinners can expect eternal torment and endless disgrace.

8.7 The Damascus Document, so called because it repeatedly refers to it having been drawn up "in the land of Damascus" located in the "desert of Judah". Amazingly, this document was first rediscovered in 1896 in a storage room of the Karaite synagogue of Cairo! Two incomplete scrolls entitled the Covenant of Damascus and recognised as Zadokite works were found, partly overlapping and with some differences in the common sections. The two fragmentary documents, conventionally referred to as

A and B which have been dated to the 10th and 12th centuries, are now known to be copies of the Damascus Document, of which parts of more than ten copies were found in 1947 at Qumran enabling the complete text to be assembled.

8.8 The Damascus Document starts with The Admonition, comprising moral instruction, exhortation, and warnings addressed to members of the sect, together with polemic against its opponents. The historical origin of the sect is set out. Intriguingly, the history starts with the Heavenly Watchers, who fell because they did not keep the Commandments and their Nephilim offspring, who were giants of men, who did their own will and incurred the wrath of God. The story then continues with Noah, Abraham, etc. The chronology concludes with a seminal event 390 years after the destruction of the First Temple (i.e. 197BC, being 390 years after 587BC). This appears to be the birth of the founder of the Qumran community, who sprouted forth from 'Israel and Aaron' as a 'planted root'. The Teacher of Righteousness emerged 20 years later to found the Community – and the Elect, the Remnant, who went to sojourn in the 'land of Damascus'.

8.9 The adoption of the name Damascus is explained in the document as derived from Amos 5:26-27: *I will exile the tabernacle of your king and the bases of your statutes from my tent to Damascus*. The 'tabernacle' is the Books of the Law; the 'king' is the congregation; whilst the 'bases of the statutes' are the books of the prophets – whose sayings were despised by the Israelites.

8.10 The second part sets out the Laws of the Community. Noteworthy is the statement that "None of the men who enter the New Covenant in the land of Damascus, and then betray it departing from the fountain of living water, shall form part of the Community nor be inscribed in the Book of Life".

8.11 The Essenes attached great importance to some texts subsequently dismissed by the Church Councils (e.g. Nicaea, AD325) – particularly the Book of Enoch and the Book of Jubilees. And it may be no coincidence that Jesus and two of his brothers, James and Jude, all quote directly from Enoch – could it be that Joseph and Mary kept a scroll of Enoch at home?

8.12 Qumran even adopted a 'pure solar calendar' derived from 1 Enoch and Jubilees – adopting a solar calendar of 364 days that divided into exactly

52 weeks. Twelve months of 30 days with an additional day of remembrance for each season. This meant all religious festivals remained on a fixed day of the week – a feature the Essenes attributed to the purity of "the certain law from the mouth of God".

8.13   But where was "the land of Damascus" specifically described as located in the "desert of Judah" – it is fairly clear that it was not the ancient city of Damascus in Syria. Other sources also confirm that 'Damascus' was a code word for what we call Qumran. It does seem very unlikely that a devout sect, bound to keep the Law in every respect, would decamp from the Promised Land and found their community in the ancient city of Damascus. Further, given the similarities between Nazarene beliefs and Qumran as evidenced by the two key documents, it seems highly likely that the Nazarene community was originally an offshoot of Qumran. Some claim a key difference – the Nazarene community rejected animal sacrifice but there is some very limited evidence for animal sacrifice at Qumran. Clearly, the harsh conditions at Qumran would mitigate against flocks and herds being maintained to support a huge sacrificial rota.

8.14   The Community Rule also required initiates to deliver all their worldly assets to the Sect, these were returned if they failed to make the grade but credited to general funds once they qualified. The early Christian Church adopted a similar rule, which was partly based on the cultural norm that once someone was imprisoned, society treated their home and chattels as open for plunder. Meanwhile, those imprisoned relied on friends and family to provide food and clothes – so donating all goods to the Church was, in effect, an insurance policy.

8.15   Another fascinating Qumran document is referred to as the Genesis Apocryphon. This is described as 'interpreting' some texts in the Torah, incorporating interpretive supplements gleaned from the Targum. Three passages stand out: – firstly, involving the parentage of Noah; secondly, the sojourn of Sarah with Pharaoh Senusret I; and thirdly, the explanation of Melchizedek.

- When Noah's mother, Bathenosh, becomes pregnant, Lamech her husband suspects the father is one of the Nephelim!! Suspicious, despite Bathenosh's denials, Lamech seeks the answer by going to his father, Methuselah – and asking him to go to paradise and seek the truth from his own father, Enoch.

- The section dealing with Pharaoh Senusret's infatuation with Abraham's wife, Sarah, also provides interesting claims – that Sarah was reported to the Pharaoh as being exceedingly sexually attractive. It would seem rather unlikely that courtiers would so describe an 80 year old woman? NB this supports the idea (noted in Part One) that the ancient rabbinical device of repeating a number for certainty has led to translations converting e.g. "40, yes 40" into "80 years old".

- Further, the Genesis Apocryphon states that Sarah spent two years living with the Pharaoh – ample time for Isaac to be fathered by Senusret and then fulfil the prophesy of pharaonic title. This also supports the Islamic view that Ismael was the (only) son of Abraham and the one whose sacrifice was ordered by El Elyon to test Abraham's faith.

- Finally, the Apocryphon describes Melchizedek as the King of Jerusalem and, as was customary, also High Priest to the 'God, Most High' – i.e. 'El Elyon' in Hebrew and Canaanite, 'Enlil' in Sumerian.

8.16   Two other fragmentary documents are noteworthy:

- One named as the Heavenly Prince Melchizedek – refers to Melchizedek in terms similar to the Archangel Michael, as head of the 'Sons of Heaven' who has taken his place amongst the gods in the divine council (referring to Psalm 82) and describes Melchizedek as executing judgment on Belial in the tenth Jubilee at the end of the Time of Jubilees in the 'end of days'. In Sumerian records, the head of the 'sons of Heaven' is Enlil.

- Another, known as the 'Son of God' fragment, includes the phrases 'son of God' and 'son of the Most High' written in the style of Daniel and scholars variously interpret as referring to a Davidic Messiah or possibly to a messianic pretender such as Antiochus Epiphanes.

8.17   The sentiments expressed in the prolific writings of the Essene community indicate the currency of terms such as 'son of God' and the re-characterisation of the Abrahamic contemporary ruler of Jerusalem, Melchizedek, as divine in the century prior to the birth of Jesus – which may well have influenced the gospel writers.

8.18 Findings at Qumran point to a fascinating possibility. Paul's conversion "on the road to Damascus" was, for political reasons, more plausibly on the road to Qumran. As there are strong indications that Jesus grew up in the Essene community in Galilee, it makes sense that Jesus would intervene to save the devout at Qumran – making his only post ascension appearance recorded in the bible. Jesus action was well targeted – turning a ruthless critic into his most effective supporter, even if Paul eventually wandered off message.

QUMRAN – THE SCROLLS REVEAL CONTEMPORARY THINKING 2000 YEARS AGO

9

Jesus 'the Nazarene'

9.1 'Nazarene' is the earliest term used to describe Jesus and his followers – the word 'Christian' was never used by Jesus or used to describe those who followed him. The term 'Christian', derived from the Greek word for 'messiah', seems to have arisen amongst Gentile followers – communities which had little understanding what the term messiah actually meant.

9.2 Many authors argue that 'Nazarene' was not just one term that was used, but the dominant term, and that it was also used to describe Jesus himself. The chief argument for this claim rests on an interpretation of the way Jesus is referred to by the writers of the gospels. The original Greek forms of all four gospels call him, in places, "Iesou Nazarene" (e.g. Matthew 26:71; Mark 1:24, 10:47, 14:67; Luke 4:34; John 17:5, 18:5, 19:19; Acts 2:22).

9.3 By comparison, the first use of the term 'Christian' is recorded as being in Antioch – at a time and in a place at least 10 and possibly 20 or more years after the death of Jesus. (Acts 11:26)

9.4 Translations of the Bible, from the fifth century Vulgate onwards, have generally rendered this into a form equivalent to "Jesus of Nazareth". However, it is not the only possible translation. Linguistically, "Jesus, the Nazarene" is at least as correct, and some critics have argued that it is more plausible given that, if it existed at the time of Jesus, Nazareth may have been only a tiny hamlet rather than a city. Nazareth is not mentioned in any contemporary history and it is not possible to prove its early existence other than by reference to Matthew 2:23 *And he came and dwelt in a city called Nazareth: that it might be fulfilled which was spoken by the prophets, He shall be called a Nazarene.* As no such prophesy appears in the Old Testament and, as we have seen, much of the early part of Matthew is unreliable, it seems quite likely this phrase was added centuries later, after Nazareth was founded, as a bit of post-facto rationalization.

9.5   Titus Flavius Josephus (AD37 to 100) thought to be a Pharisee, was a prolific writer and one-time military governor of the small province of Galilee in the late AD60's. In this role he toured Galilee, writing about each town in great detail. His report includes a stay in the town of Japha, barely 1 mile from Nazareth. It seems strange that, if it had already been established, he omitted any reference to Nazareth a place he recorded staying right next to. It is possible that following the destruction wrought by the Romans putting down the AD 66 to 70 rebellion, many Jews fled to smaller settlements and Nazareth was a beneficiary – gaining a synagogue by the time Luke was writing verse 4:16. Oddly, Luke describes Nazareth not as a village (κωμη) but as a city (πολις). But if Nazareth had been referred to in a prophesy, surely it should have existed by the time that prophesy was fulfilled?

9.6   Archaeological evidence of a settlement at Nazareth in Jesus time is sparse. Some evidence of a simple dwelling of a type used by poor farmers (only clay and chalk vessels were found, but no glass or imported materials) which may date from that period, was uncovered in 2009. Some caves in which evidence of human burials and signs of habitation have been found might be contemporaneous but Jews would not live in a place used for burials. Other evidence points to Jesus family being 'middle class' – the more accurate translation of Joseph's trade is not a carpenter but a master craftsman, a term applied to metal workers, an elite position in the community and unlikely to exist in a tiny hamlet. That Joseph may have been a skilled metalworker also fits very well with Jesus uncle, Joseph of Arimathæa, being known as a wealthy businessman who traded internationally in metals – tin and lead. So, even if Nazareth existed as an obscure village, it seems unlikely to be the place where Jesus grew up.

9.7   Fascinating new archaeological research was published in 2020 by Dr Ken Dark of the University of Reading. In his book, *Roman-Period and Byzantine Nazareth and its Hinterland*, Dark concludes that the archaeological evidence recently unearthed indicates that at the end of the first century Nazareth may have been supported a population of up to 1000. Of particular interest is evidence that indicates the village was religiously very conservative and also politically very anti-Roman. These two traits often went together as the foreign influence of Greek and Roman culture was seen as undermining religious purity.

9.8 It is not clear what the population was at the time Jesus was born, but the evidence suggests strong growth of the settlement during the 1st century. Its religious conservatism may have attracted, or have been accentuated, by an influx of some Jewish religious leaders reported to have fled to Nazareth after the Jerusalem Temple was destroyed by the Romans in AD70. The 24 leaders of the Temple were exiled to Galilee and the High Priest chose Nazareth as his official residence. The relocation of senior priests to Nazareth is reinforced by the discovery of a number of tombs equipped with very rare life-size glass copies of the *shofarot* – goats horn musical instruments used in services in the Temple.

9.9 Archaeological finds from Nazareth reveal that they only used ceramic and other artefacts regarded as ritually pure, while in neighbouring town of Sepphoris such religious rules appear to have been less strictly applied. Recent excavations in Nazareth yielded only ceramic and hewn stone utensils which would have been regarded as ritually pure. Findings of numerous fragments of stone bowls and cups are indicative of religious conservatism. Stone vessels were regarded as immune to ritual and spiritual impurity in ways that wooden and ceramic vessels were not – thus stone vessels were preferred. Use of such stone vessels for ritual washing is referred to in John 2:6 reporting on the wedding at Cana – only 8 kilometres north east of Nazareth. Strict Jews in the first century would avoid use of manufactured utensils in case they had been rendered ritually impure during their manufacture – e.g. by being placed close to non-kosher food, near a dead body or having been handled by a woman during menstruation. Therefore, it is noteworthy that all the fragments of pottery archaeologists found around Nazareth are of a single type of rough ware made in Kefar Hananya, a Jewish village 30 kilometres north of Nazareth. Presumably, Nazarenes were confident that such pottery came from Jewish source that would have kept the products ritually pure during their manufacture.

9.10 The religious conservatism also points to a degree of self-isolation – the

PART THREE: JESUS, THE NAZARENE

people of Nazareth would steer clear of mixing with those in surrounding towns that they felt were impure and unclean. At the same time, the inhabitants of the nearby towns who had adopted the contemporary Greek culture may have avoided Nazareth as being a community of old-fashioned religious extremists. This might also explain the absence of Nazareth in the chronicle of Galilean towns catalogued by Josephus.

9.11 Josephus, the Pharisee and later military governor of Galilee, referred to in 9.5 above, wrote of his stay in Japha (nowadays 'Yafa') a mere 1 mile from the centre of Nazareth and indeed now forms a suburb. Japha is an ancient town dating back at least to the 14th century BC. Japha is referred to as under the jurisdiction of Megiddo in one of the Amarna Letters (Egyptian correspondence regarding their administration of the wider Levant) written from 1360BC up to 1332BC. Japha is reputed to have been the home of Zebedee, whose two sons, James and John, were amongst Jesus first recruits.

9.12 Another indicator identified was the absence around Nazareth of use of human excrement as a fertiliser – forbidden under Judaism but widely practised in the fields of other local villages including nearby Sepphoris. Whilst mainstream Jews viewed excrement as unpleasant rather than ritually impure, their only prohibition was on praying within 4 cubits of its usage. By contrast, the Essenes viewed excrement as spiritually unclean, as well as physically unpleasant, and required all excrement to be buried underground so as not to offend God's 'divine rays of light'.

9.13 These findings support other suggestions that given some of his preferences, Jesus may have been brought up in an Essene community, and also links with ideas that there was a satellite community of Qumran near the Sea of Galilee.

9.14 The indications of anti-Roman sentiment found in the excavations suggest it may have been an active cell of the Zealots. The excavations found a sizeable network of underground hiding places and tunnels which could have sheltered at least 100 people – dating to the first century AD. The Zealots were aligned with hard-line religious thinkers.

9.15 Sepphoris, 6 kilometers north west of Nazareth, was known as the jewel of Galilee at the time of Jesus birth, but was attacked by Zealots in 4BC who destroyed its military arsenal and government treasury. The damage to Sepphoris was so bad that the new ruler, Herod Antipas, a son of Herod and one of the Tetrarch (rulers of a quarter) appointed after Herod's death, in 4BC, set up his capital at Tiberius on the shore of the Sea of Galilee. Herod Antipas ruled from 4BC to AD39, being the Herod that was tricked into murdering John the Baptist.

9.16 If Jesus grew up in Nazareth, the hard-line religious views of the locals, especially when compared with his teaching may have led to his observation that a prophet is never recognised in his home town. That Jesus was really sensitive to this rejection by his local townsfolk is reflected in his statements recorded in all four surviving gospels:- John 4:44; Luke 4:16-30; Matthew 13:54-57 and Mark 6:1-6.

9.17 As noted in paragraph 5:21 above, it is also noteworthy that another Bethlehem existed in Jesus time a mere 10 kilometres from Nazareth – a more plausible donkey ride for a heavily pregnant Mary, and a journey which female relatives essential for a birth might also have accompanied. Such a journey sounds rather more credible than the 175 kilometres to Bethlehem in Judea for her husband to attend a Roman census. Such a census would only have been for male heads of households who were Roman citizens – and detailed Roman administrative records make no reference to any census taking place at this time.

9.18 Returning to the time Jesus grew up, if he had come from Nazareth it would likely have still been quite small and hardly known even in Galilee. Therefore, it is unlikely that the appellation of Jesus would refer to a tiny hamlet, as in *"Jesus of somewhere no one has ever heard of"* but *"Jesus, the Nazarene"*.

9.19 So, from where did the term 'Nazarene' originate? Various possibilities have been put forward:

- The Hebrew word 'nazir' refers to a man who is consecrated and bound by a vow to God, symbolized by avoiding cutting his hair, not eating meat or drinking alcohol. Such a man is usually referred to as a Nazirite in English translations, and there are a number of references to Nazirites in the Old Testament (e.g. Numbers 6:13; Judges 13:5). But a Nazarite was not allowed to drink wine or even eat grapes – so if Jesus had been a Nazarite his actions would be seen as repudiating the Mosaic Law.

- The Hebrew word 'netzer' meaning 'branch' or 'off-shoot'. This could in turn refer to the claim that Jesus was a descendant of David.

- But, the most plausible explanation is that the name derives from a contemporary description of the Essenes as being 'Nazrie ha Brit' (The Keepers of the Covenant), from which the label Nazarenes may have evolved. Historical records refer to members of the Essenes as usually betrothed at 12 but only married at 30 – whilst being vegetarian and rejecting animal sacrifices. In Acts 24:5 it is written that Paul was brought before the Roman Governor at Caesarea and accused by the High Priest of being a ringleader of the Nazarenes. Epiphanius (C4th Bishop of Cyprus) wrote "Jesus the Nazarene, whose followers were called Nazarenes until Pentecost".

9.20 The Dead Sea scrolls have revealed that the Qumran community existed as the head of a series of settlements following the strictly observed Essene rules. There are strong indications that Jesus himself was raised in a satellite Essene community, including the highly significant events when he was aged 12 (visiting the Temple) and 30 (attending the wedding at Cana prior to starting his ministry).

9.21 Josephus wrote that John the Baptist was an Essene, and that it was common for Essenes to bathe several times daily for purification. Intriguingly, as noted earlier, the main Essene community at Qumran referred to their settlement as 'Damascus' leading to suggestions that Paul's conversion happened on his way to Qumran?

9.22 After the word 'Christian' had become established as the standard term for the followers of Jesus, there appear to have been one or more groups calling themselves 'Nazarenes', perhaps because they wished to lay claim to a more authentic and more Jewish way of following Jesus.

9.23 We have descriptions of groups called Nazarenes from two 4th century church fathers – Epiphanius and Jerome. Epiphanius gives the more detailed, although thoroughly disapproving, description, calling the Nazarenes nothing less than Jews pure and simple. He mentions them in his Panarion (xxix. 7) as existing in Syria, Decapolis (Pella) and Basanitis (Cocabe). According to Epiphanius they dated their settlement in Pella from the time of the flight of the Jewish Christians from Jerusalem, immediately before the siege in AD70. He describes them as those "... *who accept the Messiah in such a way that they do not cease to observe the old Law*". Jerome (Epistle 79, to Augustine) says the Nazarenes used the Aramaic

Gospel of the Hebrews, also known as the Gospel of the Holy Twelve, whilst adhering to the Mosaic law regarding circumcision (John's gospel not yet being written) and the Sabbath, but *ate only vegetarian foods*, and, they refused to recognize the apostolicity of Paul. (Jerome's Commentary on Isaiah, ix. I).

9.24 Other early church fathers such as Justin Martyr, Origen and Eusebius mention other groups who, to varying extent, 'accepted Jesus as a Messiah while continuing to observe the Jewish Law' – which just reveals their depth of ignorance about what the term Messiah means. It is obviously inconceivable that any Jew recognising Jesus as a Messiah would not at the same time continue to observe the Law. It is often suggested that these are the same as the groups identified by Jerome and Epiphanius as Nazarenes – the descendants of survivors of the two Roman genocides during the 1st and 2nd centuries. One such group were the Ebionites, referred to in second century writings.

9.25 The label Nazarene to describe followers of Jesus has indeed survived until current times. The Qur'an refers to Christians as Nasrani, the Aramaic equivalent of Nazarenes, a description also persisting amongst the St Thomas Christians in India.

10

Jesus views on Judaism

10.1 A fundamental issue is whether Jesus ever referred to Yahweh as God and worshipped Yahweh as God. Jesus is frequently reported as referring in reverent terms to his 'father' (Abba), whilst he also states on a number of occasions that God is Spirit. One may deduce Jesus was talking of his spiritual father rather than his biological father – which, as discussed in chapter 4 above, is incompatible with other teaching. One may presume Jesus was expressing his relationship with God as filial to teach us to think of our ultimate Creator in parental terms. By comparison, few would consider Yahweh to be a loving father figure.

10.2 Reading Biblical texts, Jesus appears to be a devout Jew – but our deduction is based mainly upon the fact that he frequently went to the Temple to teach. However, in Jesus time, the Temple complex was also the seat of learning and the seat of the self-governing Roman province of Judah. The available evidence indicates that it is very likely Jesus associated with the Essenes. However, whilst Essenes were known to strictly follow the Law, and in one reading Jesus is said to have claimed that he had fulfilled the Law – something which later led Paul to declare that the Law was then obsolete (Galatians 3:16-25). Jesus summarised the Mosaic Law by saying all people need to do is to love God and love others as themselves. This neatly replaced not only the 613 mitzvot extracted from the Torah but also the vast collection of priestly interpretative rulings – the halakha and the midrash. The vast majority of the immense web of priestly laws had little or no connection with love and this may the basis on which Jesus dismissed them.

10.3 Jesus teaching seemed to focus on moving away from the almost box ticking practise of following the Law and all its interpretations to focus on a simple edict judging the heart. It seems obvious now that the Creator of the universe would not dwell in a portable tent or a temple and in Acts 17:24-28 we have Paul declare that *"God does not dwell in temples built by man"* – so here **Paul is also declaring that Yahweh is not God**. Jesus own repeated statement that "God is Spirit" explains how a Spirit, can naturally dwell in people's hearts. Whilst we associate the heart with love and emotions, it does not seem the most appropriate organ – the heart is purely a mechanical device to pump blood around. However, the 'soul' being detectible as carrying an electrical charge – which disappears from the body at death – is the more likely candidate. Alternatively, our brains are the organs which think and which direct our actions and could house our soul.

10.4 The Essenes (with some justification) viewed the Jewish practise of animal sacrifices as pagan – and the indications are that Jesus did too. He is never referred to as offering sacrifices (even on behalf of others) or telling sinners to do so. Indeed, the action of clearing the moneychangers from the outer court of the Temple would have effectively stopped worshippers from offering sacrifices – because of a clever priestly ruse whereby everyone had to change their money into Temple coinage to buy sacrificial birds and animals. It is noteworthy that history records the followers and descendant offshoots of Jesus original church as being vegetarian – the Nazarene church (see 16.10) as described by Epiphanius and Jerome in the 4th Century and the Cathars of southern France in the 12th Century.

10.5 Jesus clearly had limited sympathy for the Sabbath laws (working miracles and allowing his disciples to gather food from the fields) and told followers that the Spirit of God was indwelling in them – not resident at the Temple.

10.6 Jesus also ignored the purity laws – being upbraided for allowing his disciples to eat and pray without fulfilling ritual hygiene procedures. Jesus ridiculed the food laws – calling his apostles 'dumb' for believing that creatures God had designed to evolve could be evil for them to eat – rather, that evil was something that came from men's hearts (brain or soul?) than entering through their mouths. Paul also picks this up, going on to question why believers should hesitate to eat meat, even if they think it has been dedicated to a 'pagan' god. If one does not believe a pagan god is real then its dedication is unreal as well – so just eat and enjoy God's provision. It should make one wonder….apologists try to justify the food laws of Yahweh by saying that in the old days, before people had refrigerators, it was best to avoid foods that could easily go bad in a hot climate. True, but there were no mass-market refrigerators until 70 years ago. Certainly, between the time of Abraham and the time of Jesus there were zero changes in the hygiene of food preservation – so why is there such a huge gulf between the teaching of Yahweh and the teaching of Jesus – the answer can only be because one is completely fake.

10.7 Now let's turn to some big points – where Jesus directly contradicts the Old Testament. Yes, according to Genesis 3:8-10 Adam and Eve saw El Elyon and in Exodus 33:17-23 Moses saw Yahweh, at least his hand and his back. Enoch must also have seen God, as Genesis 5:23 says he 'walked with God for *300 years*'. Job 42 says Job saw God. In Genesis 32:30, Jacob claims he saw God face to face – after wrestling with him all night and after being told his name was to be changed to Israel. According to 2 Kings 2:11, Elijah went up to heaven in a whirlwind to see God. However, Jesus is recorded as stating, in John 1:18, that no man has ever seen God and in 1 John 4:12 that no man has ever seen God but if we love each other, God (as spirit) lives in us. Further, Jesus is recorded as declaring in John 3:13 that 'no man has ever ascended to heaven'. These statements are extraordinary – either Jesus was mistaken or John misquoted Him; or Jesus was clearly pointing out that the Torah and the Prophets contain stunning errors – or that they were not talking about God the Creator but what we term pagan gods – i.e. El Elyon and Yahweh, originally known (certainly to Abraham when in Ur) as Enlil and Shamash. Some theologians seek to interpret "No one has seen" as "no one has fully known", meaning that only Jesus fully understood God whilst the earlier prophets, as mere mortals, could not. This sounds like a fudge and also gets bogged down in the fanciful explanations of the Trinity. Moreover, in 1 John 4:12, John records Jesus as more emphatic "No one has ever seen God, but if we love one another, God lives in us and his love is made complete in us".

10.8 So, it is worth thinking about – do you personally choose to believe Jesus, as recorded by John, or, stories about El Elyon and Yahweh in the OT? Consider, this series has shown that reliance on biblical inerrancy is not credible, which means we have to personally take responsibility for ensur-

PART THREE: JESUS, THE NAZARENE

ing there is a robust foundation for our beliefs.

10.9 Where Jesus' statements are recorded (in red letters) supposedly being direct quotes – then his hallmark is plain speaking. If Jesus wanted to avoid getting stoned to death too early in his ministry, he might still have spoken plainly in the company of the Apostles. For such an extraordinary confection as the explanation of the Trinity – surely Jesus would have put pen to papyrus and explained for posterity? John records many statements, some are used to support arguments both ways:

- John 10:30 "I and the Father are One". I have two explanations, the most compelling is that 'Father' is not referring to God – this is explored in Part Four. Alternatively, if 'Father' is a reference to God, perhaps it is indicating total alignment of purpose. Could Jesus be God's galactic representative throughout the Milky Way. That would be a divine role beyond our comprehension – there are c300 billion stars in our galaxy. Note: the current estimate for the *number of galaxies* in our universe is c10 billion. This may sound silly – but I strongly recommend you write out these numbers – only then may an appreciation of God be truly glimpsed.

- John 8:58 "before Abraham was, I am" – please refer to Chapter 19.

- John 20:28 "My Lord and my God" a statement attributed to Thomas. Apologists claim Jesus did not correct Thomas, so that means Jesus is God. Sorry, but this is very weak – perhaps the reply was not recorded, would you expect Jesus to clarify, "technically, I am a God class 2"? From a human standpoint, Jesus and God may be indistinguishable – but our knowledge base has expanded exponentially in the past 2,000 years – and consider the next quote:

- John 14:28 "The Father is greater than I" – in which Jesus clarifies (a) he is separate from the Father and (b) that he, Jesus, is junior to the Father – and that is before we even consider if the Father is himself God.

10.10 Furthermore, *if no man has seen God*, then Jesus, seen by multitudes, is clearly telling us that he is not God. Also, if one presumes Jesus has seen his Father, then again Jesus is telling us that his Father is not God.

10.11 Maybe you are hesitating – so let us consider the argument that really clinches it. Think: what in Jesus time made a Jew a Jew? What identified someone as a member of the Chosen People, a mark demanded by Yahweh as a sign of the covenant granted by Yahweh? Circumcision. So, does Jesus say anything about this – yes – and it is devastating for Judaism and for Yahweh.

10.12 The impact of Greek culture on the nations conquered by Alexander the Great in 332BC cannot be understated. For the Jews, the biggest issue was circumcision – and this issue raged during the three centuries leading up to the time of Jesus. The following notes are derived from a web article by Michael Glass entitled *"The New Testament and Circumcision"*. The Greek standard of beauty – and male decency – was a foreskin that completely concealed the head of the penis. For Greeks, a man could appear naked in public games as long as the head of his penis was covered. The Greek words for circumcision (*peritome* – cutting round) and mutilation (*katatome* – cutting down) were related – so the Greek hostility to circumcision is reflected in the language in which the New Testament was written.

10.13 The greatest clash between these two cultures over circumcision is found in the Books of Maccabees. These books give a gruesome account of a clash between the Jews and the Greek conquerors of Palestine. Between about 175BC and 134BC the Greeks insisted that all people they had conquered follow their religious customs. In addition, they tried to stop the Jews from circumcising their infants. This led directly to the butchery of mothers who circumcised their infants (1 Maccabees 1:60-61, 2 Maccabees 6:8-11). Reprisals of the Jewish zealots included forcible circumcision of boys (1 Maccabees 2:45), and massacres on both sides (1 Maccabees 1:29-38, 1 Maccabees 5:22, 28, 35, 49-51). The fight was dirty and bitter. The Greek authorities ordered the Jews to keep their sons uncircumcised (1 Maccabees 1:48) and put to death the women who had their children circumcised, their families and those who circumcised them; hanging the infants from their mothers' necks (1 Maccabees 1:60-61).

10.14 Maccabees reveals that many Jews wanted to adopt Greek ways. The zealots regarded these Jews as renegades, who had joined with the Gentiles and become debauched (1 Maccabees 1:11, 15). The first counter-attack against the Greeks was to turn against those they regarded as traitors in their own ranks: *'And Mattathias and his friends went around and tore down the altars; they forcibly circumcised all the uncircumcised boys that they found within*

PART THREE: JESUS, THE NAZARENE

the borders of Israel' (1 Maccabees 2:44-46)

10.15   Given this controversy about circumcision, Jesus teaching around 150 years later would have been revolutionary. When Jesus was criticized for healing a man on the Sabbath day, He responded: 'Moses... gave unto you circumcision (not because it is of Moses, but of the fathers;) and yet on the Sabbath day you circumcise a man. If a man on the Sabbath day receive circumcision, that the law of Moses should not be broken; are you angry at me, because I have made a man every whit whole on the Sabbath day?' (John 7:22-24).

10.16   Jesus contrasts the circumcision of Moses and the fathers with his 'making men whole'. However, this phrase is sharpened. It says, I have made a man *'every whit whole'* ('whit' means 'particle, least possible amount'). In this context, the phrase could hardly be more pointed and the point would not be lost on the largely Greek and uncircumcised readership. John's Gospel was written in Greek. For most Greek speakers, circumcision was a mutilation, so a comment contrasting circumcision with making a man 'every whit whole' would be seen as an attack on circumcision.

10.17   However, Jesus said something far more radical about the origin of circumcision: 'Moses gave you circumcision (it is, of course, not from Moses, but from the forefathers)' (John 7:22a). This is striking as Genesis claims circumcision was ordered by El Elyon (Genesis 17:9-14) and Leviticus claims it was demanded by Yahweh (Leviticus 12). When Jesus attributed circumcision to the patriarchs, he downgraded the importance of this ancient ritual from a command that comes from God to a custom of the patriarchs. Customs of the patriarchs may be overturned; a command from God is not so easy to ignore. Describing circumcision as an ancient custom undermines the belief that circumcision came from God. In a religious context, Jesus is almost calling circumcision a pagan ritual. Given the words Jesus used, one must presume he was aware of its Egyptian origin – as a practice followed by their pharaonic gods more than a millennium prior to the supposed time of Moses. It was quite a risky thing for Jesus to say (see John 7:25). Again, Jesus is clearly saying the Torah contains false premises.

10.18   John's gospel records Jesus attacking circumcision in three ways:

- It contrasts Jesus' healing, which makes a man every bit whole, with circumcision, which chops a bit off.

- It downgrades circumcision from a command of God to a practice of the ancestors.

- It does so in the Greek language and therefore in a cultural setting that saw circumcision as an obscene mutilation.

10.19 Paul, a learned Pharisee, started with absolute belief in Judaism, it is recorded in Acts 16:3 that soon after meeting Timothy, whose father was Greek, *'Paul circumcised Timothy'*.

10.20 Paul's thinking changed progressively. In what most believe is the earliest epistle we have, he wrote: *"...I, Paul, am telling you that if you let yourselves be circumcised, Christ will be of no benefit to you. Once again, I testify to every man who lets himself be circumcised that he is obliged to obey the entire law. You who want to be justified by the law have cut yourselves off from Christ; you have fallen away from grace."* (Galatians 5:2-4). In this astonishing use of imagery, Paul says that those who cut off their foreskins cut themselves off from Jesus! If this was not clear enough, he said plainly that they have fallen away from grace. The core of Paul's teaching is that belief in Jesus leads to salvation through grace. Paul is turning the law in the Torah upside down – *"Any uncircumcised male who is not circumcised in the flesh of his foreskin shall be cut off from his people; he has broken my covenant."* (says El Elyon in Genesis 17:14) But Paul is saying that circumcision cuts the believer off from Jesus – a powerful indication of the separation of the new faith from Judaism.

10.21 Later, in Philippians 3:2 (dated around AD62), Paul accused circumcisers of being sexually deviant mutilators: *"Beware of the dogs, beware of the evil workers, beware of those who mutilate the flesh! For it is we who are the circumcision, who worship in the Spirit of God..."* The term 'dog' in this context links to the Hebrew term for male prostitutes, as in Deuteronomy 23:18: 'You shall not bring the fee of a prostitute or the wages of a male prostitute (Hebrew: *a dog*) into the house of the LORD your God'.

10.22 The attitudes and statements identified in this chapter indicate that, according to the canonised gospels, Jesus seemingly showed little loyalty to Judaism. Virtually all the key tenets of Judaism were dismissed by Jesus as either fake or man-made. Very clearly Jesus did not regard the texts of the Old Testament as inerrantly 'God's Word' – so maybe those believing in the inerrancy of the Bible should question why they do.

10.23 Looking at various strands of evidence, I wonder if it is possible that the

PART THREE: JESUS, THE NAZARENE

gospel record has been edited to change Jesus apparent stance on at least some aspects of Judaism. Consider Paul's teaching on his early missionary journeys and the initial reaction by the church leaders in Jerusalem as in Acts 16:21-26.

10.24 Paul returns from an early missionary trip across modern Syria and Turkey to find James and other leaders of Jerusalem church tell him they have heard his teaching is false – and he must purify himself. Four elders will accompany Paul, do penance with him and help him to purify himself to atone for sins Paul has committed with false teaching. This seems a very strong rebuttal of Paul's view that the Gentiles need not follow the Torah rules on circumcision and food purity.

10.25 The original Nazarene church maintained the laws and ritual of the Torah as it spread outside the Roman Empire – across Mesopotamia, Iraq, India to the east and across North Africa, Portugal and across to Ireland and England. This was the first break between the church and Paul. Paul seemed more in tune with Jesus teaching – at least according to the surviving gospels. But it would be very informative to know what position was held by the numerous texts that were systematically destroyed by the Roman Church?

10.26 I find it rather puzzling that Paul is accused of teaching dogma different to what James and other leaders of church had understood from Jesus. Why would Paul, a self-described devout Jew, have decided to junk most tenets of Judaism, was he really just trying to 'package' the gospel into a form more digestible for Gentiles?

10.27 The reaction of the apostles led by Jesus brother, James, strongly suggests that despite having travelled with Jesus for three solid years, they had not understood that Judaic law had been repealed. At face value this suggests Jesus did support the Law – but the surviving gospels say the opposite? My conclusion is that if we had the texts that were ruthlessly destroyed and original transcripts of Jesus teaching we might find the record differs from that in the included in the NT canon today.

10.28 In his epistles, Paul always prefaces quotes from the Torah with the formula 'as it is written'. Paul applies the same formula to a quote from the Gospel of Thomas – implying he saw it as equally authoritative. This suggests the role and status of Thomas was far greater than conventional Christianity recognises, although the Catholic Church has recently begun to reappraise his role. So, it is significant that the Gospel of Thomas records Jesus apparently dismissing the Jewish scripture in Saying 71 *Jesus said, "I shall destroy this house, and no one will be able to build it"*. Whilst obscure to people today, the key lies in the use of the term 'house', 'bet' in Hebrew – well known as the first letter of the first word of the Torah. In the lexicon of the Gospel of Thomas the use of the word 'house' is also highly significant as a divisive term separating the inside from the outside – and division was the key issue Jesus came to erase from human society.

10.29 On the other hand, whilst not proof, it is significant that the gospels recording Jesus denial of Judaic rituals were all written (i) years after Paul was upbraided by James and the other leaders; (ii) all constitute the small sample of survivors of the Roman purge of the original texts; and all contradict the continued adherence to Judaic ritual recorded as practices in Ireland and India, respectively 800 and 1400 years later.

11

Did Jesus associate with the Zealots?

11.1 There are many indications of Jesus associating with the militant factions operating in Israel during his Ministry – however well disguised in the gospel accounts and however embarrassing for Christian tradition.

11.2 Surprisingly, given the conventional view of Jesus, there seems to have been a number of freedom fighters amongst his disciples. One Apostle is named Simon Zelotes, now recognised in some bibles as Simon the Zealot. John names another Simon, Simon Bar Jonah, usually taken to mean Simon son of Jonah – but elsewhere this Simon's father is named as Zebedee. 'Bar Jonah' is probably a mis-translation of the Aramaic word 'barjonna' meaning 'outlaw' or 'anarchist'. Of all the Simon's, the most important was Simon Peter but the gospels make clear his name was Simon *called Peter*. Peter is a nickname meaning rock-like or tough – today he might have been nicknamed 'Rocky'. Given the involvement of the other two Simon's, one begins to wonder if Jesus most important Disciple, chosen to found his church, was also a Zealot? Yet another disciple may also have been a Zealot – Judas is described in the synoptic gospels as Judas Iscariot. For centuries, baffled by Greek appellations, biblical commentators suggested the name should be Judas of Kerioth but, as Professor Brandon has argued, Judas Iscariot now seems more likely to be a corruption of Judas the Sicarius (the daggerman) or Zealot. In addition to Simon, Judas and Peter, another two of Jesus's disciples, James and John, are given the nickname "Sons of Thunder" which some New Testament scholars suspect may link them, too, to the insurrectionists. This suggests that maybe half the 12 disciples were outlaws or renegades

PART THREE: JESUS, THE NAZARENE

if not identifying with the Zealots.

11.3 In the gospels, there are glimpses of Jesus showing a militaristic side at odds with conventional images. In Matthew 10:34, Jesus says *"Think not that I am come to send peace on earth: I came not to bring peace, but a sword"* – which some explain as referring to the Word or the Truth. However, in Luke 22:36, Jesus is unequivocal, he instructs those of his followers who do not possess a sword to get one, selling their clothes if necessary. In Gethsemane, at least one of his followers is armed with a sword and cuts off the ear of an attendant of the High Priest. It is difficult to reconcile such references with the tradition of a mild, pacifist savior.

11.4 As discussed above, Jesus entry into Jerusalem seems a bold and calculated political act to establish his status as King Messiah. His 'cleansing' of the Temple, overturning the money-changers tables thereby disrupting commerce must have caused a minor riot. Neither money-changers, bystanders nor Jesus own followers are likely to have stood idle or engaged in theological debate with loose coins rolling in all directions. These two acts resemble calculated provocation and both incidents make it clear that Jesus had a sizeable following.

11.5 Corruption in the process of translation has obscured more than names. Whether by design or accident, it has also served to obscure information of historical importance. One example relates to Jesus arrest at Gethsemane. For most people the image of the scene is of a small band coming to arrest Jesus – derived from the Gospel account and traditional representation. When asked how many came to arrest Jesus, most people estimate between 10 and 30 – why? Because in the KJV, John 18:3, uses the Greek word 'speiran' to describe the party arresting Jesus which is translated as "a band of men" or in other versions "a number of men" – a vague and unspecified but modest number. However, in the Vulgate it doesn't say a "band of men" but a 'cohort' – today carrying an imprecise but larger value than a band – but to early Christians it was a very precise term. A cohort was a unit of 600 Roman soldiers, one tenth of a legion. The Gospel text also includes Temple Officers in the party – these were the armed guards of the Temple (i.e. the local government). So, Pilate sanctioned a huge armed unit to enable the Temple to arrest Jesus – surely a case of overkill if Jesus was merely a peace-loving prophet?

11.6 It seems unlikely that Jesus was part of the anti-imperial resistance – he believed in paying taxes ('Render unto Caesar... '), while the Zealots did not. He also pointedly criticised the Pharisees, who were in some ways the theological wing of the Zealots. Another reason why Jesus is unlikely to have been a Zealot is that his disciples were not arrested after his execution. Had they been known insurrectionists, the Roman forces would almost certainly have moved in to mop them up. There may have been a sprinkling of anti-imperialist militants among the disciples, but there is no record of Roman authorities seeking out Nazarenes before AD48.

11.7 Indeed, reading the gospel accounts leaves one mystified as to why Jesus was crucified. It was certainly not because he claimed to be the Son of God. Jesus makes no such claim in the Gospels, except once, implausibly, in Mark's trial scene. Taken in a literal sense, the title 'Son of God' would almost certainly have resulted in Jesus's being stoned to death on the spot for blasphemy, which was presumably one excellent reason why he did not make such a claim. In any case, it seems very unlikely that Jesus believed he was literally the Son of God – because no one talked of a virgin birth at that time. Maybe, with divine knowledge, he foreknew the false story about a virgin birth would be invented and for posterities sake kept referring to himself as the Son of Man? Indeed, as we shall explore in Part Four, 'Son of Man' as used by Jesus has a very specific meaning – which the Church almost manged to obliterate for posterity.

11.8 Only the Romans held power of execution, and they took no interest in the theological squabbling of their colonial subjects. Or rather, they took an interest only if they threatened to breed political consequences. They would certainly have been put on the alert by Jesus being acclaimed as the King Messiah and therefore a rightful claimant to the Jewish throne. As such Jesus constituted a challenge to the social order of a Roman province and a magnet for insurrection. The evidence of the Gospels themselves suggests Jesus neither claimed to be God nor was thought to be God by the Jews – the Jews acclaimed Jesus as their rightful Davidic, anointed King. "Away with the House of Herod – imposters from Nabatea and Edom" the people cried – whilst Herod's father had extensively added to the second Temple, the family also built shrines to a number of other gods. When the Pharisees disowned Jesus, intimating he was a claimant to the throne and a threat to the stability of the Roman appointed government, the Romans concurred that he was a threat to public order.

Judas the Sicarius

11.9 Despite evidence in the Gospels themselves, Christian tradition claims the convergence between Jesus life and OT prophesy was 'coincidental' – not calculated on Jesus part but occurring spontaneously, in accordance with a divine plan. Today, this assertion is untenable, modern scholars recognise Jesus was steeped in biblical writings and prophesies. Jesus was not conforming to the prophesies by 'miraculous accident', on the contrary he is carefully, often methodically and painstakingly, modelling his career and his activities according to the statements of the prophets. Jesus himself often says so!

11.10 Zechariah made many prophesies which were of particular interest and relevance to Jesus:- his triumphal entry into Jerusalem; His piercing and killing; and the allegorical good shepherd sold for 30 shekels of silver. It seems Jesus planned deliberately for all these prophesies to occur. For this He needed a betrayer. All four Gospels dwell on the Last Supper, Jesus declares quite openly *"his time has come"*, *"it is time for the prophesy to be fulfilled"*, *"one of you will betray me"*. Judas is openly picked – *"to whom I pass this piece of bread"*, *"go and do quickly what must be done"*. It all sounds openly planned and decided, not a clairvoyant resignation but issuing an explicit instruction, and no one present attempted to stop the process.

11.11 It seems less that Judas actively betrayed Jesus, rather that Judas was selected to carry out the distasteful task – in order that prophesy might be fulfilled.

11.12 An alternative hypothesis was put forward by Jakob Lorber, who wrote voluminous tracts between 1840 and 1864. Born to a poor peasant family in a remote corner of the then Austrian Empire (today Slovenia), Lorber claimed to hear an inner voice telling him to write. After he came to the notice of society in Graz, many sought to catch him out but were left puzzled. His writings cover many subjects which seem quite outside his possible experience. An assessment by a German philosopher, E.F. Schumacher in 1977 concluded: *"Lorber's books are full of statements on scientific matters which flatly contradicted the sciences of his time and anticipated a great deal of modern physics and astronomy. There is no rational explanation for the range, profundity and precision of their contents."*

11.13 According to Lorber, Judas was a wealthy owner of a pottery factory when he signed up as a disciple. Retaining his business commitments, Judas was not continuously with Jesus during his ministry and therefore not closely knit with the other disciples. As a witness of Jesus teaching and powers, Judas was keen for Jesus to take over Judea and restore Israelite sovereignty. Many times, particularly in the Temple, the Jewish authorities had sought to eliminate Jesus or at least arrest him, but according to Lorber, Jesus merely immobilised those seeking to act against him – carrying on with his teaching and calmly departing. Judas had the idea of getting Jesus apprehended with the aid of Roman muscle, which he thought would then force Jesus to exercise his powers to take over – removing the hated royal imposters and the Romans as well.

12

The Church founded by Jesus followers

12.1 The three synoptic canonised gospels focus on the figure of Jesus and his teaching but it seems were all written by authors without any first hand witness of Jesus. Acts, by contrast, reflects an endeavour to preserve a historical record in its context. It seems to have considerably less editing and reflects a first-hand experience of the events it describes – composed shortly after the events described by someone who played a role in them. The period covered by Acts begins after the Crucifixion and ends around AD62. Acts does not mention the incredibly significant events of AD70, which would have been extremely relevant and prophetically important and would surely have been referred to. Acts is a book of history concerning the Christians and the Jews. The fact that the destruction of Jerusalem and the temple are not recorded is very strong evidence that Acts was written before AD70. Nor does Acts mention Nero's persecution of the Christians in AD64 or the deaths of James (AD62), Paul (AD64), and Peter (AD65). At the earliest, Acts cannot have been written prior to the latest firm chronological marker recorded in the book – Festus's appointment as procurator (24:27), which, on the basis of independent sources, appears to have occurred between AD55 and 59 – hence the conclusion that it must have been written between AD57 (see next paragraph) and AD62.

12.2 The author if Acts identifies himself as Luke and modern scholars concur that he is also the author of the eponymous gospel, accepting Acts 1:1 as referring to the Gospel of Luke. Luke's account is primarily an account of Paul and we learn a great deal of the Nazarenes from Acts.

PART THREE: JESUS, THE NAZARENE

In Acts 21, during Paul's last visit to Jerusalem in AD57, is recorded the upbraiding of Paul by the Nazarenes accusing Paul of departing from Judaic beliefs and ordering that he be purified. It is believed to be a reliable historical record of Paul's dispute with the Nazarenes – which would culminate in nothing less than the creation of an entirely new religion.

12.3   In AD35, a Samaritan Messiah led an uprising in Samaria that was brutally put down. This triggered widespread unrest leading to Stephen's martyrdom by stoning in Jerusalem, in which Paul was a participant – causing many Nazarenes to flee the city. Paul, acting on behalf of the Pharisee priesthood and armed with arrest warrants from the High Priest ventures as far as Antioch in northern Syria to round up Nazarenes. This indicates two points – the Nazarenes must have spread rapidly after the crucifixion and Rome must have been sufficiently concerned to authorise armed Jewish authorities to operate far outside Judea. By AD38, an administrative hierarchy had been established by the church in Jerusalem and Jesus was openly proclaimed to be a Messiah – not the Son of God but a rightful and anointed Royal Messiah (i.e. king). Peter was its most famous member but James, Jesus brother, although conspicuously neglected by later tradition was its official head. Clearly some principle of dynastic succession was at work and James was referred to as Zadok.

12.4   Neither Jesus, James nor any Nazarene had any intention of starting a new religion – they would have been horrified by such blasphemy. The Nazarenes were devout Jews, preaching within the context of established Judaism – certainly not to compete with it. However, both the Jewish and the Roman authorities saw the new Church as subversive. By AD44, Peter, then John, then all the other disciples had been arrested and flogged (Acts 12:1-2). James, the brother of John, was arrested and beheaded – a form of execution which only the Romans were allowed to perform – suggesting James had been linked to the Zealots, as preaching the Nazarene form of Judaism would hardly warrant a death sentence from the Roman authorities.

12.5   Guerrilla activity by the Zealots continued, flaring up in AD48 when there are reports of indiscriminate killings of Zealots and Nazarenes by Roman troops – seemingly they were associating the two groups. Disturbances took a new turn from AD54 when the Zealots begun assassinating the Sadducees, starting with the High Priest and then several other Sadducees accusing them of aligning with the Roman authorities. In AD58, a new Messiah arose from the Jewish community in Egypt and quickly gained a strong following, he marched on Jerusalem but was quickly defeated by Roman troops.

12.6 In AD62, James, Jesus brother, and head of the Nazarene Church was seized and executed by the Sanhedrin the following year. Whilst a death sentence required Roman approval, Ananus ben Ananus, the high priest, exploited a temporary vacancy to act fait accompli. As Josephus reports "Festus was now dead, and Albinus was but upon the road." This suggests the Romans might have blocked James execution.

12.7 Once again, a dynastic principle of succession seemed to be applied, with Simeon – who was identified by Eusebius ('History' p3:11) as a cousin of Jesus. Initially, Simeon maintained the Nazarene administration in Jerusalem but in AD65 he evacuated the leadership to Pella – on the east side of Jordan, escaping from Roman jurisdiction. Some evidence suggests that they continued to migrate north east, settling in the Tigris-Euphrates valley. Divorced from what was fast becoming mainstream Christianity, they continued to survive and preserved traditions for centuries – with small, persecuted communities surviving through to current times – e.g. the Christians of the Syriac Church and the Assyrian Church – both in the news for being slaughtered by Isis during 2016 and 2017.

12.8 In Corinthians (1Corinthians 9:5), Paul clearly indicates Jesus' brothers were married: "and the right to take a Christian woman around with us, like all the other Apostles and the brothers of the Lord". It is reasonable to assume James had children as he was described as a fervent adherent of the Law, of which a key demand was to go forth and multiply. For Jude, or Judas Thomas, there is confirmation of a bloodline, the Nazarene hierarchy at the beginning of the second century was directed by two brothers, James and Jude, who are specifically identified as grandsons of Jesus's brother. According to Eusebius, quoting an earlier authority, "the grandsons of the Lord's brother were informed against and brought before Emperor Domitian (AD81 – 96), who asked if they were descended from David, to which they answered yes".

12.9 Descendants of Jesus family, known as Desposyni, survived to become leaders of various Nazarene communities, Eusebius traces descendants until Emperor Trajan, AD 98 – 117, whilst a Roman Catholic authority traces Jesus descendants through to the audience before Constantine in

AD318.

12.10 In AD318, the Bishop of Rome (Pope Sylvester) reported meeting Nazarene Desposyni – i.e. leaders directly descended from Jesus family. Malachi Martin, a Catholic priest, writes in *'Decline and Fall of the Roman Church'* (page 42) that church manuscripts record a deputation of eight Desposyni leaders, each heading a branch of the church meeting at the Lateran Palace. The Desposyni requested bishops appointed by Rome to Jerusalem, Alexandria, Antioch and Ephesus be replaced by appointments of Desposyni and that the Jerusalem Church be regarded as the Mother Church. (Quite where the Jerusalem Church was located is not recorded, as no Jews had been allowed to enter Jerusalem since AD144 on pain of death.) Eusebius, writing around the same time, attacked the Nazarenes and Ebionites for being heretical as they rejected Paul's writings and labelled Paul as a renegade from the Law. Around AD400, another leading church father, Epiphanius attacked both Nazarenes and Ebionites for denying the virgin birth and Jesus divinity – whilst also denouncing Paul.

12.11 Ironically, the Roman church went on to label followers of Jesus original church, the Nazarenes and derivative descendant groups, the Nestorians, the Ebionites, etc., as heretics – with inevitable consequences for their adherents.

Nazarene expansion eastwards

12.12 The Theological School of Antioch founded circa AD200, flourished until AD489 and was a major centre of theological training. The Nazarene teaching of Antioch – that Jesus was a man who became God, not God who became man, being the Son of God not by birth but through adoption by God. Consequently, Mary was neither a virgin nor the mother of God but merely human. Paul Samasata, Bishop of Antioch c AD260 was a major influence upon Arius and Nestorius. The School of Antioch had many highly regarded theological professors whose influence was widespread but begun to wane following the Council of Nicaea (AD325) and the later Council of Constantinople (AD381) which adopted the Trinitarian concept – backed by explicit threats of excommunication.

12.13 Antioch's importance reflected the belief that its church was founded by the Apostle Peter as the first Gentile Church and was recognised by its inclusion as one of the three original Patriarchs – the others being Rome and Alexandria, later expanded by the creation of the Constantinople and, as a gesture, the Jerusalem Patriarch. Alexandria came under the sway of Athanasius and, based upon the Egyptian pantheon, came up with the solution to Constantine's aversion to Christians having a Jewish senior God by proposing the idea of the Trinity. In contrast, Antioch was a centre of Nazarene Christianity. The subsequent history of the Antioch Patriarchy is very interesting. Having broken away from Rome after the Council of Chalcedon in AD451, it continued to be aligned with Constantinople during the period leading up to the schism (the Patriarch of Constantinople was served a Papal Bull of excommunication in the middle of Mass in AD1054). Antioch was conquered by Franks in AD1098 during the First Crusade and forcibly converted to the Latin Rite, however, Antioch then succumbed to Moslem rule in 1268 and the Latin Patriarchy fell to being a nominal sinecure within the Catholic Church – until finally, as late as 1964, the Office was abolished!!

12.14 The Nestorians were so named after Nestorius, who was appointed Patriarch of Constantinople in AD428. Soon after his enthronement, Nestorius made his position clear "Let no one call Mary the mother of God, for Mary was but human." This was seen as scandalous and Nestorius was duly excommunicated. In AD435, Nestorius was exiled to the Egyptian desert but his influence was widespread. When Rome declared Nestorius a heretic in AD451, the Egyptian Church refused to recognise the edict – triggering the first schism leading to the separate Coptic Church.

12.15 The Nestorians, calling themselves the Assyrian Church, did missionary work across Asia – claiming their Church had more members than Rome by the 11th Century. However, they later lost ground in Asia to Islam and Buddhism whilst suffering massacres from the Mongols and later during the pogroms during the fall of the Ottoman Empire. However, a few survived and they maintained a seminary in Nisibis (eastern Turkey near the border with Syria) into the 20th Century. Their adherents number around 300,000 today.

12.16 In the 1960's some ancient Arabic manuscripts dating from the tenth century were found in an Istanbul library by Professor Schlomo Pines. These included long verbatim quotes from 5th or 6th Century texts in Syriac attributed to Nazarenes that had been found at a monastery in Khuzistan (south west Iran). These texts reflect the original Nazarene beliefs:- Jesus is stated to be a man not a god; his treatment as divine is rejected; the importance of Judaic law is stressed; Paul is castigated and his followers are said to have abandoned the religion of Jesus – turning to the doctrines of the Romans. The Gospels are dismissed as unreliable, second hand accounts containing only a little of Jesus teaching.

12.17 There has been speculation that Mohammed's father was a member of a Nazarene community and that Mohammed, PbuH, was himself raised in Nazarene traditions, two or three of his wives also appear to have Jewish Nazarenes (who had to convert to Islam) – and certainly the treatment of Jesus in the Koran is essentially Nazarene. The Koran treats Jesus not as divine but a most holy prophet.

Nazarene expansion westwards

12.18 Alexandria, Egypt, was arguably the major world centre of learning in the early centuries, supporting a wide range of competing schools of thought. It was a major refuge for Jews escaping from Roman suppression of uprisings in Israel – it is estimated that by AD100 around a third of the population was Jewish. The great library was the most famous and comprehensive in the known world and made Alexandria a natural centre of study. Nazarene Christianity flourished before the Pauline version arrived. Even the esteemed church father, Clement of Alexandria, held many Nazarene beliefs.

12.19 It is widely believed that the great library was burnt by Christians on the orders of the Pope – to erase the great store of heretical works held there. Resistance to Rome continued, with the Egyptian Church refusing to accept the charge of heresy against Nestorius (AD451) who had been banished to the Egyptian desert – a move which led to the start of the monastic movement and dozens of monasteries being set up across the Egyptian deserts. Indeed, a comparison has been made likening the Roman church hierarchy under Constantine to the Sadducees and the new Egyptian religious communities in the desert to the Essene community of Qumran.

12.20 From Egypt and from Syria, Nazarene thought begun to spread following the seaborne trading routes – along the North African coast, to Spain and out into the Atlantic spreading to Galicia from which it filtered across the Pyrenees into Gaul and became established in Aquitaine, and to Ireland and parts of Scotland. One of the most important figures in early Spanish Christianity was Priscillian.

12.21   Priscillian held a range of views – some Nazarene, some mystical and gnostic. A rich nobleman, Priscillian preached across northern Spain attracting a large following. He demanded adherence to Judaic law, observed the Sabbath on Saturdays and denied the Trinity. He used many Nazarene texts, including Acts of Thomas, and taught that Judas Thomas was Jesus twin brother. The Spanish bishops were split – some supporting him and some against him, nevertheless he was elected Bishop of Avila in AD380. His opponents accused him of a wide assortment of heretical beliefs, even appealing to the Roman emperor to have him executed. After years of legal argument, he was convicted of practising magic and became the first heretic to be executed at the behest of the Roman Church. Priscillian and four supporters were executed at Trier but his key Church ally, Bishop Instantius, was banished to the remote Scilly Isles (off Cornwall).

12.22   Here a short digression which will fascinate those familiar with geography of the UK. In Roman times, the Scilly Isles were known as Scillonia Insula, a single large island with an extensive fertile and low lying central plain. In addition to the inexorable slow rise in global sea levels since the end of the Younger Dryas period, the continental shelf under the south west area of the UK has been gently subsiding. The large central plain of Scillonia suffered inundation creating the large number of separate small islands known today. According to a website sponsored by the Trium MBA, supported by NYU Stern, LSE, HEC Paris and the Financial Times, the gradual inundation occurred between AD400 and AD500 – soon after Bishop Instantius banishment. I wondered if the bishop had been banished to the priory on what became the island of Tresco – but it appears that it was founded only in AD946.

12.23   Priscillian's body was carried back to Spain where he was celebrated as a martyr and his grave became a shrine for pilgrimages. His martyrdom greatly strengthened the Nazarene tendency in Spain. Soon afterwards, the Vandal invasions crossing the Rhine in AD406 and the Pyrennes in AD409, inhibited Rome's ability to suppress the Nazarene church in Spain. Professor Henry Chadwick holds that Santiago de Compostela is in fact Priscillian's grave. The Pauline church in Rome seems to have downplayed James role as the original leader of Jesus church in Jerusalem, he is barely mentioned in the Gospels, and is a background figure in Acts. But his (Santiago) church in Compostela became the second most important shrine and centre of pilgrimage in medieval Christendom. According to Spanish tradition, James had visited Spain and preached widely there, and after his execution in AD62 his body had been transported to Spain and buried at Compostela. No real evidence has been found for these claims and the earliest record of these traditions dates only to the 7th Century. However, Compostela can be regarded as a shrine to the survival of Nazarene thought. Today visiting Galicia and Northern Portugal one can see many churches dedicated to St Iago – Saint James, Jesus brother, as head of the Nazarene Church.

12.24 The survival of the Nazarene tradition found its fullest expression in the Celtic Church in Ireland. In the early centuries of Christendom, Ireland was largely isolated from the religious and military turmoil convulsing continental Europe and England as the Western Roman empire declined and the Dark Ages began. Indeed, Ireland became the main centre of learning for Europe from the 5th to 7th centuries. Vast numbers of manuscripts were sent to Ireland for safe keeping from the ravages of war across Europe. Irish monasteries attracted ecclesiastic students from all over the Christian world to immerse themselves in the teachings of the past – free from rigid hierarchical priesthoods. During this period, Rome's contact with Ireland was difficult and tenuous – Rome had little means of implementing her decrees and no method of enforcement.

12.25 It is not known when Christianity first reached the British Isles but by AD200 Tertullian wrote that it was well established not only in Roman England but in parts of Britain inaccessible to the Romans. By AD314, there were 3 British Bishops at the Council of Arles. In AD431, Palladius was appointed Ireland's first Bishop, soon after a Northumbrian monk arrived – known nowadays as St Patrick. St Patrick ministered along the south east coast of Ireland and did missionary work in northern parts. However, he was deemed 'unfit' to be ordained as a priest – due to his Arian beliefs. It is significant that his extensive writings make no reference to a Virgin Birth. Discoveries indicate there was little influence from Rome before the Synod of Whitby (AD664), the main influences on the Celtic Church being from Spain, Egypt and Syria. Irish monks were known to have visited Egypt and vice versa. There are extensive Egyptian inspired motifs and decorations adorning monastic buildings and tombstones. A few monasteries showed their Egyptian inspiration by their inclusion of 'desert' in their names – such as Desertoghill, Desertegny and Bolhendesert. Prisicillian texts were used in Ireland and from AD569 it was organised under the Bishopric of Bretoña, in Galicia, Spain. The

Celtic Church also became established in Brittany, Cornwall, Wales and the Scottish Highlands.

12.26 When Nestorius studied at the School of Antioch, his mentor was Theodore of Mopsuetia. At the Fifth Ecumenical Council in AD553, Theodore and all his works were declared heretical – and most of his works have vanished. The sole source of his writings available today is from commentaries of ancient Celtic monasteries. The prestige of some monasteries was such that their abbots were known as mitred abbots and even had bishops under their authority.

12.27 The Synod of Whitby in AD664 focused primarily upon differences between 'Ionian' (Celtic) and Roman calculations to determine the date of Easter. But the ruling in favour of Rome started the decline of Celtic independence. In deciding upon the authority of Rome, the Synod made reference to trifling differences in procedures for church appointments and services between Roman and Celtic observance but was silent on matters of doctrinal differences. However, these differences were significant, its liturgy and mass differed significantly, even the version of the Bible used was deemed heretical. The Celtic Church glossed over the Trinity and did not promote the Virgin Birth. Whilst for Rome the OT had become less important and the Mosaic Law superfluous, in Ireland both were highly regarded and Mosaic Law widely promoted. Usury was forbidden in Ireland and marriage laws were based on strict application of Mosaic Law. The Judaic Sabbath was observed as was the Passover and ritual killing of animals. Once Rome appointed bishops it quietly arranged for the withdrawal and destruction of offending texts. Many Irish monasteries were devastated during the Viking raids of the 8th Century but some of the manuscripts were transported to Wales for safekeeping and may yet, at some future date, yield original texts for study.

12.28 Thus sadly, the church (founded by Jesus and led by His brother) was effectively hounded to extinction by the Roman church. As a result, the beliefs of the original followers of Jesus: that he was born of two human parents and had divine authority granted by God; were eventually suppressed and replaced by the myths of a virgin birth, that he was the Son of God and a constituent of a Trinity.

12.29 So, on the one hand we have the beliefs of Jesus own church as noted immediately above, subsequently led by his brother, then by his cousin, together with the Antioch church founded by Peter, whose beliefs were passed down by Nazarenes, Nestorians and the Celtic churches. Whilst mainstream Christianity has followed Roman political decisions to invent the Trinity to accommodate Constantine and adopt Sol Invictus dogma – changing the day of worship (to the weekly festival for the sun), the annual festival of Sol Invictus as Jesus birthday (December 25, instead of late September) and the adoption of a priestly tonsure.

THE CHURCH FOUNDED BY JESUS FOLLOWERS

13

The Sign

13.1 In the NT canon there is a single letter from James (describing himself as the brother of Jesus) and a single letter from Jude – who some suppose might be Jesus brother of that name. However, some scholars believe Jude was written by Jude the grandson of James.

13.2 The Gospels make it clear that Jesus had a brother named Jude, Judah or Judas. It is curious that there is no reference to this Jude in Acts or any other NT canon. In fact, there are references but he is referred to by another name...

13.3 Under the successive Greek and later Roman occupation, the Jews had high expectations for a Messiah that would deliver them and restore the Davidic monarchy which they had been promised would endure forever. The leading members of Jewish society watched the noble families descended from the House of David hoping for a sign that would mean the arrival of this Messiah – Jesus was identified at birth by a special sign and underwent the key ceremonies at appropriate ages of 12 and 30, whilst the gospel record includes claims of having being duly anointed – although not by the acting High Priest and not with the correct oil.

13.4 Most Christians today believe the Jewish expectation was for a *single* Messiah to appear – a descendant of the House of David who was to reign as king in a messianic kingdom over the entire earth. These expectations are based on a dozen or more texts in the Hebrew Prophets that predict the reign of such a future scion of David (Isaiah 11, Micah 5, Jeremiah 23:5-

6). Conventional Christian belief is that Jesus is this Davidic Messiah or King.

13.5 However, in declaring Jesus to be the King Messiah, early Christians had to answer the question:- who had anointed Jesus with oil? Traditionally this was to be done by a Prophet but generally by the High Priest. John the Baptist might be a candidate but we have no record of any such ceremony. Luke has Jesus "anointed of the Spirit," picking up on Isaiah 61, rather than the traditional anointing with oil. Ebionites declared that Jesus was adopted "Son of God" at his baptism by the Voice from heaven. But there is another surprising possibility some have suggested.

13.6 Examination of Jewish texts, including the Dead Sea Scrolls, reveals that contemporary expectations during the centuries before Christ commonly refer not to one but two Messiahs who are to usher in the Kingdom of God. One is to be a kingly figure of the royal line of David, but by his side will be a priestly figure, also a Messiah, of the lineage of Aaron from the tribe of Levi. As explored in section 6 above, the term "messiah" means one who is anointed. In ancient Israel both the kings and the high priests were anointed with oil and were thus called messiahs. The verb *mashach* means to 'smear with oil', and a *moshiach*, or messiah in English, is one so smeared or anointed. Technically speaking the 'first' messiah was Aaron, brother of Moses, anointed with oil by his brother Moses in a formal ceremony that made him the Priest of Israel (Exodus 29:7). The first anointed king was Saul, anointed with oil by the prophet Samuel (1 Samuel 10:1). When Saul lost favour with Yahweh, David was likewise anointed by Samuel – as king (1 Samuel 16:13; 2 Samuel 2:4). Both priest and king were accordingly messiahs or anointed ones. This means that the notion of *two messiahs* was the norm in ancient Israel and this norm, of *dual* messiahs was projected into the future once the nation began to be dismantled by the Assyrian and Babylonian invasions in the 8th to 6th centuries BC.

13.7 Zechariah, the 6th century BC Hebrew prophet, foretold of a man called 'the Branch' who would bear royal honour and sit on his throne, but he adds, *"There shall be a priest by his throne with peaceful understanding between the two of them"* (Zechariah 6:13). Here is a clear picture of the Davidic King and his counsellor, the anointed Priest. Zechariah refers in another vision to *"two sons of fresh oil"* (i.e., anointed ones or messiahs) who *"stand before the Lord of the whole earth."* He likens them in his vision to two "olive branches" that stand before the Menorah, the seven-branched oil lamp that symbolized God's Spirit and presence (Zechariah 4). Note: the prophesy is for two messiahs to stand before God, not for one of the messiahs to be God!

13.8 This ideal vision of two messiahs became a model for many Jewish groups that were oriented toward apocalyptic thinking in the 2nd to 1st centuries BC. The *Testament of the Twelve Patriarchs*, dating from the 2nd century BC puts things succinctly: "For the Lord will raise up from Levi someone as high priest and from Judah someone as king." (*Testament of Simon* 7:2). Throughout this influential work there is an emphasis that salvation for Israel will come jointly from the tribe of Levi and from the tribe of Judah, the tribe of King David. The Priest Messiah receives more attention than the King Messiah and, in many ways, he stands superior to the Davidic figure. In fact, the patriarch Judah himself declares, "For to me the Lord gave the kingship and to him the priesthood, and he set the kingship under the priesthood" (*Testament of Judah* 21:1-2). The book of *Jubilees*, coming from about the same period, pronounces a perpetual blessing upon Levi as the progenitor of the priests, and Judah as the father of the "prince" who will rule over the Israel and the nations (*Jubilees* 31). It seems, based on these texts, that the notion of "Two Messiahs" was the ideal structure of Jewish leadership. It is for this reason that in the Maccabean period 2nd century BC, the Hasmonean dynasty claiming only marriage into the Levitical priestly bloodline, were never really able to establish themselves in the eyes of the populace as kings, despite massive political and military power. Ingrained in the Jewish imagination was an idealised future in which both a Priest and a King would rule together.

13.9 John the Baptist identified himself as the "messenger" who was to prepare the Way based on a prophecy from the book of Malachi. The version we read in our modern Bibles today is as follows: *"Behold I am sending my messenger to prepare the way before me, and the Lord whom you seek will suddenly come to his temple. The messenger of the covenant in whom you delight—indeed, he is coming says Yahweh of hosts, but who can endure the day of **his** coming, and who can stand when **he** appears?"* (Malachi 3:1-2).

13.10 This translation is based on the standard Hebrew Masoretic text which dates only to the 9th century AD. We now have a version of this very passage from Malachi found among the Dead Sea Scrolls. This scroll dates to the 1st century BC, so it is a thousand years older than our standard

Hebrew text. Notice carefully the differences in the pronouns: *"Therefore, behold I send my messenger, he shall prepare the way before me. And they will suddenly come to his temple, the Lord whom you seek and the messenger of the covenant, whom you desire; behold he himself comes, says Yahweh of hosts, but who can endure **them** when **they** come?"*

13.11 This ancient version of Malachi has two figures that are to come jointly—a messenger of the covenant who prepares the Way, but also one called "the Lord whom you seek." The word translated "Lord" (*'adon'*) is not the Hebrew name for God – Yahweh, but a word that means a "master" or ruler. It may well be that Jesus and John the Baptist were familiar with this version of Malachi with the plural pronouns, and identified themselves accordingly. This was certainly the understanding of the sectarian community that wrote the Dead Sea Scrolls. (See the *Standard English Translations of the Dead Sea Scrolls* by Geza Vermes).

13.12 In one of the oldest founding documents of the Dead Sea Scrolls, *The Community Rule*, the community is expecting the coming of a prophet they called the Teacher, but also the "Messiahs of Aaron and Israel." They imagined a future in which the Priest Messiah would preside over a "Messianic banquet," with the King Messiah of Israel, whom they call the "Branch of David," as his companion. There are many references in the Dead Sea Scrolls to their expectation that two Messiahs would appear. As important as the "Branch of David" was to be, they nonetheless had the extravagant hopes for the coming priest. In a text called the Testament of Levi we read the following: *"He will atone for the sons of his generation and he will be sent to all the sons of his people. His word is like a word of heaven and his teaching is according to the will of God. His eternal sun will shine, and his fire will blaze in all the corners of the earth. Then darkness will disappear from the earth and deep darkness from the dry land"* (4Q541).

13.13 If John the Baptist was the Priest Messiah, this amazing text seems to match the high view in which Jesus held John the Baptist where he addresses him as rabbi (teacher) saying that "among those born of women there is none greater than John" and that he was not just a "prophet" but "much more than a Prophet" (Luke 7:26-30). It is the very opposite of the theological overlay that our New Testament gospels in their final edited forms project in their effort to make Jesus greater than John. It certainly supports the historical probability that Jesus did view John as his teacher as well as the priestly Messiah of Aaron of whom the prophets had spoken. For those reasons Jesus would have deferred to John's leadership and direction, a point completely lost in our gospels other than in the collection of Jesus' earliest teachings that scholars refer to as "Q".

13.14 Biblical scholars see no reason to doubt Luke's assertion that Jesus and John were first cousins. It is accepted that Mary and Elizabeth were sisters. Luke makes clear that John was descended from the priestly dynastic succession of Aaron – which means that Jesus was too. Thus, Jesus could claim to be both the Priest Messiah and the Royal Messiah

13.15 In the apocalyptic atmosphere of the time, devout Jews were anxiously awaiting the advent of two Messiahs – and they would have had their eyes fixed on a limited number of families. Thus, Jesus baptism by John in the Jordan would have taken on great significance. Following John's execution, Jesus lineal heritage qualified him to take on both roles – which would explain Luke's statement in Acts 2:36 that Jesus is **both** Lord and Christ (i.e. both King and High Priest). It is noteworthy that Jesus embarked upon his ministry immediately following his baptism and John's death.

13.16 Accounts of Jesus ministry do not question his lineage and thus eligibility for Messiahship, whilst glossing over his anointment by a baptism of water would not have been questioned by Gentiles ignorant of Mosaic Law. It was only when all the official records were burnt during the destruction of the Temple in AD70 that it suddenly became important to try to re-create a record as proof of Jesus dynastic right to Messiahship – hence the late inclusion of clearly erroneous genealogies in Luke and Matthew. Paul appears to have been aware of the creation of various genealogies and wrote in his epistles advising people to ignore them.

13.17 This also explains the late inclusion (i.e. post AD70) in Gospel accounts of incredible signs – such as the 'star' that stayed still in the sky and shone down on Bethlehem long enough for shepherds and magi to locate Jesus. Unless this was a spacecraft in geosynchronous orbit, the story is not credible. But there seems to have been a far more believable event that would have been seen as a sign from God.

13.18 The principal of dual Messiahs also opens up an even more provocative idea – plainly hidden in the Gospels themselves. A figure whose naming is hidden to contemporary readers may have held a profoundly important role but later found to be inconvenient, if not embarrassing, during the development of Pauline Christianity. Doctrinal difficulties may have led this character to be largely redacted from the gospels – whilst retaining a significant role in other highly regarded texts.

13.19 The successful birth of live twins without modern obstetrics and of twin boys by a descendant of the royal house would have been seen as such a sign. What, you may wonder, am I referring to? In Aramaic the word 'Thomas' means twin. The disciple Thomas is referred to in John 20:24 as 'Thomas Didymus', or 'Thomas called Didymus' – as didymus also means twin in Greek, this results in the name "Twin called Twin" – clearly the feature is of paramount importance.

13.20 All four Gospels and Acts make reference to Thomas but nothing of any consequence is ascribed to him. In John 11:16, it is recorded that upon hearing of Lazarus death, Thomas rather oddly, urges everyone to go to Lazarus home "so that we may all die with him". The story of Lazarus may have been a late addition, drawing heavily upon ancient Egyptian beliefs – see Part Four. Again, in John, Thomas initially doubts Jesus bodily resurrection – which historical research indicates is likely to be a fake story dating to the 4th century (also explored in Part Four).

13.21 However, outside canonical books, Thomas role is much more significant. According to Eusebius, writing his Ecclesiastical History in the AD290's, Thomas travelled north east, evangelising the Parthians, who occupied the region from the Tigris-Euphrates basin through modern day Iran, before taking the Gospel to India. In India he died, pierced by lances and the tomb in which he was buried was soon afterwards found to be empty. A similar tradition exists amongst the Nasrani, a Christian sect centred in Kerela, on the south western coast of India, who claim to have been converted by Thomas – who they record as having been killed at Mylapore, near Madras.

13.22 The Indian government designates members of the community as "Syriac Christians", a term originating with the Dutch colonial authorities (who governed up to 50 coastal cities dotted around the sub-continent between 1615 and 1825) to distinguish the Saint Thomas Christians, who used Syriac rites from others newly evangelized by the Portuguese Catholics who followed Latin rites.

13.23 The Jewish settlement at Cochin is known to have existed in the 1st Century AD, perhaps visited by Thomas. The earliest known source connecting the Apostle to India is the *Acts of Thomas*, thought to have been written in the 3rd Century.

13.24 Although little is known of the immediate growth of the church, Bar-Daisan (AD154–223) reports that in his time there were Christian tribes in North India which claimed to have been converted by Thomas and to have books and relics to prove it. But at least by the year of the establishment of the Second Persian Empire (AD226), there were bishops of the Church of the East in northwest India, Afghanistan and Baluchistan, Pakistan, with laymen and clergy alike engaging in missionary activity.

13.25 In addition to Eusebius, a number of 3rd and 4th century Roman writers also mention Thomas' trip to India, including Ambrose of Milan, Gregory of Nazianzus, Jerome and Ephrem the Syrian whilst Eusebius records his teacher, Pantaenus of Alexandria visited a Christian community in India using the Gospel of Matthew written in Hebrew in the 2nd Century. Pope Benedict XVI publicly announced that research by the Catholic Church confirmed that Thomas had reached southern India.

13.26 These, seemingly well documented activities, mean that Thomas was one of the most active disciples, certainly travelling as far afield as Paul did to Italy and Spain but over far more challenging terrain. Differing from Paul, Thomas message was that of Jesus original Nazarene Gospel – hence their name Nasrani and their subsequent use of Syriac rites – a term presumably dating from the migration of the original Jerusalem church to Pella after the execution of James.

13.27 If all these writers were aware of Thomas work – why is there so little reference in canon to someone who must have had a forceful and determined character? What is being clumsily concealed – what was the name of this Twin and whose Twin was he? These questions are partly answered in the apocryphal *Gospel of Thomas*, a very early work thought to date before AD100. Here Thomas is identified as Judas Thomas, which of course means 'Judas the Twin'. In the *Acts of Thomas*, thought to date from early 3rd century, the issue is clarified with Thomas also named as 'Judas Thomas'. And when Jesus appears to a young man "he saw the Lord Jesus in the likeness of the Apostle Judas Thomas... the Lord said to him: "I am not Judas who is also Thomas, I am his brother". Note particularly the words *'also Thomas'* meaning Jesus stated he was also a

PART THREE: JESUS, THE NAZARENE

twin!!

13.28 In another, fragmentary record, named as the Gospel of St Bartholomew, Jesus twin is explicitly called Messiah by Jesus himself:- Jesus, approaching Simon Peter and Judas Thomas, addresses them "Greetings my venerable guardian Peter, greetings twin, my second Messiah".

13.29 Whilst the evidence of Jesus and Judas being twins is quite strong, that of his twin, Judas, assuming the role of Priest Messiah is very thin.

13.30 In the ancient world the birth of twins was seen as a significant portent – the Divine Twins, Castor and Pollux played a key role in the development of Greek mythology, Romulus and Remus were revered as the twins who founded Rome. Edessa, modern Urfa, in Turkey is noteworthy – it lies a mere 5km from Göbekli Tepe and a 30 minute drive from Harran. Edessa was the centre of another twin cult – Momim and Aziz – until replaced by a cult devoted to Jesus and Judas as twin Messiahs. It is at Edessa that the Acts of Thomas is believed to have been written. It is in Edessa that the oldest church was built, which was destroyed in AD201. There is evidence of Judas Thomas visiting there and preaching to convert the local king, Abgar V (AD13 – 40) – who it is claimed wrote to Jesus seeking healing and received a written reply. Indeed, some references claim correspondence extended to seven letters between the two. The seminary of Edessa was attacked in AD489 for teaching heretical views but the scholars and many manuscripts were successfully moved to establish a new Nestorian School in Nisibis – which continued in existence until the 20th Century.

13.31 Nowadays, the suggestion that Jesus had a twin brother sounds outrageous, even blasphemous but it is actually one of the oldest and most persistent "heresies". It is important to bear in mind that for early Christians the texts in which Judas is described as Jesus brother were widely used by Christian congregations, not only in Israel, Egypt and Syria but further afield in India, Spain and Ireland. During the Renaissance the idea surfaced repeatedly – it is conspicuous in certain of Leonardo's works, and in Poussin. At Rennes-le-Chateau, work commissioned by Berenger Sauniére in 1896 shows Mary and Joseph each holding a Christ child, i.e. each holding a Messiah.

13.32 To summarise, there appears to be significant evidence that Jesus had a twin brother who made a huge contribution to spreading the Gospel. To contemporary Jews, anticipating two Messiahs, the birth of twin boys by one of the key families that also combined lineal descent from the dynastic lineage of both Aaron and David must have been seen as a very auspicious sign of potential Messiahship.

13.33 However, for the Church having adopted the dogma of Jesus having been fathered by the Holy Spirit and later struggling to accommodate Emperor Constantine's demands – such information was no longer acceptable – hence neither the *Gospel of Thomas* nor the *Acts of Thomas* could be considered as canon – and ruthless actions were initiated to eradicate such ideas.

13.34 Consider for a moment, if the Roman authorities could decide to ruthlessly eradicate all texts that clearly stated Jesus had a twin brother, and possibly that Judas was a twin messiah, surely something they would have believed as an intervention by God, could they also have decided that a text authored by Jesus himself was too dangerous to allow in circulation?

14

The Transfiguration

14.1 As described in the gospels, the Transfiguration was an incredible event, eclipsed only by the resurrection. Previously, in John 6:46, Jesus is quoted as stating that "no one has ever seen God except me" – which invalidates a lot of Old Testament claims. John recognises the profound importance of this statement by referring to it in his introduction, John 1:18 "No one has seen the Father except the one sitting at his side" and again in 1 John 4:12. Elsewhere there are OT references to walking with, talking with and even arm wrestling with God as well as warnings of the danger of seeing God's face but Jesus is emphatic – 'no one has seen God'. Even more profound, particularly for Trinitarians, this clearly indicates that someone seeing Jesus has not seen God.

14.2 The descriptions of the transfiguration event as told in Matthew 17:1-8, Mark 9:2-8 and Luke 9:28-36 are almost identical – Jesus took Peter, James and John up a mountain to pray. While praying, Jesus personal appearance was changed into a glorified form, and His clothing became dazzling white. *(Jesus might have explained that the purity of his image enabled his spirit to be seen.)* Moses and Elijah appeared and talked with Jesus about His death as an event that would soon take place. Then a cloud enveloped them and a voice said, "This is My Son, whom I have **chosen**, whom I love; listen to Him!" The cloud lifted, Moses and Elijah had disappeared, and Jesus was alone with His disciples who were still very much afraid. Jesus warned them not to tell anyone what they had seen until after His resurrection.

14.3 As all these accounts are believed to have been written some 30 years after the event, the common source must be attributable to the master document known as "Q". None of the authors of the synoptic gospels had been present at the transfiguration whilst, of those three who were present, only Peter makes clear reference to the event. Peter makes no mention of Moses or Elijah. Luke refers to the discussion between Jesus and the two patriarchs as relating to Jesus imminent departure from Earth; Matthew and Luke refer to Elijah, to which Jesus seems to hint that John the Baptist was a reincarnation of Elijah. However, John is silent about this amazing event – which does seem rather odd? Some claim John 1:14 is "alluding" to the Transformation but given the mass of other detail in John, it is surprising he does not report this amazing event. John 1:14 also betrays late glossing by including a reference to Jesus being *"the only begotten of the Father"* – the term *"begotten of the Father"* only being invented during the Council of Nicaea in AD325.

14.4 Why were James, John and Peter told to keep the event to themselves, particularly when Jesus must have known they were blown away by what they believed they had witnessed? If the purpose was revelation and reassurance given what was soon to come – why keep it secret from the other nine disciples? Indeed, why go up a mountain, why not just share the supernatural image when all the disciples were gathered together? Moreover, how did the three disciples recognise Moses and Elijah – it does not recount any introduction? And, apart from indicating to the Jews the rarefied company Jesus kept, why involve Moses and Elijah in the event? Given the strong evidence, set out in Part One of this series, that Moses is a composite fictional character – his inclusion rather undermines the credibility of the purported event.

14.5 The words attributed to the voice from the cloud is revealing – of contemporary views between AD 33 (when the transfiguration is reported to have occurred) and AD 80 (when these gospels were written): the voice, which the text implies is God, stating: 'this is my son, whom I have chosen'. 'Chosen' implying 'adoption' for a purpose, a role, an inheritance perhaps – but not His only son and not equal and certainly not the same as God as in the Trinitarian concept.

THE TRANSFIGURATION

15

The Apostolic Mission to Britain

15.1 This chapter begun as an attempt to catalogue what happened to the original 12 Apostles. The NT does not give much detail concerning the work of the original Apostles following Pentecost but reports of their travels persist in tradition. Many have written of where the original Apostles travelled after Pentecost and, for those particularly interested in this, I recommend two researchers who provide detailed references concerning their sources which I believe lend credibility to their writing. McBirnie writing in *'The Search for the Twelve Apostles'* has collated very interesting snippets of information from a wealth of ancient sources; whilst Mitred Archpriest Dmitri Ross of the Orthodox Church has drawn upon sources used by few others. My personal view is that there is so much information that at least some of it must be based upon historical facts, however, for me it is impossible to discern which events actually happened and which have been invented.

15.2 Scholars of the past have not hesitated to show where the original apostles travelled. Socrates Scholasticus in his *Ecclesiastical Historie*, states that the Apostles agreed amongst themselves to travel to certain nations (Bible Research Handbook, serial 52d).

15.3 However, my research begun to reveal truly amazing details concerning the early arrival of the Gospel in Britain. The evidence is fragmentary but very extensive and taken together appears to be convincing. Over the centuries what may have been fact became distorted and exploited for political purposes and utilised for myths which then resulted in the underlying truths being totally discredited. The results collated here no doubt contain some embroidered myths but amongst the evidence there seems to be clear corroboration of some real facts. I trust you enjoy this chapter and I predict you will conclude that at least some of the details are true. I'll start by identifying the source of some of the myths.

15.4 Whilst Jesus personal ministry is recorded as mainly focusing on the Jews, there are many instances of him preaching to Gentiles. Both Matthew 15:21 and Mark 7:24 record Jesus as being in the Phoenician cities of Tyre and Sidon, where he is quoted as saying "I was sent only to the lost sheep of Israel". Contemporaries would have understood this as a reference to the Ten Lost Tribes of Israel having been deported to Nineveh as distinct from Judah exiled to Babylon. In Matthew 10:6, Jesus very clearly instructs the disciples: "Do not go among the Gentiles or enter any town of the Samaritans. Go rather to the lost sheep of Israel. As you go, preach this message." Early Christian writers had no doubts where the lost tribes had spread to, the disciples may have shared the same contemporary understanding.

15.5 The following paragraphs reveal a wide range of early sources identifying where the disciples travelled to spread the gospel. I am surprised to find many references to Jesus' disciples visiting Britain, recalling things my Mother told me – some 60 years ago – specifically I remember her linking Joseph of Arimathæa with Glastonbury. At the time, it sounded to me an extraordinary claim but she was an avid reader of history and I would love to know, and now read, her sources.

15.6 The conventional view is that the early history of Christianity in Britain is highly obscure. Some claim that 'medieval' legends concerning the conversion of the island under King Lucius or from a mission by St Philip or Joseph of Arimathæa have been discredited; they seem to have been pious forgeries introduced in attempts to establish independence or seniority in the ecclesiastical hierarchy formalized following the Norman conquest of England.

15.7 My research has revealed some intriguing details. The early writings which tell of early visits by disciples seem to have been hijacked in the 18th and 19th centuries by speculative writers who postulated that the British and American peoples were descendants of lost tribes – specifically Ephraim and Manasseh – and thus brought ridicule down upon those

15.8 The belief Britons descended from Israelite tribes can be traced from a French Huguenot, Loyer, who published *The Ten Lost Tribes* in 1590, attributing his arguments to easy conversions of early Britons to Christianity as being 'preaching to the converted' those knowingly descendants of the Israelite host. The British admiral, Sir Francis Drake, promoted the idea whilst King James I (ruling as the first king of unified England and Scotland from 1603 to 1625) delighted at being crowned king of England at Westminster Abbey seated upon the Stone of Scone (aka Stone of Destiny). The Stone of Scone had been used for centuries at coronations of Scottish kings but had been stolen by King Edward I from Scone Abbey after the Battle of Dunbar in 1296 and then used for English coronations. The legend is that the sandstone slab was used by Jacob as his pillow when he dreamt of a spaceship landing near him and Yahweh descending down its ladder. James I was motivated to commission what became the King James Version of the Bible partly on his belief that having been crowned upon the Stone of Scone he had somehow inherited the title 'King of Israel'.

15.9 From the 18th to early 20th centuries the idea that the British were the descendants of the lost tribes gained wide publicity, partly no doubt as a rationale for its success in developing a global empire. It was probably quite satisfying to link the 'burden' of globe girdling sovereignty to biblical prophesy. Many argued that because very few exiles from Judah had returned to Jerusalem in 538BC, the majority of both Judah and of Israel had migrated across Europe and many settled in Britain. Americans also entered into the spirit of the argument and postulated that they too were direct descendants of the lost tribes – the Brits were, it was claimed, descendants of Ephraim and the Americans descendants of Manasseh. The allocation was never quite explained, nor the mongrel composition of both resident populations. Nevertheless, both rabbinical and Christian writers became excited by OT references that could be deployed to support their contention. Joseph's descendants, it was said, were to be especially blessed – like a fruitful vine with a never-ending supply of water, ensuring their constant growth. Their populations would multiply rapidly. They would expand to lands beyond their original borders, grow militarily strong and reap the choicest physical blessings of the earth. They would produce and prosper. These were the 'birthright' blessings

(1 Chronicles 5:1-2) God promised to Joseph's descendants. Because of these divine blessings, Joseph's descendants were to stand out among Israel's other tribes (Genesis 49:22-26). To the people of England in the 19th Century it was obvious that these attributes must be foretelling the British Empire. Many influential people came to believe these arguments.

15.10 Sadly, early historical evidence suggesting early apostolic conversions in Britain became totally discredited – and largely written out of conventional history. But, by reviewing the minutes of Church Councils – fortunately maintained by the Catholic Church – the evidence points to the special status of the early British Church, which in turn points to something concerning its foundation. So, let's look at the historical evidence and what Church records point to.

15.11 Safe travel and an excellent road network across the Roman world would have made possible the rapid spread of the gospel. Evidence indicates that significant numbers of the early British people professed Christianity. This seems to be a fact that is generally overlooked by modern historians who maintain that Augustine was the first to preach the gospel in England, after arriving in AD595 – nearly two centuries after the Romans had departed.

15.12 In fact there is clear evidence that Christianity, of the Nazarene version, had reached Britain even before the Romans incorporated England into their empire. Julius Caesar invaded in 55BC with 10,000 troops but withdrew after a few months. He tried a second time the following year with 27,000 troops but again had to withdraw after only 3 months. The next attempt was under Emperor Claudius – who sent 40,000 troops in AD43 plus 20,000 reinforcements the following year, establishing Roman rule that lasted until AD410. After the Roman withdrawal, raids by Angles and Saxons increased and gradually they established rule over the eastern half of England by around AD550. Christianity in Britain suffered from the withdrawal of Roman military forces with the pagan Angles finding early British Churches rich and defenseless – they became targeted and a great many destroyed.

15.13 Now let us review the surprising volume of evidence pointing to early Apostolic missions to Britain – I'm sure you will be surprised!

THE APOSTOLIC MISSION TO BRITAIN

Joseph of Arimathæa

15.14 The conventionally accepted information about Joseph is that he was the uncle of Jesus mother, Mary, specifically the Talmud records Joseph as the younger brother of Mary's father. However, no one has identified the location of 'Arimathæa' and it has been suggested that it is a corruption of a title conveying high status – derived from the Hebrew *ha rama* and the Greek *Theo*, meaning 'the Highest of God'. Gospel references certainly convey high status. Luke 23:50 states Joseph was a member of the ruling council, the Sanhedrin. He was regarded as wealthy (Mark 15:43) and indeed owned his own sepulcher – in which he placed Jesus body. He was brave and or influential enough to request the Roman Governor, Pilate, to give him Jesus body.

15.15 There are numerous extra-biblical records concerning Joseph of Arimathæa – let's start with evidence from the Vatican Library!! Cardinal Caesere Baronius (1538 – 1607), who was twice almost elected Pope, wrote *'Annales Ecclesiastici'* on the history of the church whilst he was **Curator of the Vatican Library**. When published, this work was acclaimed as the most important historical reference on the church since Eusebius. Quoting from ancient manuscripts in the Vatican Library, Cardinal Baronius wrote that following Pentecost, Joseph of Arimathæa *gave up his work(*)*. One manuscript told of Joseph of Arimathæa, Lazarus, Philip, Martha and Mary landing at Marseilles in AD35. At Marseilles, they split into two groups – one group led by the Apostle Philip stayed in the vicinity of Marseilles. The other, which included Joseph, travelled north. Because of his familiarity with Britain, Joseph was chosen by Philip to cross the Channel and take the gospel to Britain. With 11 or 12 associates, he sailed along the north shore of Cornwall and Devon and landed on the Somerset coast. At Glastonbury, Joseph established the first missionary base in the British Isles.

15.16 Cardinal Baronius does not specify which Mary. By the time he wrote Mary Magdalene had long been demonised but we know Jesus mother Mary travelled with John and lived at Ephesus (although Eastern Orthodox belief is that she was buried in Jerusalem). However, there are traditions backed by a lot of circumstantial evidence that Mary Magdalene lived in Provence and even founded the city of Orange. Both Hegesippus (an early Christian chronicler cAD110 to 180, who wrote against Gnosticism and Marcion) and Josephus Flavius (Romano-Jewish historian

PART THREE: JESUS, THE NAZARENE

AD37 to 100) record Mary travelling by ship with Joseph of Arimathæa, Lazarus, Martha and a number of others landing at St Maries de la Mer, close to Marseilles.

15.17 (*) *'Gave up his work'* is noteworthy because elsewhere there are strong traditions concerning his work. The circumstances which led to Joseph of Arimathæa choosing Britain to build the first church and start preaching are interesting. There exist a number of entirely independent traditions both in France and Britain that Joseph of Arimathæa was a wealthy and successful tin merchant. The richest tin mines in the world at that time were in Cornwall. Whilst the Mendip Hills in nearby Somerset contained rich deposits of copper and lead, which form useful alloys with tin. It is of course well known that a metal trade between Britain and the Near East existed for many centuries and that merchants from Phoenicia and Palestine came regularly to Cornwall and Somerset for tin, lead and copper. This is mentioned by such classical writers as Herodotus, Homer, Pytheas and Polybius, whilst the historian Diodorus Siculus (c90BC to c20BC) gives the details of the trade route in his *Bibliotheca Historica*. Siculus gave detailed description of the Jewish managed trade bringing tin from Cornwall. After the tin was mined it was shaped into slabs or blocks, taken to a small island, Ictis, which at low tide was connected to the mainland by a narrow path. This little island is now known as St. Michael's Mount (near Marazion, Cornwall). The tin and other metals were taken by boat from the Isle of Ictis to Morlaix, thence transported overland across France to Massilia, (now Marseilles) and then shipped to Tyre, close to the Palestine border. Stories of Joseph of Arimathæa exist at separate places all along this ancient trade route.

15.18 The story is still told "at Marazion in Cornwall of St. Joseph coming there to trade with tin miners" (Glastonbury – Her Saints, page 66 by the Rev. Lionel Smithett Lewis, MA). In the Guide to Penzance (Ward, Locke and Co.) it is stated; "There is a tradition that Joseph of Arimathæa was connected with Marazion when he and other Jews traded with the ancient tin miners in Cornwall". Marazion means 'bitter Zion'. Its other name is still Market Jew. The origin is said to be derived from the fact that it was a colony of Jews, who traded in tin. 'Jew's houses', 'Jew's tin', 'Jew's leavings', 'Jew's pieces' are still common terms in the Cornish tin mines. The oldest pits containing smelted tin are called "Jew's houses" – *(Glastonbury Her Saints, p66)*. "Amongst the old tin workers, who have always observed a certain mystery in their rites, there was a moment when they ceased their work and started singing a quaint song beginning 'Joseph was a tin Merchant;." *(Joseph of Arimathæa at Glastonbury, pp 23-24)*

15.19 It is agreed by most authorities that Mary was widowed while Jesus was just a youth. It is also generally considered that Joseph of Arimathæa was the uncle of Mary, and took special care over Jesus. Naturally, Jesus would be interested in the accounts that his uncle would give of Britain – a land free from the oppression of Rome, and free from ecclesiastical fanaticism such as was prevalent in his own country. It is not altogether surprising therefore to find in different parts of Somerset and Cornwall, four independent ancient traditions tell that on one of his visits Joseph of Arimathæa brought the boy Jesus with him to Britain. These are summarised as follows in the Revd C.C. Dobson's book, 'Did Jesus Visit Britain as they say in Cornwall and Somerset?'.

1. The first is found in Cornwall and is recorded in Baring Gould's *"Book of Cornwall"* where he writes; "Another Cornish story to the effect that Joseph of Arimathæa came in a boat to Cornwall, and brought the boy Jesus with him ... ".

2. The second is found in Somerset of the coming of Christ and Joseph in a ship of Tarshish, and how they came to the Summerland (Somerset) and sojourned in a place called Paradise.

3. The third tradition is to be found in the little village of Priddy on the top of the Mendip Hills to the effect that Jesus and Joseph stayed there.

4. Finally, traditions associate Jesus with Glastonbury.

15.20 In connection with Paradise mentioned above, it is noteworthy that on old Ordinance Survey maps the district around Burnham in Somerset was still called Paradise. Even at Burnham today there is a Paradise Farm. The old well close to the shore of the fine natural harbour at the mouth of the River Camel (in Cornwall) at which the boat conveying Jesus might have called, is still known as Jesus Well. In bygone days it was regarded as a holy well, and traces of the Chapel erected over it remain to the present day.

15.21 There are even indications that Jesus came to Britain twice. On the

PART THREE: JESUS, THE NAZARENE

second occasion it is told that he came not as a boy but as a young man, and not as a mere visitor, but resided at Glastonbury in the Isle of Avalon for a considerable period. That Jesus built for himself a little wattle house for prayer and meditation, near a well at the foot of the hill known as Glastonbury Tor, and that it was subsequently used by Joseph of Arimathæa and his associates as a private chapel (as distinct from the church they erected beside it for public worship) is referred to in the following extract from the report which Augustine sent to Pope Gregory I (he of the Gregorian chant) during his mission to Britain at the end of the sixth century: "In the western confines of Britain there is a certain royal island of large extent surrounded by water, abounding in all the beauties of Nature and necessaries of life." Regarding this, the Revd C.C. Dobson commented; "Having been taken as a boy by Joseph on this voyage and visited Glastonbury, Jesus noticed the beauty and quiet of this island. Seeking a quiet retreat in which to spend years alone before his ministry he returned here as a young man, erected his own small abode ... and then in prayer and meditation prepared for his work". *(Did Jesus Visit Britain? pps 26-27)*. This absence of Jesus from Judah would explain the Bible's silence regarding the early manhood of Jesus.

15.22 Taliesin, the Prince-Bard and Druid, wrote *"Christ, the Word, from the beginning our Teacher and we never lost His Teaching."* To quote C.C. Dobson again *"Here is an island unconquered by the Romans, and remote from Roman influence and authority. The attempt to conquer it by Julius Caesar had proved abortive. Here was a faith propagated by profound oral teaching, enshrining the truth of the coming Christ, under the very name Jesu, and the principle of the Atonement. Do we wonder that Jesus came to reside in a land ripe to receive his truth?"* In Britain, Jesus would be free from the tyranny of Roman oppression and the superstition of Rabbinical misinterpretation and the grosser aspects of pagan idolatry, and its bestial, immoral customs. This forcefully brings to our mind the words of Jesus near the very end of his Ministry, "The Kingdom of God shall be taken from you (in Judea) and given to a nation bringing forth the fruits thereof" Matthew 21:43.

15.23 So when Joseph of Arimathæa returned to, still independent, Britain to proclaim the Gospel he was welcomed by Druids already familiar with the name Yesu. It is a remarkable fact that Druidism never opposed Christianity, and eventually became voluntarily merged into it. It is recorded that Druidic belief even named one aspect of God, Yesu! Procopius of Caesarea wrote in AD530 *'Bel, Teranis and **Yesu** – One only God – All*

Druids acknowledge one Lord God alone'. The Druids believed Yesu was the present, the sustainer and the son, and his was also the name the Druids expected to be the Messiah and healer, the curer of all ills known as the branch, and symbolised by the mistletoe. Therefore, it was claimed, many British people never had to actually change the name of their God, for they had been worshipping the same one all along.

15.24 In view of the above, we can understand why, after his expulsion from Palestine in AD35, Joseph of Arimathæa was eager to bring the Gospel to Britain and take up residence at Glastonbury already hallowed by the home of Jesus there. According to some records, Joseph lived in Britain for the remainder of his life. The Welsh poet, Maelgwyn of Llandaff (AD450) records that on Joseph of Arimathæa's grave at Glastonbury the epitaph read as follows: (Translated) "I came to Britain after I buried Christ. I taught. I rest." Serenus de Cressy (c1605 – 1674), a Benedictine monk and historian, tells us that Joseph of Arimathæa died at Glastonbury on 27 July AD82. Maelgwyn also describes the exact position of the grave with meticulous care.

15.25 Revd C.C. Dobson gives the following interesting account of Joseph's body: "The Vicar of Glastonbury tells us that Joseph's body remained buried here until 1345, when Edward III gave his licence to John Bloom of London to dig for it, and the Abbot and monks consented. There is the statement of a Lincolnshire monk in 1367 that his body was found. They placed it in a silver casket let into a stone sarcophagus, which was placed in the east end of Joseph's Chapel, and it became a place of pilgrimage. There is a written record of the sarcophagus being still in position in 1662 when the Chapel had become partially ruined. Owing to fear of Puritan fanaticism prevalent at the time it was secretly removed by night into churchyard of the Parish Church, and its identity was concealed by the pretence that the initials on it, J.A., stood for John Allen. In 1928 the present Vicar of Glastonbury found it half buried in the soil, and had it removed into the Church, and its construction bears out the accounts of a silver casket which could be raised and lowered, and shows other marks of identity."

15.26 The Cronica Sive Antiquitates Glastoniensis Ecclesie (Chronicles of the Glastonbury Church) over 500 years of records collated by a Benedictine monk, known as John of Glastonbury in the 1360's gives a record of the meeting of Joseph of Arimathæa and Arviragus, a British King: *"Joseph*

PART THREE: JESUS, THE NAZARENE

*then counselled the King to believe in Christ: King Arviragus refused this, nor did he believe in Him. Arviragus the King gave him **twice six hides at Glastonia**. Joseph left the rights with those companions in the XXXI year after the Passion of Christ. These men built a church of wattles."*

15.27 The early English historian William of Malmesbury (1080 – 1143), wrote of Joseph of Arimathæa, accompanied by eleven missionaries, came to Britain from France, having been sent by Phillip the Apostle, and that the British King gave them Ynys- vitrin (Glastonbury) and **twelve Hides of land**. Amazingly, this is confirmed in the Doomsday Book of 1086 (a recording of the assets of the English for tax purposes) which contains the following entry: *"The Church of Glastonbury has in its own rule twelve Hides of Land, which have never paid tax."* (Doomsday Survey, p.249b).

15.28 In J.W Taylor's work, *The Coming of the Saints*, the journey of Joseph of Arimathæa is followed place to place from Palestine to Marseilles, through Gaul into Britain (The Early British Church, p.9, by Rev. L.G.A. Roberts). That Joseph of Arimathæa was the first to preach the Gospel in Britain is also reported by St. Gregory, a Roman historian and Bishop of Tours (538 – 594) in his History of the Franks, and by Eleca (864 – 902) Bishop of Zaragoza in his *Fragments*.

15.29 For a long time Glastonbury ("Isle" of Avalon) was regarded as the most sacred spot in all Britain. It was widely believed that the original Church made of wattles erected by Joseph of Arimathæa and his companions was the site upon which Glastonbury Abbey was built, at the direction of King Ine of Wessex in 712. By 1086, the Doomsday Book recorded Glastonbury Abbey as the richest monastery in the country. However, it was mostly destroyed in 1539 during Henry VIII's dissolution of the monasteries. Regarding its antiquity as such, note the following extracts from the various authorities:

- Sir Henry Spelman: *"It is certain Britain received the faith in the first age from the first sowers of the Word. Of all the Churches whose origin I have investigated in Britain, the Church at Glastonbury is the most ancient".*

- Archbishop Ussher: *"The British National Church was founded AD36, 160 years before heathen Rome confessed Christianity. The Mother Church of the British Isles is the Church in Insula Avallonia, called by the Saxons, Glaston".*

- Fuller: *"If credit be given to ancient authors, this church at Glastonbury is the senior church of the world".*

15.30 Most of the most highly regarded of the early Church fathers – Tertullian (AD155 – 240); Origen (AD185 – 254); Eusebius (AD263 – 339) and Jerome (AD347 – 420) all wrote of the British Church being established by Joseph of Arimathæa in AD36 or AD37.

15.31 I conclude this section on Joseph of Arimathæa by calling your attention to what may be more than a coincidence. Matthew 15:21 and Mark 7:24 record Jesus preaching in Tyre (see 15.4 above) which was so successful that a church was founded there within two years of the crucifixion. We also find descriptions of the trade conducted by Joseph of Arimathæa – importing tin and lead from Britain using Phoenician ships which brought the metals to their port at Tyre (see 15.17 above).

The Apostle Simon Zelotes

15.32 After Joseph of Arimathæa, the next well-known missionary to Britain was Simon Zelotes, one of the twelve apostles. Dorotheus, Bishop of Tyre, AD303 wrote that Simon Zelotes went to Britain after Joseph of Arimathæa. He says Simon preached Christ all along the north coast of Africa and then crossed to Britain where he was martyred. (*Synopsis de Apostol 9*, Simon Zelotes). Nicephorus, Patriarch of Constantinople in AD758 also wrote that his martyrdom was in Britain. The Greek Orthodox Church agrees and recognizes his saint's day as May 10th, the date of his martyrdom.

15.33 Simon made at least two trips to Britain, the first in 44 and the second in 60 according to Eusebius and Cardinal Baronius. On his last trip he went into the south of Britain, an area not yet protected by Roman troops and considered dangerous. He preached fiery sermons and was arrested by a Roman Prefect Catus Deciannus (aka Caius Decius) and put to death on 10 May 61 by in the town of Caistor in Lincolnshire according to Cardinal Baronius in *Annales Ecclesiastici* quoting Vatican documents. The same information was recorded by Nicephous, Patriarch of Constantinople in 758.

15.34 Hippolytus, Bishop of Rome, writes that Simon was the first bishop in Britain. According to William Cave (1637 – 1713), Simon Zelotes preached the gospel in Egypt, Cyrene, Africa, Mauritania, and Libya. He then went to Britain and was crucified and buried there. Several early writers attest to his visit to Britain but there is some doubt that he was martyred there, with one tradition that places the tomb of Simon the Zealot in the Cimmerian Bosphorus.

Aristobulus

15.35 Aristobulus was one of the seventy Apostles (Luke 10:10) sent out to preach, according to Eusebius and Hippolytus. He is mentioned by Paul in Romans 16:10 and is identified with Zebedee, the father of the disciples James and John and the brother of Barnabus. He later became a bishop to the Celts of northern Spain and Britain and is known as the Apostle of Britain. Hippolytus (who had heard the lectures of Irenaeus who was a pupil of Polycarp, the pupil of John) writing in AD160, in the *Martyrologies* of the Greek Church states that he was chosen by Paul to take the gospel to Britain. He ministered in what is today Wales, building several churches and ordaining priests and deacons before being martyred in AD59.

15.36 The Jesuit historian Michael Alford (1587 – 1652) in volume 1 of his *Regia Fides* states, "It is perfectly certain that before St. Paul had come to Rome, Aristobulus was absent in Britain". Haleca, Bishop of Augusta also informs us as follows: "The memory of many martyrs is celebrated by the Britons, especially that of St. Aristobulus, one of the seventy disciples". "Aristobulus, Cyndav and his son, Mawan, men of Israel, came from Rome with Bran the Blessed to teach the faith of Christ to the race of the Cymry (the Welsh).

15.37 Hippolytus (170 – 235) and the records of the Orthodox Church both identify Astrobulus as introducing Christianity to Britain in AD42. Dorotheus of Tyre writing in AD303 also identified 'Aristobulus, who is mentioned in Romans 16:10, was sent by the Bishop of Tyre who appointed him as Bishop of Britain'.

15.38 The Celtic Saint Prydain in his *Genealogies of the Saints of Britain* writes Aristobulus was Paul's forerunner in Britain, sent by the apostle to the Gentiles to prepare the way for his own particular mission, which was to follow later and to be separate from Joseph of Arimathæa's work at Avalon (Glastonbury). In the early stages, Aristobulus was associated with Joseph but never attached to the group at Glastonbury. He laboured in the part of Britain now known as Wales; and the district of Arwystli in Montgomeryshire on the River Severn.

15.39 The Eastern Orthodox Church regards him as the first bishop of Britain and honours him as the Saint of the British Isles.

15.40 Ado, archbishop of Vienne (800-874), states in the *Adonis Martyrologia*, that Aristobulus was Bishop of Britain, brother of St. Barnabas the apostle, by whom he was ordained Bishop. He was sent to Britain, where after preaching the truth of Christ, and forming a church, he was martyred on 17 March AD59.

15.41 Haleca, Bishop of Augusta, wrote "The memory of many martyrs is celebrated by the Britons, especially that of Saint Aristobulus, one of the seventy disciples" *(Halecae Fragmenta in Martyrologia)*. The *Adonis Martyrologia* of St. Ado, Archbishop of Vienne in Lotharingia, under March 17 reads, "Natal day of Aristobulus, Bishop of Britain, brother of St. Barnabas the Apostle, by whom he was ordained bishop. He was sent to Britain, where, after preaching the truth of Christ and forming a Church, he received martyrdom."

The Apostle Peter

15.42 Peter was slated for execution and while in prison was miraculously delivered by an angel. After being delivered we read, "…And he departed, and went into another place" (Acts 12:17). Josephus, who lived in the early second century, wrote that in his day there was a large Jewish colony in Babylon (Ant., XV, ii, 2), descendants of the very large majority of Exiles that never returned in 538BC. This certainly explains why Peter's first epistle was written from Babylon (1 Peter 5:13).

15.43 Roman emperors seemed to regularly expel Jews from Rome: the first recorded in 139BC triggered by Jewish missionary preaching, repeated in AD19 by Tiberius. Emperor Claudius also expelled all Jews from Rome in the period AD49 to 53, as recorded by the historian Suetonius and in Acts 18:2. It has been suggested that this expulsion led to Peter travelling to Gaul, where he preached and established a church, before sailing to Britain.

15.44 While in Britain he became acquainted with the two branches of the royal Silurian house of Arviragus and Caractacus. He was taken into the home of the Pudens at the Palatium Britannicum. The visit of both Paul and Peter to the Pudens are recorded in 2 Timothy 4:21. Linus, who was ordained first Bishop of Rome, is believed to have been a Briton and the

PART THREE: JESUS, THE NAZARENE

son of Pudens and Claudia. The Pudens also had a property in Rome, at which both Peter and Paul stayed during visits to Rome. The importance of the Puden family to the early church is reflected by the Roman basilica of Santa Pudenziana, built in the 4th century dedicated to Saint Pudentiana, sister of Saint Praxedis and daughter of Saint Pudens.

15.45 The Venerable Bede wrote of a *"British king, Lucius"*, writing to Pope Eleutherus in AD171 requesting instruction in the Christian faith. Lucius is thought to have been born in Wales and achieving fame in supporting Christianity within Roman realms he died in Chur (CH) and was later sanctified. Lucius may have been a local leader in Wales but there is no record of him as a British king. However, there are references to Lucius building a church in AD179 at Cornhill, London, and dedicating it to St. Peter in commemoration of his evangelizing work in Britain. The London historian John Stow, writing at the end of the 16th century, reported *"there remaineth in this church a tablet whereon is written,...that King Lucius founded the same church to be an archbishop's see and chief church of his kingdom"*. The tablet seen by Stow was destroyed when the medieval church was burnt in the Great Fire of 1666 but not before a number of writers had recorded what it said: *"Be hit known to al men, that the yeerys of our Lord God anno clxxix [AD 179]. Lucius the fyrst christen kyng of this land, then callyd Brytayne, foundyd the fyrst chyrch in London, that is to sey, the Chyrch of Sent Peter apon Cornhyl, and he foundyd ther an Archbishoppys See, and made that Chyrch the Metropolitant, and cheef Chyrch of this kingdom."* Rebuilt after the Great Fire by Sir Christopher Wren, the church is still named 'St Peter upon Cornhill'.

15.46 Another indication that Peter was in Britain may be found at Whithorn, in Galloway in the Scottish Borders. A stone 4 feet high, 15 inches wide with the Latin inscription "Locvs Sancti Petri Apvstoli" (The place of Peter the Apostle) has been excavated there.

15.47 Tradition says Peter made several visits to Briton and Gaul, including one shortly before his death. Simeon Metaphrastes (c900 – c984) a Greek historian of the Byzantine Church, wrote that Peter not only travelled in the western parts of the Mediterranean, but spent a long time in Britain where he converted many to the faith.

The Apostle Andrew

15.48 Andrew is traditionally linked to Scotland and is said to have preached there. I did not find any credible conjecture to support this, however he is the patron saint of Scotland. In addition, Andrew has been identified in Scythia, near the Black Sea, as well as in Greece or Macedonia, and Asia Minor. Another tradition places him in the foothills of the Caucasus Mountains where he preached to the Scythians, even as far as the Caspian Sea.

Paul

15.49 Paul's commission included preaching to the Gentiles, to kings, and to the children of Israel (Acts 9:15). Paul tells us in the book of Romans that he intended to go to Spain (Romans 15:28). "So, after I have completed this task and have made sure that they have received this fruit, I will go to Spain and visit you on the way". But he was imprisoned (house arrest) and prevented from visiting Spain at that time.

15.50 The question arises why Spain? Because there were colonies of Jews living there, some were slaves and others had been imprisoned by Herod Antipas.

15.51 Bede and other early historians say Paul was sent to Rome in AD56 and at some stage spent two years under house arrest. But the years from AD61 to AD65 are unaccounted for in Paul's life. Eusebius, John Chrysostom and Jerome all write that Paul went to Spain after being released from his house arrest. The Muratorian Fragment, the earliest known list of canon dating from around AD175, states that Paul had journeyed to Spain (v39). Jerome wrote: "Paul was dismissed by Nero, that he might preach Christ's gospels in the west". Jerome explained that "at this time Nero's wickedness had not yet broken forth". Paul was put to death in the 14th year of Nero reign.

15.52 Clement, the third bishop of Rome (himself a disciple of Paul), also states that Paul visited Spain and that he went to the extremities of the west of the Roman empire to preach the gospel there just before his martyrdom. Theodoret (393 – 457), bishop of Cyprus, wrote, "Paul, liberated from his first captivity at Rome, preached the gospel to the Britons and others in the West. Our fishermen and publicans not only persuaded the Romans and their tributaries to acknowledge the Crucified and His laws, but the Britons also and the Cymry." *(De Curandis Graecorum Affectionibus Lib.IX)*. Clement of Rome wrote that Paul went to the utmost bounds of the West. **Irenæus, Tertullian, Origen, Eusebius and Athanasius all confirm that Paul preached in Britain** – a hugely important endorsement that is impossible to ignore. In his *History of the Apostles*, Capellus wrote, "I scarcely know of one author, from the times of the Fathers downwards, who does not maintain that Paul, after his liberation, preached in every country in Western Europe, Britain included".

15.53 Bishop Burgess writing his *History of the Apostles*: in the early 19th century "Of St. Paul's journey to Britain we have as satisfactory proof as any historical question can demand." Tradition says he resided in Siluria, South Wales and preached as far north as the banks of the River Clyde according to the "Triads of Paul the Apostle" handed down in ancient Welsh.

15.54 The *'Sonnini Document'*, is a manuscript purporting to be Acts chapter 29, written in Greek and discovered by D.S. Sonnini, in Constantinople in the time of Louis XVI and published in London in 1801. The part that deals with Paul's visit reads as follows: "And having departed out of Spain, Paul and his company found a ship in Armorica (Brittany) sailing to Britain, and went therein, and passing along the south coast they reached a port called Raphinus (the Roman name for Sandwich, Kent). Now when it was noised abroad that the apostle had landed on their coast, great multitudes of the inhabitants met him, and they treated Paul courteously and he entered in at the east gate of their city (i.e. London) and lodged in the house of a Hebrew and one of his own nation. And on the morrow he came and stood on Mount Lud (now Ludgate Hill, upon which stands St. Paul's Cathedral) and the people thronged at the gate, and assembled in the Broadway, and he preached Christ unto them, and many believed the word and the testimony of Jesus." The manuscript also records a meeting with some of the druid priests who showed him some of their rites which they maintained were descended from the Jews.

15.55 The names of a British prince and princess who had become Christians, are mentioned in the New Testament by Paul in 2 Timothy 4:21. *"Do your best to get here before winter. Eubulus greets you, and so do Pudens, Linus, Claudia and all the brothers"*. Pudens was a Roman noble and son of a Roman Senator and Claudia was his wife according to Tacitus. At the time that verse was written all three of them were living in Rome. Pudens has the distinction of being the only name mentioned in the Bible known to be from Britain. Their son, Linus, was subsequently installed by Paul as the first bishop of Rome (according to Eusebius and Iraeneus, it was Linus, not Peter, who was the first bishop of Rome).

15.56 There are a couple of interesting inscriptions on stones that have been found. The first was a stone found among Roman remains at Chichester in 1723. The stone is on exhibit outside the Council House at Chichester. Pudens is mentioned in connection with the erection of a Roman Temple. He had been stationed there while a Roman soldier and this was before his conversion to Christianity. He married Claudia, daughter of Claudius Cogidunus (or Caractacus) a British King in AD53 in Rome. The names Pudens, Claudia and Cogidunus are also all mentioned in an epigram written at Rome by Marital. Martial writes of his friend Pudens: "Oh Rufus, my friend Pudens marries the foreigner Claudia" and "Claudia Rufina has sprung from the azure Britons". He also says Linus was their son, the same Linus that was installed as the first bishop of Rome by Paul.

15.57 The second is an inscription on a memorial on the church of St. Pudens in Britain. It was written following the execution of Praxedes in the 2nd century, who was the last surviving member of the original Christian family of Claudia and Pudens. "In this sacred and most ancient of churches, known as that of Pastor (Hermas), dedicated by St. Paul, formerly the house of Sancus Pudens, the Senator, and the home of the holy apostles, repose the remains of three thousand blessed martyrs which Pudentiana and Praxedes, virgins of Christ, with their own hands interred". Interred here was the last surviving child of Pudens and Claudia.

15.58 It is believed that Paul spent his last house arrest in the house of Pudens in Rome *(International Standard Bible Encyclopedia)*.

15.59 Several prominent Roman Catholic historians have admitted Paul was in Spain and Britain, including Cardinal Baronius and historian Mary Sharp who writes that Paul's ministry was recorded by Luke in Acts, except for his ministry to Spain, which is alluded to by Clement and recorded in the Muratori fragment. Mary Sharp also notes that Paul's martyrdom outside the Ostian Gate, shortly after his return to Rome, occurred on the same day Peter was martyred.

15.60 But perhaps the one of the most compelling evidences that Paul was in Britain comes from a pope. Pope Pius XI said in a speech to English Catholics that it was not Pope Gregory, but St. Paul himself who first introduced Christianity into Britain. An article in the London Morning

PART THREE: JESUS, THE NAZARENE

Post of 27 March 1931 reads: "The Mayors of Bath, Colchester, and Dorchester, and the 150 visiting members of the Friends of Italy Society, were today received in special audience by the Pope. His holiness, in a specially prepared address, advanced the theory that it was St. Paul himself and not Pope Gregory, who first introduced Christianity into Britain."

15.61   The *'Sonnini Document'* referred to in 15.54 above, appearing to be a 29th chapter of Acts is obviously a late addition but is at least in part based upon understanding at the time it was written, maybe 4th or 5th Century. It provides supporting evidence of Paul's travels and may have helped trigger speculation concerning some Lost Tribes migrating to Britain. The additional chapter includes: *"And Paul, full of the blessings of Christ, and abounding in the spirit, departed out of Rome, determining to go into Spain; for he had a long time purposed to journey there, and he was minded to go from thence into Britain. For he had heard in Phoenicia that certain of the children of Israel, about the time of the Assyrian captivity, had escaped by sea to the 'isles afar off' as spoken by the prophet, and called by the Romans: Britain. And the Lord has commanded the gospel to be preached far hence to the Gentiles, and to the lost sheep of the House of Israel".*

15.62   Bede, in his *Ecclesiastical History of the English Nation*, said that in AD 665 Pope Vitalian sent the relics of Peter and Paul to Oswy, King of Britain.

Other references to very early Apostolic visits

15.63   Even as early as the second century AD, Tertullian wrote that the extremities of Spain, parts of Gaul, and the regions of Britain which had never been penetrated by Roman arms (i.e. Ireland, most of Scotland and much of north Wales) had already received the religion of Christ.

15.64   The church historian Eusebius (AD265-340) no less, said, "The Apostles passed beyond the ocean to the isles called the Britannic Isles." Delegates from the British church participated in all the earliest church Councils, being present at Elvira (AD300), Arles (AD314), Nicaea (AD325) and Rimini (AD359).

15.65   In AD402, John Chrysostam, Patriarch of Constantinople, wrote that throughout British Isles "you hear men everywhere discoursing matters out of the Scriptures".

15.66   The British historian Gildas (AD516-570) recounts the oldest British record of life under the Romans in his work *'De Excidio et Conquestu Britanniae'* providing the only substantial source for history of this period written by a near-contemporary. Gildas wrote that Christianity was introduced into Britain in AD38, during the last year of the reign of Tiberius Caesar. The date of AD38 corroborates other references to the arrival of Joseph of Arimathæa that year.

15.67   Augustine was sent to Britain by Pope Gregory I in AD595 to establish the Catholic Church and appointed the first Archbishop of Canterbury in AD597. When Augustine came to convert the pagan Saxons, the British Churches refused to accept him. Their argument was that they could not depart from their ancient (Nazarene) customs. His conversion work was directed at the Angles and Saxons, after these had killed many of the British Christians (Frederick Haberman, *Tracing our Ancestors* p142). The history of the flourishing Celtic Church was buried under the waves of heathen Saxons, Danes and Romanised Norman influence.

15.68   The Synod of Whitby, in 664, sought to reform churches across Britain to conform to Roman dogma. However, prolonged resistance to change continued for the next 400 years, particularly in Ireland and was only eradicated under the Norman kings following their successful invasion of England in 1066.

15.69   The Venerable Bede (670-735) wrote, "The Britons preserved the faith which they had received, uncorrupted and entire, in peace and tranquility until the time of the Emperor Diocletian" (*Bede, History of the English Church and People*, bk. 1, chap., 4).

15.70   Freculphus, the French bishop of Lisieux from 823 to 850, in his *Twelve Books of Histories* wrote that Philip sent Joseph of Arimathæa and his companions to England from France, and that they landed in Glastonbury.

15.71   The tradition of Church Councils repeatedly affirms that, surprisingly, Britain was almost the first country to receive the gospel in Europe, the British Church being the most ancient. The Council of Pisa (1409) recorded an argument during the council that the churches in France and Spain must yield precedent to the British Church because Joseph of Arimathæa founded the British Church not long after the crucifixion of Jesus. The Councils of Constance (1414), Sienna (1424), and Basle (1434) upheld this view. Since the British Church was founded more than 550 years before the time of Augustine, British pre-eminence was taken for granted until 1409. The Council of Pisa had been convened by concerned cardinals and bishops seeking to resolve the 'Great Schism' under which two competing Popes based in Avignon and Rome were recognized by different national churches. Both Popes were considered unworthy and both widely regarded as greedy and obstinate monarchists blocking calls both for unity and reform. The Council elected a new Pope, Alexander V, who eventually succeeded in reuniting the two church bureaucracies in Rome. Recognition of the precedence of the British Church may also have been related to its support for Rome during the schism whilst France and Spain supported Avignon.

15.72 In 1558, Cardinal Pole (the last Roman Catholic Archbishop of Canterbury) in his address to Philip and Mary (King Phillip II of Spain and Mary, Queen of England), stated that Britain was first of all the countries in Europe to receive the Christian faith.

15.73 Cardinal Baronius (1538-1607), the distinguished Catholic scholar and curator of the Vatican library, wrote (possibly using sources unavailable to the rest of us) in his *Ecclesiastical Annuls* that Joseph of Arimathæa, along with others, was exiled in AD36. After preaching the gospel in Marseilles, he and his companions went to England.

15.74 So, claims that Christianity was introduced into England by Augustine refer only to Latin rites. The record shows fierce independence from Rome continued for many centuries. The Celtic Church in Ireland denied Roman bishops had authority anywhere outside the Roman Empire. There are no extant facts to support the idea that St. Patrick visited or represented Rome. Nowhere in his writings does he refer to Rome. As late as AD634, the Churches in Ireland and northern England were independent of the churches on the continent that were subject to the bishoprics within the Roman Empire. Not until Ireland was partly conquered by Henry II of England (1154-1189) was the Celtic Church forced to be subject to Rome.

15.75 In conclusion, I suggest that whilst quite a few of the references in this chapter represent over-enthusiastic patriotic wishful thinking – there remains sufficient authoritative evidence that many of those identified as preaching in Britain in the first century really did so. The reports that Augustine made back to Pope Gregory during his mission in the years following AD595 probably made difficult reading for the Vatican. The likelihood that Britain had received so much early apostolic attention – focused on the teachings of the Nazarene Church – would have been a very inconvenient truth. It seems to have taken another 500 years until Henry II's reign to secure Roman dogma through control of the appointment of Catholic bishops. That key elements of the evidence above comes from the Vatican archives, courtesy of Cardinal Baronius, together with the endorsement of Pope Pius XI, add considerable weight to the argument.

16

Evidence of the split between Nazarene and Pauline theology

16.1 The split between the original Jerusalem Church, initially led by James (from the crucifixion in AD33 until his martyrdom cAD62), and Paul grew out of doctrinal differences. These arose as Paul developed his theology increasingly separate from Judaic beliefs as he sought to convert Gentiles, and some echo of this can be found in Paul's epistles and also in the writings of early Church leaders. The Nazarene Church wrote to the Corinthians telling them to ask Paul for written proof of his backing by the Christian leaders, which has been preserved in 4.35 of the Recognitions of Clement (3rd bishop of Rome) *"Wherefore observe the greatest caution, that you believe no teacher, unless he bring from Jerusalem the testimony of James, the Lord's brother, or of whomever may come after him. For no one, unless he has gone up thither, and there has been approved as a fit and faithful teacher for preaching the word of Christ – unless, I say, he brings a testimonial thence, is by any means to be received. But let neither prophet nor apostle be looked for by you at this time, besides us."* And, from 11.35 of the Homilies of Clement: *"Wherefore, above all, remember to shun apostle or teacher or prophet who does not first accurately compare his preaching with that of James who is the brother of my Lord, and to whom was entrusted the administration of the Church of the Hebrews in Jerusalem".*

16.2 The seriousness of the split is partly disguised as we only have one side of the argument preserved in the NT texts – in Acts, written by Paul's friend Luke and in Paul's own writing. Paul either fails to see James objectives or refuses to cooperate. In 2 Corinthians 11:3-4, Paul states explicitly that Nazarene emissaries of James are promulgating *"another Jesus"*, a different Jesus from the one he is promoting. For Paul, instead of trying to make converts to Judaism, he preaches that what matters is simply a profession of faith in Jesus as a divinity sent by God – which is all that is required for salvation. The basic requirements of Judaism – the observance of the laws set out in the Torah, particularly circumcision and adherence to the dietary laws are abandoned. Jesus, James and the Nazarenes in Jerusalem advocated worship of God, in the Judaic sense, Paul replaces this with worship of Jesus as a God, distinct from the Father. This substitution was regarded as blasphemous by the Nazarenes.

16.3 Arguably, one of the best sources for discerning Jesus original teaching must be the foundation document (referred to by scholars as 'Q') which it is believed to be one of the sources used by each of the writers of the Synoptic gospels. Early Church fathers referred to a text of Jesus teaching written by Matthew in Hebrew – this could have been written by Matthew (one of the original 12) and suggests a first hand and therefore authoritative account of Jesus actions and sermons. All the gospels are dated long after Jesus life, the earliest is believed to be Mark which, because of key references, many date to AD68 or 69. Crucially, Mark makes no reference to a miraculous birth and no attempt at Jesus genealogy. Only with the Roman destruction of the Temple in AD70, burning all the detailed records of Jewish family genealogies, did it become necessary to try to justify Jesus lineage. Most scholars believe Matthew and Luke were written between AD70 and AD90, drawing upon surviving oral tradition to draw up blatantly fabricated genealogies of Jesus. Moreover, none of the synoptic gospels were written by authors with first-hand knowledge of Jesus.

16.4 As set out in Chapter 10 above, there is evidence in the recorded statements of Jesus that he pretty much rejected every tenet of Judaism except the idea that there is a Creator. God is neither singular nor plural to Jesus but an omnipresent Spirit who can dwell in each of us.

16.5 Although probably brought up in strict accordance with tenets of the Jewish faith, Jesus teaching clearly shows that he had no loyalty to Judaism. His key rule – to love God and treat everyone as you would wish them to treat you – is universal.

16.6 Whilst we can discern a big gulf between Judaism and Jesus new teaching, his own immediate followers did not seem to. The Nazarene churches and the planted churches along the Atlantic littoral and across the

EVIDENCE OF THE SPLIT BETWEEN NAZARENE AND PAULINE THEOLOGY

Fertile Crescent and into India – all tended to retain many aspects of Judaism – the Sabbath on a Saturday, circumcision, the food and hygiene laws if not the full mitzvot and some retained animal sacrifices. It is almost as though the Nazarenes seemed to 'add' Jesus to Judaism.

16.7 Then Paul, at least 15 years after his conversion according to the consensus dating of his Letters, started to dramatically change the view of Jesus. Whilst not picking up the embellishments of the synoptic gospels – his admonition of fake genealogies (1 Timothy 1:4) shows he was aware of some circulating texts. Paul begun to radically call into question core beliefs of Judaism – being a member of the Chosen People would not save you; adherence to the Mosaic laws only identified your sins and could not lead to your salvation. During his missionary work, Paul moved progressively against circumcision, from arranging it for Timothy (in Acts) through ambivalence (Corinthians and Romans) to rejection (Galatians) and thence to outright condemnation (Philippians). [For more detail please refer to paragraphs 10.19-21 above] Paul's warning to congregations he wrote to ended by saying those who underwent circumcision cut themselves off from Christ and these people would then be denied grace – i.e. unsaved and condemned to everlasting damnation. That is quite a journey!! Paul's journey regarding circumcision would have progressively widened the gap between his teaching and the beliefs of the Nazarene church in Jerusalem. What drove the 180 degree change in Paul's position – was it divine revelation (unlikely as surely it would not change progressively but abruptly) or accommodation of Greek cultural sensitivities? Indeed, this recorded 'evolution' of Paul's views on circumcision, as embedded in canonised texts, would seem to be inexplicable for those who claim biblical inerrancy.

16.8 Some explanation for Paul's changing views may be gleaned from non-biblical sources. Epiphanius (AD310-403), Bishop of Salamis, quotes in his Panarion from Ebionite texts (now lost). The Ebionites, an early Jewish Christian sect, were vegetarian and rejected animal sacrifice, they were scattered by the Roman-Jewish war of AD66-70 but some groups survived until the 3rd and 4th Centuries. The quotations referred to by Epiphanius comprise almost our entire record of a text referred to as the Gospel of the Ebionites but we have no evidence what its title actually was. The text appears to have contained a blend of material also in the gospels of Matthew and Luke as well as other material. The Ebionites denounced Paul for preaching a distortion of Jesus teaching.

16.9   The Ebionites told of Paul travelling to Jerusalem and spending some years there studying under Gamaliel, the president of the Sanhedrin. During this period he fell in love with the daughter of the High Priest, which spurred Paul to study and gain a position in the Sanhedrin, initially as a Sadducee and later as a Pharisee. The Sadducees were religious conservatives, they tended to be more wealthy and most high priests were Sadducees. The Sadducees kept strictly to the written law, the Torah and the long held Jewish belief that the soul was lost forever at death, passing into the darkness of Sheol. The Pharisees, more working class, accepted oral tradition and interpretations of the Torah and critically the acceptance of the novel Persian idea of resurrection. In AD57, in his trial before the Sanhedrin chaired by High Priest Ananias ben Nedebeus (per Josephus), Paul exploited his knowledge of the opposing views concerning the destiny of the soul and its resurrection to sow discord amongst his accusers (Acts 23:6-8).

16.10 According to the Ebionites, Paul became so infatuated with the daughter of the High Priest that he had himself circumcised, a painful operation for an adult – but still the lady rejected him as not being born Jewish. According to Epiphanius, *"Paul flew into a rage and wrote against circumcision and against the Sabbath and the whole Jewish Law"* – looking back from the 4th Century, this description probably telescoped Paul's journey from a decade into a sudden event. In Paul's mind he may have felt he went through a very painful surgery for nothing. Being rejected would have given Paul a reason to hate Jews and women. After being rejected by his daughter, Paul then found employment in the service of the High Priest as a police informer and enforcer" – in which role he journeyed towards 'Damascus' and underwent another conversion.

16.11 One has to wonder whether Paul's series of successive conversions represented divine inspiration or opportunism? Other sources inform us that 'Paul of Tarsus' was the son of a wealthy tent manufacturer based in Tarsus (on the south coast of modern Turkey) who supplied tents to the Roman legions. Paul's father was a social climber, he had become wealthy enough to purchase Roman citizenship. This may have shaped Paul's outlook, as a wealthy young man he decided to travel. To be appointed to the Sanhedrin, Paul must have been an expert in the Torah – learning that Acts describes that he acquired from Gamaliel, recognised as the foremost teacher of the time. Jewish references indicate that Gamaliel was a Pharisee and Acts refers to Paul as being a Pharisee. If

Paul had entered the Sanhedrin initially as a Sadducee, it may have reflected his wealth and self-esteem, and possibly, to please the High Priest whose daughter he sought.

16.12 Epiphanius quotations from the Ebionite writing provides a good explanation for the fixations we find in Paul's epistles. Paul's painful experience undertaken to win the priest's daughter seems to have pitted him against circumcision and women in general. Paul promoted chastity but if a man was unable to control himself then he should take a wife merely to avoid sin. In 1Corinthians 7:1, Paul wrote: "It is good for a man not to touch a woman". He continues: "For I would that all men were even as myself… It is good for them if they abide even as I" – alluding to himself being unmarried. Paul sees marriage as a last result "But if they cannot contain, let them marry, for it is better to marry than burn" (in hell because of sinful lust). Paul and two of his disciples, Thecla and Titus, also wrote texts urging Christians to refrain from sex completely, remain unmarried and abstain from sexual relations if already married. Marcion preached chastity and despite the obvious results managed to sustain a substantial following for many centuries. Sextus even promoted self-castration whilst the Roman church adopted chastity for the priesthood at Nicaea.

16.13 Paul was so negative about women that he made up his own laws: "the wife is bound by the law as long as her husband lives" (1Corinthians 7:39). This contradicts Jewish law which permits a man to grant his wife a divorce after which she is free to remarry – Deuteronomy 24:1-2. Paul describes the purpose of marriage in terms equivalent to legalising rape, his description being focused on conjugal rights:- "The wife does not have authority over her own body but yields it to her husband" (1Corinthians 7:4) which in Paul's legalistic style goes on to repeat the same obligation for husbands. Wives may only deprive their husbands by mutual consent but only for a short time and in order to pray! Like Paul, many other church fathers showed a hostility to women – Tertullian, a 3rd Century author in Carthage, insisted on the renunciation of marriage, since it was based on the same act as harlotry. Tertullian also called women the "gate through which the devil enters man".

16.14 Circumcision seems to prey on Paul's mind, he makes frequent references to it in his epistles. According to Strong's New Exhaustive Concordance of the Bible, Paul makes no less than 40 references to circumcision (Romans 16 times; Galatians 13 times; Colossians 4 times; 1 Corinthians

3 times; Philippians twice and once each in Ephesians and Titus) whilst Acts refers to circumcision in relation to Paul nine times. Was Paul's obsession and the curse he said he laboured under linked with persistent pain from a botched circumcision? In 2 Corinthians 12:7-8, Paul writes that "I was given a thorn in my flesh, a messenger of Satan, to torment me. Three times I pleaded with the Lord to take it away from me."

16.15 Originally Paul embraced Judaism so fervently that he took up employment to track down and persecute Jewish Christians. But in his epistles Paul is frequently dismissive of the Torah:

- The Torah provides knowledge of what is sinful, Romans 3:20;

- Jesus death releases Christians from following the laws of the Torah and allows them to follow his teaching, which Paul illustrates by death allowing a widow to marry again, Romans 7:1-4;

- Jesus represents the fulfilment and therefore the end of the Torah, Romans 10:4;

- No one can fulfil the laws of the Torah, therefore none are righteous before God – but Jesus has redeemed us from the Law and faith in Jesus redeems us, Galatians 3:11-13;

- Paul warns his audience: if you allow circumcision, Jesus is of no value to you, you cut yourself off from grace. If you agree to circumcision you are committed to obey the whole Torah and grace from Jesus will not be available to you, Galatians 5:2-4.

16.16 Paul's 'invention' of original sin instigated another major departure from the beliefs of Judaism and the teaching of Jesus. In Judaism there is no original sin which Adam's descendants either inherit or are enslaved by. In Genesis 4:6-7, God tells Cain *"If you do what is right, will you not be accepted? But if you do not do what is right, sin is crouching at your door; it desires to have you,* **but you must rule over it**.*"* Moses tells the Israelites that *"what I am commanding you today is not too difficult for you or beyond your reach. It is not up in heaven, so that you have to ask, "Who will ascend into heaven to get it and proclaim it to us so we may obey it?" Nor is it beyond the sea, so that you have to ask, "Who will cross the sea to get it and proclaim it to us so we may obey it?"* **No, the word is very near you; it is in your mouth and in your heart so you may obey it.** (Deuteronomy 30:11-16). Despite his first rate training and expert knowledge of the Torah, Paul starts to teach that mankind inherited sin from Adam and is unable to control it, leading inexorably to everlasting damnation unless one accepts salvation offering through belief in Jesus. Paul even supports his new concept by quoting a clip from Deuteronomy (in Romans 10:8) but cutting off the end of the verses quoted above which contradicts his assertion.

16.17 Something that always puzzled me, is the apparent absence of early contemporary writings capturing Jesus teaching. After all, the Jews were one of the more literate peoples and many thousands directly heard Jesus teaching. Surely, to hear Jesus live, speaking to you, must have been electrifying. Regardless of his physical stature (Jesus may not have been a handsome 1m90 tanned blonde with piercing blue eyes), but his voice must have conveyed deep wisdom, sincerity and authority – those who heard, believed and followed would surely want to capture his teaching by recording his stunning and revolutionary truths. The Logia or Q manuscript may have been a collection of these early sayings. As identified, the earliest reference to a work by Matthew referred to it being a collection of the Lord's sayings written in Hebrew. Such writings would have passed around the early Nazarene Church, and after Paul's conversion he must have read some. Surely, these must have influenced Paul – but what happened to these writings?

16.18 We know from official Catholic records that there were originally at least 50 different non-canonical early Christian texts in circulation. Caches of manuscripts found in the past century mean the number of long lost texts we know of is at least 118 (see Part Four, a listing is downloadable from the website for this series www.truthpublications.co.uk). These texts were progressively banned by Church Councils starting with the Council of Nicaea in 325. From this time, the Church devoted huge resources to seizing and burning all copies of every condemned text. Such behaviour indicates the earlier writings contradicted the Roman dogma invented under Constantine, who chaired the Council of Nicaea – and the brutality with which the original beliefs were eradicated points to great fear on the part of the usurpers.

16.19 Paul's theological journey was most probably influenced by what he read of Jesus teaching in texts no longer available to us. Paul's epistles record his progressive abandonment of Judaic beliefs. Early in his ministry, Paul writes of circumcising his assistant but by the end he is decrying circum-

PART THREE: JESUS, THE NAZARENE

cision as a depraved practice, jettisoning the food purity laws and moving not only to eating anything, but abandoning kosher and approving the consumption of meat offered to idols. This becomes even more stark if it is accepted that Jesus promoted vegetarianism – some say that Jesus action against the money changers in the Temple was aimed at preventing sacrifices of the creatures purchased with the money exchanged. We have 4th Century descriptions by Church fathers Epipanius and Jerome of the 'heretical' beliefs of Nazarenes and Nestorians which include their being vegetarians (see 10.4 above); and of the Nazarene Cathars surviving to the 12th Century along the Pyrenees who were vegetarian because they believed animals had souls. Thus, whilst many who joined Jesus original church became vegetarian, Paul promoted consumption – even of meat dedicated to pagan gods. The Theological School of Antioch founded circa AD200, and which flourished until AD489, was a major centre of Nazarene theology – teaching that Jesus was a man who became God, not as God who became man, being the Son of God not by birth but through adoption by God.

16.20 Paul's view was that the Jews had been chosen and given the Torah but had simply failed to obey the rules. Thus, it is ironic that whilst Jesus direct followers clung on to most aspects of Judaism despite Jesus clear teaching, Paul managed to understand Jesus more fully and swept away the Torah for those who chose to become Christians.

16.21 What is also strange, given that Paul faithfully follows Jesus rejection of the tenets of Judaism, is the fact that in his writings, Paul makes only two indirect references to Jesus. Paul never directly quotes Jesus and never makes any reference to Jesus life or actions on Earth. Paul makes only three references to 'the Lord' which might be attributed to Jesus – two are also quoted in Luke and John, which suggests these were assembled from circulating documents written earlier. First, in 1 Corinthians, Paul quotes Jesus from the last supper, using Luke's version. Second, Paul in 1 Corinthians 8:6 says *'for us, there is but one God, the Father, from whom all things came and one Lord Jesus Christ,'* which is very close to Jesus' prayer to the 'Father' in John 17:3, *'And this is life eternal, that they might know thee the only true God, and Jesus Christ, whom thou hast sent.'* The only unique reference is hotly debated over whether it can really be attributable to Jesus – in 2 Corinthians 12:7, Paul refers to the 'Lord' refusing to release him from a demonic 'Angel of Satan', with this 'Lord' supposedly explaining the reason was that *'my grace is sufficient for thee.'* It is hard to believe Paul meant

Jesus spoke this refusal, because why would Jesus leave Paul subject to an 'Angel of Satan'? Christian scholars acknowledge this dilemma if we attribute this quote to Jesus: This verse can be read as "Paul's apostolic mission is cast under suspicion." (C. Fred Dickason, *Demon Possession and the Christian*; Crossway, 1989, p120). Likewise, David Barr relates that "12:7 is *notoriously difficult*, prompting Barrett to write *'it can hardly be in the form Paul intended it…*" (David L. Barr, *The Reality of the Apocalypse*; Society of Biblical Literature, 2006.)

16.22 So far, it seems like Paul's teaching was more faithful to Jesus views than his own Nazarene followers. However, that was only part of what Paul changed.

16.23 The most fundamental change was Paul's elevation of Jesus from a Messiah, blessed by God to a Deity himself, granted full authority by God over humanity. This is consistent with John, generally believed to have been written a few decades after Paul's death, categorising Jesus as The Word, the intermediary created by God to convey God's word to mankind. However, Paul never made Jesus equal to God nor made any reference to a Trinity. The Trinity came later as the Alexandrian school, influenced by earlier Trinities of Egyptian and Babylonian gods, made common cause with Emperor Constantine.

16.24 In 1 Timothy 6:14-16 Paul writes "keep this command… until the future appearance of our Lord Jesus, which God will bring about in his own time…*(God)…whom no one has seen, or can see*". From this it is clear that Paul does not believe Jesus is God, exactly in line with how Jesus always described himself. As subordinate to God the Creator, he frequently prayed to God, he claimed authority from God but he never claimed to be God himself or to be part of God.

16.25 Paul's second epistle to Timothy in 3:16 states "All Scripture is God-breathed and is useful for teaching, rebuking, correcting and training in righteousness". Paul being a pedantic lawyer and an enthusiastic Christian clearly exaggerates, worse his statement is always taken out of context. For Paul, a learned Pharisee, 'Scripture' meant the Torah and the Prophets it did not include the Writings (such as Daniel) and of course did not refer to any of the New Testament – which did not exist at this time (only Acts and Paul's letters had been written. Whilst Acts states it is written by Luke, there are many who doubt that it was the Luke who authored the gospel). Surprisingly, Paul is saying all of the Torah and the Prophets is 'God-breathed' – despite it being full of serious errors!! As just noted in 16.15, Paul also repeats Jesus statement that **"no one has seen God"** (i.e. neither Adam, Enoch, Noah, Abraham, Elijah – *nor anyone that met Jesus*). So here Paul clearly contradicts what he wrote in Timothy 3:16 by stating that the Torah contains many errors. Jesus had also stated that no man has been to heaven and circumcision is not commanded by God – to Jews these were huge claims. So, Paul may have been exaggerating to make a point. Perhaps Paul should have used *"Some"* instead of *"All"* scripture – unwittingly Paul may be responsible for creating the 'Inerrants'. It is also possible that Paul did not write Timothy 3.16 – modern scholars ascribe both of the letters to Timothy and the letter to Titus as written posthumously in the style of Paul – up to 100 years after his death.

16.26 For many of Jesus followers, his death did not lead to the expected end times or cataclysmic disaster – so what were they waiting for, a second coming? Paul developed a new paradigm of a spiritual world where Jesus was preparing a dwelling for his faithful followers whilst his messianic mission was transmuted from an earthly kingdom to a heavenly kingdom.

16.27 Through Paul, begins the transformation of Jesus teaching into an altogether different religion, firstly promoting Jesus to divinity; followed by John explaining Jesus was the embodiment of one of the Greek concepts of the Creator, the Logos (the Word). Then, another two centuries later, Emperor Constantine orchestrated the Council of Nicaea to manoeuvre himself into becoming a Messiah and progressively adorning Christian dogma with an array of pagan beliefs from the cult of Sol Invictus.

16.28 The divergence of Paul from the original teaching of Jesus is shown clearly in one of his earliest epistles – that addressed to the Galatians. Most academic theologians date the epistle to the Galatians as chronologically very early, being either the 1st or 2nd epistle and dating to around 48 or 49. The Galatians occupied a central area in modern Turkey, the area around Ankara. They were descendants of Celtic tribes who had moved eastwards into the area and had adopted Greek culture, the name Galatia deriving from the Roman name for the Celts – as in Gaul.

16.29 As the Roman domains spread north out of Italy in the centuries prior to Jesus, they encountered Celtic peoples right across central Europe – from

EVIDENCE OF THE SPLIT BETWEEN NAZARENE AND PAULINE THEOLOGY

the British Isles and Spain across France, Switzerland, Austria, Hungary and Romania – and the few tribes that had migrated into central Turkey whom they called the Galatians.

16.30 Focusing back on Paul, the first point to note is that, at the time Paul wrote, none of the books that made it into the New Testament had been written. This was certainly not because no one thought Jesus teaching was worth writing about but because all such writings were later destroyed by the Roman church. A number of these were discovered for the first time in the Nag Hammadi cache discovered in 1945.

16.31 The first chapter of Paul's Epistle to the Galatians brings out three key points:

- Paul acknowledges his gospel message differs significantly from the others that people are hearing and which Paul denigrates in no uncertain terms (Galatians 1:6-9). Paul's message was almost the only one to survive – it would have been far more informative for us to be able to study all the other gospels written by those apostles who travelled with Jesus on his ministry rather than be left with gospels written mainly by those who never met Jesus (this is examined in more detail in Part Four);

- Paul introduces the idea of bodily resurrection to Christianity. This originated as a Zoroastrian belief, spread during the Persian empire and gained traction in Judea during the Maccabean period (the Hasmonean dynasty ruling from 167BC to 37BC). It was refuted by the Sadducees but adopted as a doctrine by the Pharisees, of whom Paul had been a member (Galatians 1:1). None of the early texts we have recovered, that were in circulation when Paul wrote to the Galatians, refer to Jesus bodily resurrection – including the Gospels of the Ebionites, According to the Hebrews, According to the Egyptians and of Thomas;

- Paul's arrogance in explaining that he had spent years in Arabia, far away from anyone who had accompanied Jesus during his ministry, in developing his gospel message. He explained that, only after three years of study and development, had he bothered to go to meet James (appointed by Jesus as head of his church) and Peter (Galatians 1:17).

PART THREE: JESUS, THE NAZARENE

16.32 From Galatians we might conclude that the three key orthodox Christian doctrines may be traced to Paul but not to Jesus:

- The resurrection of the mortal body – which Jesus never taught. Jesus was focused on teaching us how to save our souls from the second death and, in the event that we failed, that he would resurrect our souls;

- Of Jesus crucifixion being <u>*required*</u> to save humanity from eternal damnation (or, in then contemporary terms, to redeem human souls from Sheol);

- Of salvation only requiring <u>*faith*</u> in Jesus – although exactly what one has to have faith in is never really spelled out by Paul. Paul indicates it might be faith that Jesus is the Son of God – an extraordinary claim that Jesus himself never made – see chapter 19. Jesus plainly taught that salvation comes from treating others as one treats oneself, salvation comes from works <u>*not*</u> faith – a point reinforced by James *"faith without works is dead"* (James 2:26) and moreover by Jesus statements that imply works earn salvation even without faith.

16.33 Galatians chapter 1 also indicates that Paul had, to some extent, already lost faith in Jewish scripture – describing Judaism as the *"traditions of his fathers"* (Galatians 1:14) – 'traditions' doesn't sound very holy!

16.34 In the 2nd chapter of Galatians, Paul continues to adopt an arrogant stance, when returning to Jerusalem after 14 years – he baldly asserts his superior theology – as in *"those who seemed to be something added nothing to me"* (Galatians 2:6). He then identifies the leaders of *those who seemed to be something*, as James, Peter and John as those *"who seemed to be the pillars of the church"*. Paul then arrogantly writes to the Galatians – boasting of his public humiliation of Peter (Galatians 2:11-16). Paul does not come over as a team player!!

16.35 There are also strong indications of later orthodox editing of Paul's text. As a leading student of the Mosaic Law, Paul would never have referred to Jesus as both *'Christ'* in Galatians 1:1 and as *'Son of God'* in Galatians 2:20 – knowing full well that these were mutually exclusive terms. Further the use of the term *'God the Father'* in Galatians 1:1 also sticks out as a 3rd or 4th century trinitarian phrase. So, one is left to ponder what else may have been edited into or excised from Paul's epistles.

EVIDENCE OF THE SPLIT BETWEEN NAZARENE AND PAULINE THEOLOGY

16.36 The irreconcilability of Jesus and Paul raises questions of contemporary importance. How many Christians are aware of the difference between what Jesus taught and what Paul taught? Clergy never inform their congregations of the fundamental differences between Jesus teaching and the doctrines forged at Nicaea which are erroneously taught as Christian.

16.37 Paul's epistles reveal the development of his theological thinking. In his earnest attempts to convert Gentiles to a belief in Jesus, Paul was competing with a range of existing religions. Paul's teaching drops most aspects of Mosaic Law to focus on the person of Jesus – but Paul makes no reference to many of the now questionable claims set out in the Gospels. This may just confirm the Gospels later authorship after Paul's death.

16.38 To gain traction across the Roman Empire, the responsibility for Jesus crucifixion seems to have shifted from the Roman authorities, who came to be painted as tolerant but trying to pacify Jewish religious feelings, to the Jews who ruthlessly murdered their own saviour.

16.39 Indeed, chapters 9 to 11 of Paul's epistle to the Romans, is the principal source of the belief that the majority of the Jews rejected Jesus. According to Paul, this rejection was all part of God's plan to divert the Gospel message to benefit the Gentiles and, in so doing, make the Jews jealous so that they then repent of their sins and receive God's mercy. If this sounds a bit tortuous it reflects Paul's legalistic mind creating a pathway showing a logical and sequential argument to explain why he, as a leading Jew, is preaching to Gentiles. There was certainly some initial resistance to the idea of taking the message of the Jewish Messiah to the heathen Gentiles. However, a moment's reflection makes Paul's assertion dubious. Surely, if those across the Roman Empire who were converted by the Apostles and their immediately appointed deputies, resolutely clung to the new faith when arrested and threatened with death as many did – then how much more would those who saw and listened to Jesus during his ministry, his entry into Jerusalem and his crucifixion, resist turning from Him. Ironically, it was of course the younger Paul who, as Saul, was the leading scourge of Jewish Christians (known then as the Nazarenes) – arresting and killing large numbers prior to his own conversion.

16.40 The conclusions that may be readily discerned are that the overwhelming majority of Jews that Jesus met readily followed him – recognising he was the legitimate King Messiah and feting his entry into Jerusalem. Afterwards, it was Paul himself who was the leading persecutor of Jews that believed in Jesus – so it is possible that in Chapter 9 of Romans, Paul is dissembling a rationale for his own pre-conversion behaviour. Soon after Paul was martyred, believed to be in AD64, Judah and Galilee suffered heavy Roman suppression during the Jewish uprisings between AD66 and 70, culminating with the destruction of the Temple and the siege of Masada. The even more ferocious Roman punishment metered out during the Bar Kokhba Revolt of AD132 to 135 was genocidal, deliberately trying to wipe out the Jewish population across what is today regarded as Israel. Therefore, by AD135, the vast majority of the descendants of the original Jewish Christians were dead.

16.41 The fact that the majority of Jews surviving today remain faithful to Judaism reflects the far less successful conversion rate achieved by apostles and missionaries spreading the Gospel to Jewish communities outside Israel than that achieved by Jesus direct teaching. Paul records his being chased out of some cities, sometimes by fellow Jews when he had preached in their synagogue – perhaps because they saw Paul's message as distorting their understanding of the Torah as in 16.8 above; by the wholesale dismissal of the food laws and particularly by turning circumcision from the sacred sign of God's chosen people into an act cutting oneself off from God. Thus, it may be concluded that Paul was inaccurate when in making his claim in his letter to the Romans, but during the following 100 years the Roman Legions made his Epistle appear accurate.

16.42 It has been claimed that Paul is the 'Man of Falsehood' identified in the Habakkuk Commentary, (1QpHab of the Dead Sea Scrolls) a text which a number of experts have dated to AD63. Also referred to as a 'Prophet of Falsehood' and as an Expounder of Smooth Things (i.e. a Pharisee), this person was 'a man of high eminence and authority' in the Jewish nation but taught falsehoods and the abandonment of the Law. It would be quite extraordinary if this text was an epitaph of Paul, the description certain fits Paul, and it would be ironic given the indications linking Jesus with the Qumran community.

16.43 To compete, the writers (of those gospels which survived) seem to record Jesus matching other contemporary gods miracle for miracle. The story of Tammuz, referred to in Part One, again finds echoes in the gospel accounts. Tammuz, originally Dumuzid the Sumerian king *fifth* before the

Flood, was known as the Shepherd King and had an enduring following. Ezekiel (8:14) complained about him being worshipped in the Temple and it is known that Bethlehem was an ancient cult centre for Tammuz, with a shrine surviving until Jesus time. Tammuz was born of a virgin, died from a wound in his side and after 3 days rose from the dead rolling away a rock from the entrance to his tomb. Other elements of the Gospel stories reflect the legends about Osiris, Adonis, Dionysus, Zoroaster and Mithras. Mithras, born of a union between a god and a woman, and whose beliefs include an apocalypse, a day of judgement, bodily resurrection and a second coming of Mithras.

16.44 Perhaps readers now begin to appreciate how much false dogma has been grafted onto Jesus message and the danger of assuming the Bible is the word of God rather than in reality being a collection of writings by men recording their own imaginings about God. Superficially, it seems easy to identify many passages of many books which appear accurate and therefore potentially to have been divinely inspired. However, if certain passages are divinely inspired, many other passages contain a mass of falsehoods, errors and adopted pagan beliefs and practices – why would a God who wished to inspire writers to convey his truths then permit his inspiration to be so adulterated?

16.45 Further, if God delegated responsibility for humanity to Jesus – why would Jesus have permitted the abominable process by which the books contained in the bible were selected; the huge numbers of believers harbouring newly banned books to be murdered; or, the chaotic results of having so many variants between different branches of Orthodox, Coptic, Ethiopian, Syriac, Catholic and Protestant bibles. The only logical conclusion must be that the bible is definitely not what almost all church authorities claim it to be.

17

Constantine's profound impact on Christianity

17.1 The historical record concerning Constantine (Roman Emperor from AD306 on a contested basis and fully from AD325 to AD337) and his beliefs is quite different from the conventional theological view of him leading the conversion of the Roman Empire to Christianity.

17.2 In Europe during the medieval period, kings claimed they ruled by divine right – a right conferred, ratified and legitimised by the Church. From the 8th Century, using a document referred to as the Donation of Constantine (later proved to be a fraud), the Church appropriated a power previously reserved for God and installed itself as God's mouth-piece. In accordance with Old Testament practise, kings were anointed with oil. Modern Christians would be astonished if the Church anointed a secular ruler as a fully-fledged priest-king – yet that is what the Church did with Constantine – he was anointed King Messiah by the Pope. The Church endorsed Constantine's presentation of himself as a warrior Messiah, implementing God's will with his sword. In effect the Church recognised Constantine achieving what Jesus failed to do – win political and martial battles.

17.3 Constantine is seen as a liberal and as a supporter of Christianity. His initial victory after becoming Emperor, defeating the challenger Maxentius, is seen as a victory of Christians over pagans. References to Constantine having a dream and seeing writing in the sky are taken as triggering his conversion to Christianity. It is true he was tolerant – by the edict of AD313 all forms of monotheism were approved. He donated the Lat-

PART THREE: JESUS, THE NAZARENE

eran Palace to the Bishop of Rome and decided to convene the Council of Nicaea in AD325 to force the numerous strands of Christianity to confront each other and to reconcile their differences into a unified set of beliefs. As a result, Jesus divinity was decided by a vote by the Bishops – who were told in advance what the correct answer was!

17.4 As a result of Nicaea, Rome became the centre of Christianity and the arbiter of orthodoxy. Christianity today derives less dogma from Jesus than to the dogma that Constantine established – but this is a long way from saying Constantine was a Christian or that he Christianised the Empire. Most of the popular traditions associated with Constantine are erroneous. His first dream was at a temple dedicated to Apollo and, according to witnesses, his vision prior to the battle was of Sol Invictus (known as the Sun god), following his then recent initiation into that cult. The triumphal arch erected by the Senate after his victory is dedicated to Sol Invictus. Constantine did not make Christianity the official state religion – he made Sol Invictus the god of the State and remained its Chief Priest throughout his reign. Sol Invictus was emblazoned on the coinage.

17.5 The monogram 'Chi Rho' (thought to be the first two letters of Christos in Greek), was hastily painted on the shields of Constantine's soldiers as part of his standard – the Labarum.

The Chi Rho was a device already widely used in Roman times. Ptolemy III (246BC to 222BC) used it on his coinage and in pre-Christian times it was used as a device to mark a particularly valuable or important passage in the margin of a page – being the abbreviation of 'chreston', meaning 'good'.

17.6 The first official recognition of Christianity as a permitted religion (religio licita) was the Edict of Serdica in 311 by Galerius, Emperor of the Eastern Roman Empire – this edict abolished the rules by which Christians were persecuted under an edict of Diocletian. The Emperor of the Western Roman Empire, Licinius (ruling 308 to 325) issued the Edict of Milan in 311 granting official toleration to Christians. The Edict of Milan was co-authored by Licinius and Constantine. The Edict stated *"that* it was proper that the Christians and all others should have liberty to follow that mode of religion which to each of them appeared best". The edict made the empire officially neutral, Christianity was made legal alongside all other recognised religions – it was not elevated to being the state religion. As part of its recognition, the edict also returned confiscated church property.

17.7 Licinius was defeated at Chrysopolis by Constantine in 324 and executed the following year with Constantine becoming sole emperor. As noted above in 17.4, Constantine's religion was and remained Sol Invictus and he remained the high priest to Sol Invictus throughout his reign. Interestingly, his mother, Helena was a passionate Christian and was responsible for the triangular peninsula between Egypt and Israel becoming erroneously named as Sinai – see Part One, chapter 13.

17.8 The Church seems to have concluded Constantine was a helpful patron and bent its rules to accommodate him. Sol Invictus was essentially monotheistic but had Baal and Astarte in supporting roles – one can immediately recognise these three gods as comprising the bull calf, Nannar, his son, Shamash and his daughter Inanna (using their Sumerian names; or Sin, Utu and Ishtar in Akkadian; with Inanna being known as Astarte and Ashtoreth by western Semites). Constantine's familiarity with a divine trinity may have contributed to the idea of adopting a Christian Trinity.

17.9 The Church modified its dogma to capitalise on the opportunity. When Constantine declared the venerable day of the Sun to be a weekly holiday in AD321, the Church switched the Sabbath from Saturday to Sunday. Similarly, despite the gospel account placing his birth in September, Jesus birthday was celebrated on 6th January (and still is by the Orthodox Church) – Rome moved Jesus official birthday to coincide with Sol Invictus on 25th December. The aureole of light crowning the head of the sun god became the Christian halo. Various beliefs from Mithras (Roman derivative from Zoroastrianism), upon which Sol Invictus was modelled, were also adopted – including the immortality of the soul; a future judgement and bodily resurrection. Christianity moved towards an amalgam of pagan beliefs and more distant from its Judaic roots.

17.10 According to research by Alastair Kee, published in *Constantine v Christ*, Constantine's association with Christianity was exclusively with God the Father, he saw himself as a patently successful King Messiah contrasting

PART THREE: JESUS, THE NAZARENE

with Jesus 'failures' as a Messiah.

17.11 Constantine pushed the idea of a Trinity, originally only supported by Athanasius (Bishop of Alexandria) and around 10% of the other bishops at the Council of Nicaea because he liked the idea of the Messiah being divine and part of the godhead. He saw Jesus as a Jew (a nation who, like most Romans, he hated) and as a failure whilst he, Constantine, was a highly successful Messiah – presumably in line to subsequently replace Jesus in the Trinity. Very tellingly, Constantine's conversion to Christianity only happened on his deathbed – when he also repudiated the Trinity as false.

17.12 Another 43 years were to pass after Constantine's death before Christianity was officially adopted as the state religion. This happened with the Edict of Thessalonica in 380 made jointly by the three reigning emperors that year – Theodosius I, Gratian and Valentinian II. The edict specified Nicene Christianity and condemned to persecution any adherents of Arianism, Nestorianism and all other 'heretical' sects.

17.13 Constantine's association of God the Father with the sun god even has a long pedigree in Judaism. From Akhenaten, whose Hymn to the Sun is largely subsumed into Psalm 104; Psalm 84 which equates Yahweh with Shamash (whose celestial sign was the sun); the pre-Roman inclusion of images of the sun god in many ancient synagogues (complete with surrounding 12 signs of the zodiac) provide further links to Sol Invictus.

17.14 Conventional Christianity tries to position Sunday as the day of worship by reference to Paul's frequent statements that the Law was abolished. This is highly selective and clearly inaccurate. A more accurate view might be that the 613 mitzvot were abolished – but not the Ten Commandments and therefore not the designation of the Sabbath. There are numerous examples in the gospels recording Jesus observance of the Sabbath, including:

- Luke 4:16 "…and as was his custom, he went into the synagogue on the Sabbath day, and stood up for to read"

- Luke 6:6 "And it came to pass also on another Sabbath, that he entered into the synagogue and taught…"

- Luke 13:10 "And he was teaching in one of the synagogues on the

Sabbath."

17.15 Jesus was carefully scrutinized by the religious leaders who were looking to find fault in what he did. He was accused of healing the sick on the Sabbath (Mark 3:2-3; Luke 6:6-11; Luke 13:11-17; John 9:16) because the Pharisees thought this constituted work. He was accused of Sabbath-breaking because his disciples ate a small amount of grain while walking through a field on the Sabbath day. Jesus response was that as the "Lord of the Sabbath" (Mark 2:28) He knew how to properly observe the Sabbath. Jesus told his audience that they were hypocrites, as prophesied by Isaiah, who honour me with their lips but not their hearts – and whose worship is based upon the traditions of men (Mark 7:6-8).

17.16 The Jewish priests had expanded the Law from the Ten Commandments to 613 mitzvot and built a mass of 'case law' splitting hairs to create a tangled thicket of rules. In Jesus view, such legalization resulted in the Sabbath becoming a burden rather than the joy it was intended it to be. Jesus honoured the Sabbath, demonstrating that the Sabbath was a day of physical rest and spiritual rejuvenation, a day to do good to others should the opportunity arise.

17.17 Church historians admit that not even the pagan elements which crept into the Christian church could erase from the writings of Paul his clear observance of the Sabbath. Various churches in Asia Minor, where Paul did most of his work, continued keeping the Sabbath as late as the fourth century. Acts contains various passages clearly demonstrating Paul keeping the Sabbath: Acts 13:14 *"But when they departed from Perga, they came to Antioch in Pisidia, and went into the synagogue on the Sabbath day, and sat down"*. Paul is viewed as repudiating the Law but to have attended the synagogue on the Sabbath – because repudiating Sabbath-keeping would have generated endless confusion among Christian brethren. The fact is the very act of attending the synagogue on the Sabbath is proof Paul kept the Sabbath. He did not keep Sunday as a day of worship. Acts 13:42-44 record Paul preached in the synagogue on the Sabbath, and his sermon was so powerful that the Gentiles asked Paul to preach to them on the next Sabbath. On the following Sabbath, almost the whole population came to hear Paul preach. Clearly, Paul kept the Sabbath and the Gentile converts kept the Sabbath too.

17.18 Acts 17:2 provides more proof: *"And Paul, as his manner was, went in unto them, and for three Sabbath days reasoned with them out of the scriptures"*. Again, in Acts 18:1-8, reports that *"After these things Paul departed from Athens, and came to Corinth... And he reasoned in the synagogue every Sabbath, and persuaded the Jews and the Greeks... and many of the Corinthians hearing believed, and were baptised."* Here we see Gentile converts attending the synagogue on the Sabbath day, and as a result of Paul's preaching were converted. The conclusion must be that early Christians kept the Sabbath.

17.19   Some who oppose the Sabbath do so on the grounds that there is no New Testament command to keep the Sabbath. However, reviewing Hebrews 4 in Greek reveals that there is. Paul is making a comparison between the rest that Israel received when the people entered the promised land and the rest Christians will receive when they enter the Kingdom of God. The word "rest," in verses one through eight, is from the Greek word *katapausis*, which means "a place of resting down." But when we come to verse nine, we have a change in the Greek term used. "Rest" in verse 4:9 is from the Greek word *sabbatismos*, which means "keeping of a Sabbath." The verse should be translated, "There remains therefore a keeping of the Sabbath for the people of God".

CONSTANTINE'S PROFOUND IMPACT ON CHRISTIANITY

18

Concepts of 'God's Son' and 'Only Son'

18.1 Many refer to John 3:16 as proof that Jesus is the 'son' of God, and per 3:16 the 'unique Son'. This belief is sadly typical of thinking trapped in the theory of biblical inerrancy. A moment of reflection might suggest the absurdity and arrogance of such beliefs.

18.2 John, brought up in the Hebrew faith and believing Yahweh created everything, would have found the idea of Yahweh having children rather radical – after all the God he believed in was supposed to be monotheistic. It was Jesus who appears to have kept telling the disciples that the Father was in Him, He in the Father and that He would be in them and them in Him. The only rational explanation is, as John quotes Jesus elsewhere and as Paul clearly states – God is Spirit. Therefore, a sentient force, such as a spirit, can be omnipresent – dwelling in all of us.

18.3 Jesus reference to being a Son is conventionally linked to Jewish tradition of the Son of Man seen in Heaven by Elijah but the meaning evidenced in the early Christian texts is somewhat different. Jesus is recorded in the surviving gospels as making a major distinction between himself being a Son of Man and others as "born of women" – as in Luke 7:28 and Matthew 11:11. However the true meaning of these enigmatic labels has been hidden for most of the Christian era and only revealed by the discovery of texts long thought completely destroyed. The real meaning is explored in Part Four of this series.

18.4 Jesus usually tried to communicate in terms which his audience could easily understand. His sermons emphasised the importance of relationships and the personal relationship he had with the power that had commissioned his mission on Earth. The use of the term 'Sonship' being a way of explaining to humans the desired relationship between an ultimate Creator and part of his creation. Paul emphasises this in Romans 8:14 "because those who are led by the Spirit of God are Sons of God". In a similar way, maybe at his baptism, the Spirit of God entered Jesus and he became a Son of God by adoption, through grace, just before starting his ministry.

18.5 There is a more radical and yet more simple explanation. When Jesus refers to his 'Father', he may be simply referring to love. Jesus dominant character trait is love, he could say that his mission was to teach mankind to love and his actions conformed to, and were obedient to, an overarching commitment to love others.

18.6 It seems the Creator had good reason to intervene in a very direct way to teach mankind a better way of living. Given the conclusion that the Creator instigated our universe, some 13.82 billion years ago, and that there are an uncountable number of stars, it may be more humble to suggest we are the only species to sin so profligately as to require the Creator's personal intervention. Just as, after we forgot Sumerian astronomical knowledge by the time of Hellenistic Age, and from Roman times until Copernicus, humans arrogantly believed our Sun, and indeed the rest of the universe, revolved around the Earth!! The number of stars in the Milky Way, our home galaxy, is estimated at between 200 to 400 billion – the range is wide as we know the total mass but not the average mass of the stars in our galaxy! Estimates of the number of galaxies in the Universe range from 125 billion up to as many as 2 trillion – which suggests that the number of stars in the universe could be up to 6×10^{23} (6 followed by 23 zeros). Discoveries during the last decade have led us to conclude that the typical star has a host of orbiting planets – usually with a couple in the Goldilocks zone. So, it is extremely arrogant to believe we humans are the sole purpose of creation.

18.7 Whilst it took our planet 4.543 billion years to evolve to its current time, advanced humans *(homo sapien sapien)* have only existed for about 172,000 years (based upon analysis of female mitochondria). Aeons before Earth supported life, hundreds of billions of stars had experienced their full cycle: of gravitational agglomeration; followed by the ignition of fusion producing light from a huge but dark collection of hydrogen atoms; the hydrogen fuel burning for some billions of years and then death as a supernova or sometimes contraction into a cold dark compact solid. During the lives of such stars, the gradually evolving conditions of their Goldilocks planets (basically those planets orbiting their stars at the right distance for surface water to be substantially in liquid form and/or for internal volcanic activity to maintain surface warmth for a similar result) will have offered opportunities for life, and sometimes intelligent life, to evolve. DNA appears to have been designed to support the evolution of entire ecosystems – again it would be presumptuous in the extreme for us to believe it was designed solely to cater for humanity.

18.8 Logic suggests DNA itself spread throughout the universe, triggering the evolution of millions of intelligent life-forms on millions of different planets. Our theology suggests sin occurs because God wants us to choose to love Him rather than just programming us to love Him. Therefore, God has deliberately granted us freewill – the freedom to choose between good and evil. If so, then maybe the majority of intelligent species, provided with freewill, have become sinful and then required redemption – either Jesus must be exhausted or maybe God despatches an incarnation fairly regularly?

18.9 Therefore, I conclude 'Sonship' is highly unlikely to be unique.

18.10 Whenever Jesus is quoted as referring to his Father, from whence we get the idea of his Sonship, Jesus always expresses loyalty and obedience – strongly implying a junior role. However, Jesus authority is so far above ours that for all practical purposes we cannot really differentiate Him from God. Luke 12:10 provides some clear guidance on this – where Jesus says that anyone who blasphemes the Son of Man (Himself) will be forgiven – but anyone who blasphemes against the Spirit will not be forgiven. That shows a stark difference!

19

John chapter 8 – Jesus own words debunk claims he is God

19.1 This quote in John 8:58 which, at face value in the English translation, appears to be Jesus claiming to be Yahweh (I am) and therefore God the Father, always struck me as odd – it stands out as a contradiction. Simplistic interpretation concludes Jesus meant that: (i) he had existed a long time and (ii) he was Yahweh – to the delight of the Trinitarians. However, the briefest consideration indicates otherwise. If Jesus wanted to indicate he had existed for a long time – he surely would have used a better yardstick than Abraham? Abraham had lived a mere 2000 years previously – why not use Noah (c10,700 years previously) or Adam (c172,000 years previously)? And if any message was intended for later generations, such as ourselves, why not say I was here before the dinosaurs (c300 million years previously) or, with meaning for both his immediate audience as well as us, before the formation of the Earth – some 4543 million years previously? Claiming to have lived when Abraham was around would not be much when the most knowledgeable of his contemporaries would have been familiar with texts contained in the Library of Alexandria, in a city where one third of the population was Jewish according to estimates. The most learned of the Pharisees may well have been familiar with Egyptian king lists showing original pre dynastic 'god'-kings, who were recognised as mortal, reigning around 30,000 years each.

19.2 I also suspected that the English translation producing "I Am" was a deliberate attempt to suggest Jesus was claiming to be Yahweh. Given that the characters of Jesus and Yahweh are polar opposites (love v hate) – the text stands out as fake. Jewish sources also point out that a better translation of the tetragrammaton (YHWH) is "I will be" rather than "I am".

19.3 Some detailed␣detective work by bibleanswers.org uncovers the true statement and puts it into the context of the forgoing verses of John 8. This I paraphrase and develop further, as below.

19.4 John 8:1-11 records: *But Jesus went to the Mount of Olives. And early in the morning he came again into the temple, and all the people were coming to him; and he sat down and began to teach them. And the scribes and the Pharisees brought a woman caught in adultery, and having set her in the midst, they said to Him, "Teacher, this woman has been caught in adultery, in the very act. "Now, in the Law, Moses commanded us to stone such women; what then do you say?" And they were saying this, testing him, in order that they might have grounds for accusing Him. But Jesus stooped down, and with his finger wrote on the ground. But when they persisted in asking him, he straightened up, and said to them, "He who is without sin among you, let him be the first to throw a stone at her." And again he stooped down, and wrote on the ground. And when they heard it, they began to go out one by one, beginning with the older ones, and he was left alone with the woman, where she was, in the midst. And straightening up, Jesus said to her, "Woman, where are they? Did no one condemn you?" And she said, "No one, Lord." And Jesus said, "Neither do I condemn you; go your way. From now on, sin no more."*

19.5 It seems that the Pharisees had been following Jesus, trying to entrap him, particularly concerning the, 'Law of Moses'. They were jealous of Jesus, and felt threatened by him, because Jesus was gathering a considerable following. In John 8:2, Jesus is "teaching" people in the Temple courtyard, which the Pharisees would have viewed as highly provocative. Given the highly legalised nature of Judaism, the Pharisees no doubt saw the opportunity for catching Jesus out – so that they would have grounds to accuse him of false teaching.

19.6 It is odd that in John 8:5-6 the Pharisees brought before Jesus a woman has been caught in adultery, saying they found her, *"...in the very act."* The statement implies the Pharisees knew exactly when and where to find this woman. How would they have known in advance?

19.7 The Pharisees were mean-spirited, jealous, and greedy; they knew Jesus was tender, merciful and compassionate; therefore, they appeal to the letter of the Mosaic law, saying, *"Now, in the Law, Moses commanded us to stone such women; what then do you say?"* John 8:6 says they were saying this to test him, in order that they might have grounds for accusing him. The trap was set! If Jesus let the woman go without having her publicly stoned, the Pharisees could discredit him publicly. However, if Jesus said the woman should be stoned to death, and the crowd was incited to hurl rocks at her until she was dead, the Roman government would imprison Jesus, because it was against Roman law to punish anyone by death without Roman approval. So, what does Jesus do?

19.8   Jesus stooped down, and with his finger wrote something on the ground. What did he write? Maybe it was Deuteronomy 19:15 (2 or more witnesses required to convict), or at least the commandment concerning adultery in the Law of Moses; whatever it was, it did not seem to deter them because 8:7 says, *"…they persisted in asking him."* Jesus straightened up, and said to them, *"He who is without sin among you, let him be the first to throw a stone at her."* And again (a second time) Jesus stooped down, and wrote on the ground. This time the Pharisees reacted very differently, and they began to go out one by one, beginning with the older ones.

19.9   Given the reaction of the Pharisees, it has been suggested that what Jesus wrote the second time was the names of three older Pharisees who claimed to have witnessed the naked woman in adultery. But, how did they know where to find this woman caught, *"in the very act?"* Maybe Jesus also wrote Deuteronomy 19:18-21 – if a witness is found to be false, the witness gets the same punishment, without mercy. By writing their names next to the commandment in the Law of Moses concerning false accusation, in effect, Jesus was accusing them of the very act of adultery themselves! Embarrassed, the Pharisees angrily leave the scene, then they conspire against Jesus.

19.10 Continuing in the gospel of John, verses 8:12-18 record: *Again therefore, Jesus spoke to them, saying, "I am the light of the world; he who follows me shall not walk in the darkness, but shall have the light of life." The Pharisees therefore said to Him, "You are bearing witness of yourself; your witness is not true." Jesus answered and said to them, "Even if I bear witness of myself, my witness is true; for I know where I came from, and where I am going; but you do not know where I come from, or where I am going. You people judge according to the flesh; I am not judging anyone. But even if I do judge, my judgment is true; for I am not alone in it, but I and He who sent me. Even in your law it has been written, that the testimony of two men is true. "I am he who bears witness of myself, and the Father who sent me bears witness of me".*

19.11 When the Pharisees return to Jesus, they are condemning him for accusing them of adultery without having a proper "witness" according to the terms of the Law of Moses. Under the Law, if a man accused another without having at least two witnesses, then he would be stoned to death for making a false accusation!

19.12   In John 8:17, Jesus appears to be quoting Deuteronomy 19:15-21 *One witness shall not prevail against a man for any crime or any wrong in connection with any sin he commits; only on the testimony of two or three witnesses shall a charge be established. If a false witness rises up against any man to accuse him of wrongdoing. Then both parties to the controversy shall stand before the Lord, before the priests and the judges who are in office in those days. The judges shall inquire diligently, and if the witness is a false witness and has accused his brother falsely, then you shall do to him as he had intended to do to his brother. So, you shall put away the evil from among you. And those who remain shall hear and reverently fear, and shall henceforth commit no such evil among you. Your eyes shall not pity: it shall be life for life, eye for eye, tooth for tooth, hand for hand, foot for foot.*

19.13   In John 8:13, the Pharisees jump at the chance to accuse Jesus, *"You are bearing witness of yourself; your witness is not true."* The reason for this is because the Law of Moses required at least two witnesses to verify an accusation. If what Jesus wrote in the ground was the names of the Pharisees, as the author of the article in bibleanswers.org suggests, then in terms of fleshly judgment, the only "witness" Jesus had was himself. This underscores the importance of context.

19.14   Jesus answered the accusation of the Pharisees and gave them his second "witness" in John 8 verses 16 & 18 when he told them, *"But even if I do judge, my judgment is true; for I am not alone in it, but I and He who sent me. Even in your law it has been written, that the testimony of two men is true. I am he who bears witness of myself, and the Father who sent me bears witness of me."*

19.15   Who was Jesus' witness? Jesus claimed his second witness was his Father who had sent him, a second ***man*** – note this indicates his Father was a man and not God, whom Jesus always states is Spirit. Jesus claim that he and his Father (whom they might have thought he meant God or another invisible divine power) had witnessed the Pharisees actions might have unnerved them. But this claim also proves Jesus is not purporting to be "God" in John 8:58 and clearly states that he and his Father, whether or not people assume his Father is God, represent two separate witnesses. Many more proofs emerge, this dissection may seem longwinded but I hope that you agree that this issue is rather important.

19.16 John 8:19 records: *And so they were saying to him, "Where is your Father?" Jesus answered, "You know neither me, nor my Father; if you knew me, you would know my Father also."*

19.17 Trinitarians assert that Jesus is 'God manifest in human form' (i.e. – manifest in the flesh). They use John 8:19 and John 14:9, *"... He who has seen me has seen the Father"*, to claim that Jesus is God. 'Oneness' pastors often describe that looking into the face of Jesus, we see God. They conveniently ignore the context, which always proves that Jesus is a man. Contemplate, it is important for your soul to seek the Truth without prejudice or bias. For example, in John 14:9 the Greek word for "seen" is "heoorakoós" and heoorakoós means, "to perceive; to see with *understanding*; to be acquainted with." What Jesus says in John 14:9 therefore is this, "... he that has become acquainted with me, has become acquainted with the Father. John 14:9 does not refer to Jesus as, "God," because in John 14:6 Jesus said, "I am the way, and the truth, and the life; no one comes to the Father but through me."

19.18 Back to John 8, in verses 20-24: *These words Jesus spoke in the Temple Courts, as he taught in the temple; and no one seized him, because his hour had not yet come. He said therefore again to them, "I go away, and you shall seek me, and shall die in your sin; where I am going, you cannot come." Therefore, the Jews were saying, "Surely he will not kill himself, will he, since he says, 'Where I am going, you cannot come'?" And he was saying to them, "You are from below; I am from above; you are of this world, I am not of this world. I said therefore to you, that you shall die in your sins; for unless you believe that I am he, you shall die in your sins."* Jesus is telling them that because of their sins, they shall suffer the second death and therefore their souls shall not be able to follow him – as Jesus soul is united with his Spirit, and therefore united with his ancestors, his 'Father'.

19.19 In John 8:24 Jesus says, *"... for unless you believe that I am he, you shall die in your sins?"* Both Trinitarian and Oneness advocates claim that this verse is yet another proclamation by Jesus whereby he claims to be, "God," as the great, "I am." Their argument goes like this (this is what they say): "Jesus said that unless you believe that 'I AM' (God), you shall die in your sins." Trinitarians claim that this is Yahweh of the OT speaking through Jesus human body of flesh the same way Yahweh did to Moses in Exodus 3:14 when He said, "I AM THAT I AM." Trinitarian churches say it is a simple claim to "Deity" as, "God the Son," the second person of the Trinity. Both Trinitarian and Oneness positions arrive at this by using John 8:23 out of context: because actually Jesus is quoted as saying, "I am from above," and again, "I am not of this world."

19.20 John 8:25-27 states: *And so they were saying to Him, "Who are you?" Jesus said to them, "What have I been saying to you from the beginning? I have many things to speak and to judge concerning you, but He who sent me is true; and the things which I heard from Him, these I speak to the world." They did not realize that he had been speaking to them about the Father.*

- How could Jesus be "sent" if he was God?

- Jesus told the Jews he was not referring to himself when he mentioned the One that "sent" him, but he was speaking of the Father.

19.21 John 8:28-30 continues: *Jesus therefore said, "When you lift up the Son of Man, then you will know that I am he, and I do nothing on my own initiative, but I speak these things as the Father taught me. And He who sent me is with me; He has not left me alone, for I always do the things that are pleasing to Him." As He spoke these things, many came to believe in him.*

Note in this passage:

- Jesus calls himself, "the Son of Man". This is a term that all Jews recognized from Ezekiel where it is used 83 times to describe that prophet. Jesus is claiming a very rare status that makes him almost uniquely qualified to teach mankind how to avoid death. The true meaning of the title has been successfully suppressed by the Church but it can be found in texts that were thought to be permanently lost – see Part Four. Many Jews would also have been familiar with Numbers 23:19 which clearly states that God is not human. NB some see Son of Man as a reference to Daniel 7:13-14 where it might be taken as a reference to a messiah – an office for which Jesus is very likely to have been eligible – but would never be seen as an indication of divinity. Moreover, Judaism does not recognise Daniel as scripture.

- The phrase Jesus uses, "I am he," in John 8:28 refers to him as the Son of Man, and it is the exact same words in John 8:24 when Jesus said, "For unless you believe that I am he."

- Jesus cannot be "God" in John 8:58 or anywhere in this chapter because he said in 8:28, "…the Father taught me," and in 8:29, "…He has not left me alone," and in 8:30, "…I always do the things that are pleasing to Him." If Jesus was God, who is teaching him? If he were God, would he mention being left alone? And last, but not least, how could he be God while doing what is pleasing to his Father? Is that God trying to please himself?

19.22 I am being pedantic but it shows the strength of doctrinal bias in conventional Christianity when overwhelming evidence is ignored in favour of a few obscure verses. Respect for (usually) charismatic pastors seems to close down many people's power of critical thinking!

19.23 Remember, context is always relevant when studying scripture. The key to understanding John 8:58 is found primarily in verses 40 & 53.

19.24 Jesus goes on to contrast the audiences' commitment to sin rather than follow the righteous ways of their ancestral father Abraham. John 8:31-41 records: *Jesus therefore was saying to those Jews who had believed Him, "If you abide in my word, then you are truly disciples of mine; and you shall know the truth, and the truth shall make you free." They answered Him, "We are Abraham's offspring, and have never yet been enslaved to anyone; how is it that you say, 'You shall become free'?" Jesus answered them, "Truly, truly, I say to you, everyone who commits sin is the slave of sin. And the slave does not remain in the house forever; the son does remain forever. If therefore the son shall make you free, you shall be free indeed. I know that you are Abraham's offspring; yet you seek to kill me, because my word has no place in you. I speak the things which I have seen with my Father; therefore, you also do the things which you heard from your father." They answered and said to him, "Abraham is our father." Jesus said to them, "If you are Abraham's children, do the deeds of Abraham. But as it is, you are seeking to kill me, a man who has told you the truth, which I heard from God; this Abraham did not do. You are doing the deeds of your father."*

19.25 In the passage above, Jesus makes some key points:

- Jesus tells them, if you want to know the truth I am speaking, you must abide in my word, because my word is what I hear from God. The Jews just do not understand, because their response is, *"We are Abraham's offspring."*

- Abraham is extraordinarily important for Jews, playing the original

PART THREE: JESUS, THE NAZARENE

father figure of the nation to whom God (at least El Elyon) made key promises as the chosen people. Jacob, Abraham's grandson, whose name was changed to Israel, fathered twelve sons from whence the 12 tribes are alleged to originate.

- Notice Jesus calls himself, "the son," and not the Father.

- Note in verse 37; Jesus acknowledges Abraham as the Jews' father, then rebukes them in verse 39 because they are not acting in love and faith like their father Abraham acted.

- John 8:40 is the clincher, because it proves beyond all reasonable doubt who Jesus is, when he scolds the Jews saying to them, "… you are seeking to kill me, a man who has told you the truth, which I heard from God." How can Jesus refer to himself as God in John 8:58 if he calls himself "a man" that told the truth, which he heard, "***from*** God?"

19.26 John 8:41-44 continues: *They said to Him, "We were not born of fornication; we have one Father, even God." Jesus said to them, "If God were your Father, you would love me; for I proceeded forth and have come from God, for I have not even come on my own initiative, but He sent me. Why do you not understand what I am saying? It is because you cannot hear my word. You are of your father the devil, and you want to do the desires of your father. He was a murderer from the beginning, and does not stand in the truth, because there is no truth in him. Whenever he speaks a lie, he speaks from his own nature; for he is a liar, and the father of lies. But because I speak the truth, you do not believe me. Which one of you convicts me of sin? If I speak truth, why do you not believe me? He who is of God hears the words of God; for this reason you do not hear them, because you are not of God."*

19.27 Note especially John 8:42 because Jesus makes yet another clear distinction between himself and God; he tells his audience, "If **God** were your Father, you would love ***me***…" Why? Because Jesus came from God; in other words, God sent him to the Jews. The Trinitarian position is that Jesus left his throne in heaven, and came to earth, and God became a man. This is impossible to construe from the text because Jesus says, *"I have not even come on my own initiative, but He sent me."* When Jesus states that God sent him and that that he is telling truths that he heard from God, Jesus clearly cannot be God himself.

19.28 Moving on to John 8:48-53: *The Jews answered and said to him, "Do we not*

JOHN CHAPTER 8 – JESUS OWN WORDS DEBUNK CLAIMS HE IS GOD

say rightly that you are a Samaritan and have a demon?" Jesus answered, "I do not have a demon; but I honour my Father, and you dishonour me. But I do not seek my glory; there is One who seeks and judges. Truly, truly, I say to you, if anyone keeps my word he shall never see death." The Jews said to him, "Now we know that you have a demon. Abraham died, and the prophets also; and you say, 'If anyone keeps my word, he shall never taste of death.' Surely you are not greater than our father Abraham, who died? The prophets died too; whom do you make yourself out to be?"

19.29   The current text of the above passage compounds Jewish misunderstanding of what Jesus was saying with later editing to suppress Jesus original teaching. Jesus reference to escaping death was never about bodily death but escaping the second death after which Jews believed their souls were forever abandoned to Sheol. The more learned Jews fully understood what Jesus meant as he had already referred to himself as a Son of Man, like Ezekiel and Enoch. Thus, Jesus is telling the crowd that he, Jesus, shall never taste the second death again because he had already escaped that death and came united with his soul endowing him with complete knowledge of his entire history. Jesus is telling the crowd that if they keep his word, they can avoid the second death too. Abraham, the revered father of the nation, had never referred to himself as a Son of Man and according to scripture had merely died and been buried in Hebron. This is the core of Jesus claim to be 'above', i.e. more senior, than Abraham.

19.30   So, the audience hear Jesus raise himself far above Abraham, and challenge him saying: Jesus, Abraham is the greatest of all our spiritual ancestors, and he died, just like all the other great prophets. So, if you are saying we can live forever by believing in you, then you are either crazy, OR you are claiming to be GREATER in stature and power than Abraham was. Jesus has just told them so, and now in the next few verses repeats the claim.

19.31   In John 8:54-56 Jesus answered, *"If I glorify myself, my glory is nothing; it is my Father who glorifies Me, of whom you say, 'He is our God'; and you have not come to know Him, but I know Him; and if I say that I do not know Him, I shall be a liar like you, but I do know Him, and keep His word. Your father Abraham rejoiced to see my day, and he saw it and was glad."*

- John 8:54 is yet another proof Jesus is not God, nor is he claiming to be deity, because he clearly states, *"…it is my Father who glorifies me, of whom you* (the Jews) *say, 'He is our God.'* Jesus says it very plainly, "MY

PART THREE: JESUS, THE NAZARENE

Father..." is the One you Jews say, "He is OUR God." Very clearly Jesus is telling them that God is someone he calls Father and that God is his God as well as theirs – "our" God.

- Jesus in effect tells the Jews, "I know God and you don't know Him." For proof he uses the Jews' own words against them, saying of Abraham, "Your father Abraham rejoiced to see my day, and he saw it and was glad." Conventional theologians claim this was Jesus claiming to have been alive 2000 years previously in Abraham's time – and therefore Jesus must be divine. However, in the Greek text of John 8:56 the word "it" is not found – Bible translators have erroneously inserted "it".

- What Jesus might have been saying is that indeed, Abraham did escape the second death and his descendant awareness rejoiced to see Jesus at work. But, again, it is poor translation that cause problems.

19.32 John 8:57 states: *The Jews therefore said to Him, "You are not yet fifty years old, and have you seen Abraham?"* Maybe the crowd misunderstood Jesus, maybe the text editor was confused or maybe translators changed the meaning. Jesus was not claiming to have seen Abraham but that Abraham would rejoice at what Jesus was doing. Jesus then responds in John 8:58-59 to clarify his meaning: *Jesus said to them, "Truly, truly, I say to you, before Abraham was born, I am." Therefore they picked up stones to throw at Him; but Jesus hid Himself, and went out of the temple.*

19.33 Why are they trying to stone Jesus? We know it was not because Jesus claimed to have seen Abraham. The answer is found to a great extent in the Greek; the words translated, "was born," are better translated, "existence" (i.e. – meaning to exist). Also, the word translated as, "before" is the Greek word, "prín" from a root word "pros" meaning "superior; first in rank or title."

19.34 Therefore, John 8:58 is more accurately translated as, **"Truly, truly I say to you, I exist as superior in rank to Abraham's existence."** The Greek text reads, "prín Abraám genésthai egoó eimí". In other words, Jesus is telling these Jews that his rank before God, as a Son of Man who escaped the second death, is greater than that of their father Abraham. Once he said this, the Jews took up stones to stone him to death. Note: in making this statement, Jesus is a long way from claiming he is God (part of a Trinity) or even that he is divine.

JOHN CHAPTER 8 – JESUS OWN WORDS DEBUNK CLAIMS HE IS GOD

20

Comma Johanneum and Matthew 28:19

20.1 There are two passages in the NT which are taken as the basis for the idea of the Trinity – Matthew 28:19 and 1 John 5. However, a little research quickly shows both are fraudulent changes made long after the two books were originally written. The change to Matthew was made after a few centuries, that to 1 John relatively recently – around AD1220. I touched on this in Part One but here I lay out very extensive evidence that the "Trinity" is a purely human invention.

1 John 5 – known as the Comma Johanneum

20.2 1 John is generally believed to have been written between AD80 and AD95. The original text of verses 6 to 8 is well documented as:

6 This is the one who came by water and blood—Jesus Christ. He did not come by water only, but by water and blood. And it is the Spirit who testifies, because the Spirit is the truth. 7 For there are three that testify: 8 the Spirit, the water and the blood; and the three are in agreement.

However, mid second millennium versions of the Catholic Vulgate suddenly appear as:

6 This is the one who came by water and blood—Jesus Christ. He did not come by water only, but by water and blood. And it is the Spirit who testifies, because the Spirit is the truth. 7 For there are three that testify in heaven: the Father, the Word and the Holy Spirit, and these three are one. 8 And there are three that testify on earth: the

Spirit, the water and the blood; and the three are in agreement.

20.3 This change, made to justify the invention of the Trinity, results in logic failure when reading the preceding verses:

1: "Everyone who believes that Jesus is the Christ is born of God" 'is the Christ' meaning is the Messiah come to save humanity from sin; 'is born of God' meaning true believers become God's children; being 'born of God' is the source of love.

6-8: "⁶This is the One who came by water and blood, Jesus Christ, not with the water only, but with the water and with the blood. It is the Spirit who testifies, because the Spirit is the truth. ⁷For there are three that testify: ⁸the Spirit, the water and the blood: and the three are in agreement."

20.4 All commentators discern water and blood relate to Jesus – water as purifying and blood as redemptive atonement for the sins of humanity. Some link water and blood to baptism and crucifixion; others as two sacramental liquids flowing at crucifixion. As the passage is focused on Jesus himself the most likely meaning of the Spirit may be the Spirit of God indwelling in Jesus – maybe from the time of the baptism by John.

20.5 None of the above identifies Jesus as himself being God, but perhaps as the adoptive Son of God. However, the reference to three elements (water, blood and spirit) resulted in some over-enthusiastic Trinitarians to insert additional text in the 16th century (based on a scribbled margin note on a 10th century manuscript) at the beginning of verse 1 John 5:8 *"in heaven the Father, the Word and the Holy Spirit, and these three are one. And there are three that testify on Earth,"*

20.6 The above insertion is widely debated and referred to as the "*Comma Johanneum*".

20.7 It is noteworthy that even a fairly fundamental evangelical organization, the Bible Studies Foundation, sponsored a new online version referred to as the New English Translation in 2005 which reverts to the original non-Trinitarian text shown in many hundreds of first millennium manuscripts:

5:7 For there are three that testify, 5:8 the Spirit and the water and the blood, and these three are in agreement.

However, the conventional Trinitarian reading was introduced to the English-speaking world through the King James Version:

5:7 For there are three that bear record in heaven, the Father, the Word, and the Holy Ghost: and these three are one. 5:8 And there are three that bear witness in earth, the Spirit and the water and the blood, and these three are agree in one.

Overwhelming evidence, both external and internal, proves the text was corrupted.

20.8   Turning firstly to the external evidence. The more recent longer reading is found only in eight late manuscripts, four of which have the words in a marginal note. Most of these manuscripts (2318, 221, and with minor variations 61, 88, 429, 629, 636, and 918) originate from the 16th century; the earliest manuscript, codex 221 (10th century), includes the reading in a marginal note that was added sometime after the original composition. Thus, *there is no sure evidence of this reading in any Greek manuscript until the 1500s;* each such reading was apparently composed after Erasmus' Greek NT was published in 1516. Indeed, the reading appears in *no Greek witness of any kind* (either manuscript, patristic, or Greek translation of some other version) *until AD 1215* (in a Greek translation of the Acts of the Lateran Council, a work originally written in Latin). This is all the more significant, since many a Greek Father would have loved such a reading, for it so succinctly affirms the doctrine of the Trinity. The reading seems to have arisen in a fourth century Latin homily in which the text was allegorized to refer to members of the Trinity. From there, it made its way into copies of the Latin Vulgate, the text used by the Roman Catholic Church.

20.9   The Trinitarian formula made its way into the third edition of Erasmus' Greek NT (1522) because of pressure from the Catholic Church. After his first edition appeared, in 1516, there arose such a furor over the absence of the *Comma* that Erasmus needed to defend himself. He argued that he did not put in the *Comma* because he found no Greek manuscripts that included it. Once one was produced (codex 61), rather conveniently written by one Roy or Froy at Oxford in 1520, Erasmus apparently felt obliged to include the reading. He became aware of this manuscript sometime between May 1520 and September 1521. In his annotations to his third edition he does not protest the new rendering which suddenly appears in his text, as though it were made to order; but he does defend himself from the charge of indolence, noting that he had taken care to find whatever manuscripts he could for the production of his Greek New Testament. In the final analysis, Erasmus probably altered the text because of political, theological and also economic concerns: he did not want his reputation ruined, nor his *Novum Instrumentum* to go unsold.

20.10 Thankfully, many bibles now in print exclude the *Comma Johanneum*.

Matthew 28:19 – the Great Commission

20.11 Controversy has long raged over the accuracy of the received text used in this clause. There is strong evidence that this clause was clumsily edited in the 4th Century with Jesus instruction to *"go out and spread the gospel, baptising believers in my name"* – changed after the adoption of the Trinity dogma at the Council of Nicaea in AD325 to *"go out and baptise in the name of the Father, Son & Holy Spirit"*. The mistakes are legion in the grammar and titles, and jar when compared with many other references in the gospels where Jesus tells the disciples to baptise *"in my name"*.

20.12 The following three excerpts are quoted by Eusebius as coming from an unaltered book of Matthew that could have even been the original or an early copy of the original of Matthew. Thus, Eusebius informs us of the actual words Jesus spoke to his disciples in Matthew 28:19.

"With one word and voice He said to His disciples: Go, and make disciples of all nations in My Name, teaching them to observe all things whatsoever I have commanded you," (Proof of the Gospel by Eusebius, Book III, chapter 6, 132 (a), p. 152)

Eusebius even tells us when the Trinitarian formula was first used in baptism – AD348 – see 20.62 below.

COMMA JOHANNEUM AND MATTHEW 28:19

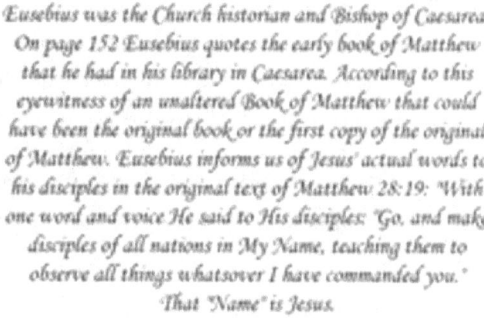

Eusebius was the Church historian and Bishop of Caesarea. On page 152 Eusebius quotes the early book of Matthew that he had in his library in Caesarea. According to this eyewitness of an unaltered Book of Matthew that could have been the original book or the first copy of the original of Matthew. Eusebius informs us of Jesus' actual words to his disciples in the original text of Matthew 28:19: "With one word and voice He said to His disciples: 'Go, and make disciples of all nations in My Name, teaching them to observe all things whatsoever I have commanded you."
That "Name" is Jesus.

The Demonstratio Evangelica" by Eusebius

"But while the disciples of Jesus were most likely either saying thus, or thinking thus, <u>the Master</u> solved their difficulties, <u>by the addition of one phrase, saying</u> they should triumph "<u>In MY NAME</u>". And the power of His name being so great, that the apostle says: "God has given him a name which is above every name, that in the name of Jesus every knee should bow, of things in heaven, and things in earth, and things under the earth," He showed the virtue of the power in His Name concealed from the crowd when He said to His disciples: "<u>Go, and make disciples of all the nations in my Name</u>." He also most accurately forecasts the future when He says: "for this gospel must first be preached to all the world, for a witness to all nations." – (Proof of the Gospel by Eusebius, Book III, ch 7, 136 (a-d), p. 157)

"Who said to them; Make disciples of all the nations in my Name." – (Eusebius, Proof of the Gospel, Book III, Chapter 7, 138 (c), p. 159)

20.13   In Book III of History, Chapter 5, Section 2, Eusebius tells of the Jewish persecution of early Christians, quoting: *"relying upon the power of Christ, who had said to them, Go ye and make disciples of all the nations in my name."*

20.14   And in his Oration in Praise of Emperor Constantine, Chapter 16, Section 8, we read, *"Surely none save our only Savior has done this, when, after his victory over death, he spoke the word to his followers, and fulfilled it by the event, saying to them, "Go ye and make disciples of all nations in my name."*

20.15 Eusebius was present at the council of Nicaea and was involved in the debates between Arias and the pagan views (based upon earlier Egyptian gods) of Athanasius that became the trinity doctrine. If the manuscripts he had in front of him read *"in the name of the Father, and of the Son and of the Holy Spirit,"* he would never have quoted instead, *"in my name."* So, it appears that the earliest manuscripts read *"in my name,"* and the phrase was enlarged to reflect the orthodox position as Trinitarian influence spread.

20.16 The King James Bible, 1611, quotes Matthew 28:19 as *"Go you therefore, and teach all nations, baptising them in the name of the Father, and of the Son, and of the Holy Ghost:"*

20.17 Trinitarians invariably claim this verse supports their belief. However, this verse in no way affirms the Trinity doctrine that states that the Father, Son and Holy Spirit are three co-equal, co-eternal beings that make up *one God*. Whilst conventional Christianity is based upon the existence of a Father, a Son and the Holy Spirit – this verse does not provide evidence of a Trinity as claimed. This verse refers to three powers but never says they are one and says nothing about their personality. It does not say they are three beings, it does not say they are three in one or one in three, it does not say these three are the Godhead, it does not say these three are a Trinity, it does not say these three are co-equal or co-eternal beings, it does not say that these three are all God, and yet some draw the conclusion that this supports their belief in the trinity which is clearly not so. They are concluding something from this verse that it simply does not say.

20.18 One might also ask that, if this verse were genuine, why do all the Apostles consistently disobey Jesus instruction? Every single biblical quote concerning baptism is in breach of the injunction stated in Matthew 28:19. There are numerous references to baptism in the New Testament – but every reference states that new converts were baptised into the name of Jesus only:

Acts 2:38 *Then Peter said unto them, Repent, and be baptised every one of you in the name of Jesus Christ for the remission of sins, and you shall receive the gift of the Holy Ghost.*

Acts 8:12 *But when they believed Philip preaching the things concerning the kingdom of God, and the name of Jesus Christ, they were baptised, both men and women.*

Acts 8:16 *For as yet he was fallen upon none of them: only they were baptised in the name of the Lord Jesus.*

Acts 10:48 *And he commanded them to be baptised in the name of the Lord.*

Acts 19:5 *When they heard this, they were baptised in the name of the Lord Jesus.*

Acts 22:16 *And now why tarriest you? Arise, and be baptised, and wash away your sins, calling on the name of the Lord.*

Romans 6:3 *Know you not, that so many of us as were baptised into Jesus Christ were baptised into his death?*

1 Corinthians 1:13 *Is Christ divided? was Paul crucified for you? or were you baptised in the name of Paul?*

Galatians 3:27 *For as many of you as have been baptised into Christ have put on Christ.*

20.19 So do you personally conclude that Matthew 28:19 originally read *"baptising them in the name of the Father, and of the Son, and of the Holy Ghost"* or *"baptising them in My name"*?

And based on your conclusion, which of the following is correct?

Colossians 2:12 *Buried with the Father, Son and Holy Spirit in baptism, wherein also you are risen with them through the faith of the operation of God, who has raised them from the dead.*

or:

Colossians 2:12 *Buried with Him in baptism, wherein also you are risen with Him through the faith of the operation of God, who has raised Him from the dead.*

20.20 In isolation, Matthew 28:19 does not prove or disprove the Trinity doctrine but Scripture certainly strongly indicates that baptism should be in the name of Jesus as all examples reveal.

20.21 The reason we are baptised in the name of Jesus is because we are baptised *"into"* Jesus. Baptism is a symbol of His death, burial and resurrection. Even if the Trinity doctrine was true, Christians believe only Jesus died, was buried and rose again. When we are baptised in the name of Jesus, we affirm we are Christians. Paul argued this point in 1 Corinthians 1:13 when he said, *"Is Christ divided? Was Paul crucified for you? Or were you baptised in the name of Paul?"* The obvious answer to this rhetorical question is, *"No. You were baptised in the name of Jesus because He was crucified for you."*

20.22 Consider also Mark 16:16 *"He that believeth and is baptised shall be saved"* and whose name do we call upon in order to be saved when we are baptised? *"Arise, and be baptised, and wash away your sins, calling on the NAME of the LORD."* Acts 22:16

It does not say *"calling on the name of the Father, Son and Holy Spirit"*. We are told that there is only one name under heaven whereby we can be saved? We do NOT call on the name of the Father or Holy Spirit to be saved in baptism. These verses also point to Matthew 28:19 being altered, indicating that originally the reference was only to the name of Jesus: *"for there is NO other NAME under heaven given among men, whereby we must be saved."* Acts 4:12

Whose name did Peter say we were to be baptised in? *"Peter said unto them, Repent, and be baptised every one of you in the name of Jesus"* Acts 2:38.

20.23 We cannot prove this verse has been tampered with by the Catholic Church but we do know:

(i) The Catholic Church confesses to changing it

(ii) Most theologians also agree that they did change it

(iii) Initially, few followed this supposed instruction and all were baptised in the name of Jesus ONLY!

(iv) Other Scriptures say we are baptised and saved by calling on the name of the Jesus ONLY

(v) Eusebius who saw the earliest manuscripts when he quoted this verse wrote that it said "In His name"

I think most will agree that the weight of evidence is overwhelming that Matthew 28:19 should read *"in My name."*

20.24   Before his death in AD560 Pope Pelagius said: *"There are many who say that they baptise in the name of Christ alone and by a single immersion."* Henry Burrage quotes Pope Pelagus in a work published in 1879, describing the early practice of baptism in the name of Jesus alone was still very popular until AD560, despite severe persecution from Theodosius and his Trinitarian mentors who legislated mass persecution between AD380 and 395. See image below.

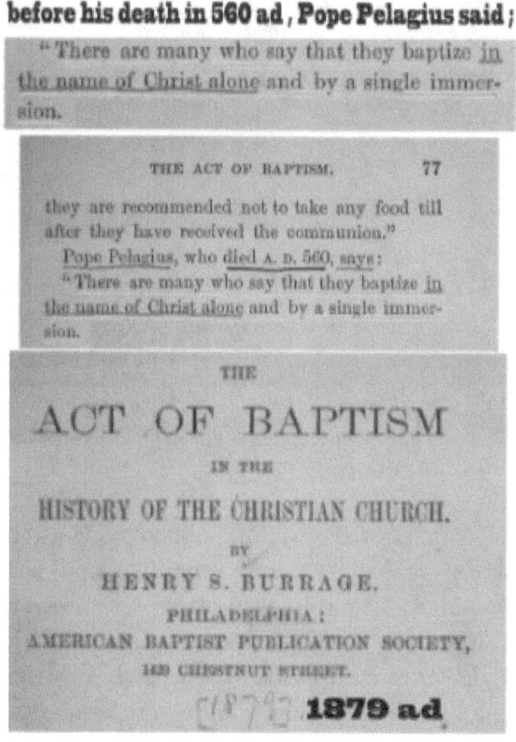

20.25   In the Catholic Catechism (extract below), the Catholic Church declares that the baptismal formula was changed from the name of Jesus to the Trinitarian formula in the fourth century. Everyone in the Bible that was baptised, from the day of Pentecost to the Ephesian disciples (the last recorded baptism in the book of Acts), was baptised in the name of Jesus. So, we have official evidence that every Christian for the first 300 years was baptised in the name of Jesus.

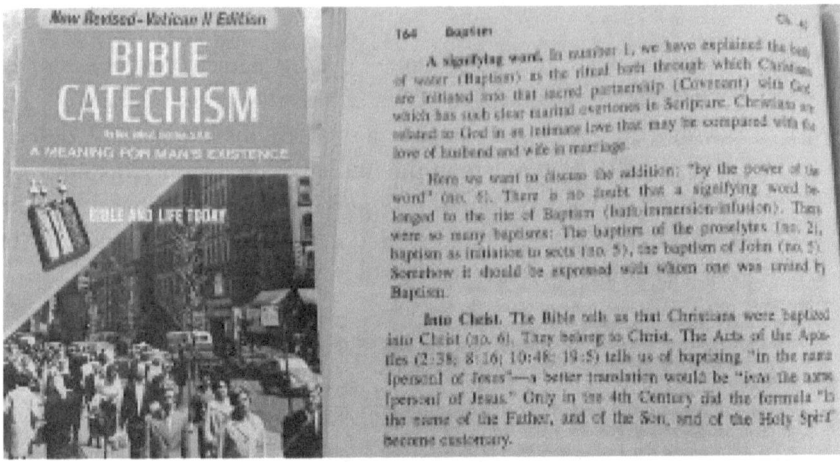

In the Catholic Catechism above you will see the following paragraph.

*"**Into Christ.** The Bible tells us that Christians were baptised into Christ. They belong to Christ. The Acts of the Apostles (2:38; 8:16; 10:48; 19:5) tells us of baptising "in the name (person) of Jesus." – a better translation would be "into the name (person) of Jesus." Only in the 4th Century did the formula "In the name of the Father, and of the Son, and of the Holy Spirit" become customary."* Bible Catechism, Rev. John C Kersten,

20.26   The authenticity of the traditional text of Matthew 28:19 has generated significant research. A comprehensive analysis from both a historical and a theological standpoint has been assembled under the title 'The 28:19 Forgery', by the Church of the Living EL, Jerusalem, who describe themselves as Apostolic Christians, whose creed appears distinctly Nazarene – i.e. based upon Jesus own teaching rather than 4th Century Catholic dogma. Their very detailed paper on Matthew 28:19 examines the evidence from early biblical manuscripts, from writings of early Church fathers and applies ten tests concluding with seven main conclusions. Their analysis is exhaustive and the conclusions are compelling – a detailed summary follows:

20.27   Questioning the authenticity of Matthew 28:19 is not a matter of determining how easily it can or cannot be explained within the context of established doctrinal views. Rather, it is a matter of discovering what

Jesus actually said and whether the concept of the Trinity was revealed by God or merely invented in the 4th Century for political reasons.

20.28 This question is extremely relevant to the Christian faith. The amount of information supporting the conclusions presented may seem overwhelming and pedantic, but for the serious seeker of truth, the search is well worth effort.

20.29 However, it must be remembered that no manuscripts remain that were written in the first, second or even the third centuries. There is a gap of **three hundred years** between when Matthew wrote his epistle and our earliest manuscript copies.

20.30 Considering the fact that all of the scriptures from Genesis through Malachi make no reference to a Trinitarian God, and that from Mark through to Revelation we also find no evidence for a Trinity, we must consider the possibility that all the existing manuscripts may have one or more textual errors in common.

20.31 According to the Biblical historian Dr. C. R. Gregory: *The Greek manuscripts of the text of the New Testament were often altered by the scribes, who put into them the readings which were familiar to them, and which they held to be the right readings.*

20.32 F.C. Conybeare wrote: *"Just as with the manuscripts, all extant Versions, containing the end of Matthew, also contain the Triune name. But, of course, there is more to be considered than what is present in a document. One must also take into consideration what is absent. Again, quoting from the Encyclopedia of Religion and Ethics: "In all extant versions the text is found in the traditional Trinitarian form ... though it must be remembered that the best manuscripts, both of the African Old Latin and of the Old Syriac Versions are defective at this point."* By defective, it is describing **absent – the key page having been torn out.**

20.33 So, although many early Versions contain the traditional Triune name in Matthew 28:19, **the earliest of these Versions do not contain the verse at all.** And curiously, not due to omission, but due to **removal**! We cannot be certain of the motives why these pages were destroyed, but we can consult the early historical writings.

20.34 F.C. Conybeare writing in the Hibbert Journal states *"In the course of my reading I have been able to substantiate these doubts of the authenticity of the text of Matthew 28:19 by adducing evidence against it, so weighty that in the future the most conservative of divines will shrink from resting on it any dogmatic fabric at all, while the more enlightened will discard it as completely as they have its fellow-text* (i.e. 1John5) *of the 'Three Witnesses'."*

20.35 Relevant evidence may be gleaned from numerous early Church fathers, either via quotations from their writings, or as commented upon through the writings of their contemporaries: (i) Eusebius of Caesarea, author of the Vulgate amongst many other books; (ii) The unknown author of De Rebaptismate, (iii) Origen, (iv) Clement of Alexandria, (v) Justin Martyr and (vi) Macedonius.

20.36 The writings of these early church fathers all indicate that they witnessed copies of Matthew, that are no longer available, in an original form without the trinitarian formula.

20.37 Eusebius of Caesarea, also known as Eusebius Pamphili, was born around AD270, and died around AD340. He lived in times of rampant doctrinal change and in later life assisted in the formation of the Nicene Creed. However, regarding inquiry into Matthew 28:19, Eusebius is the key witness. Therefore, to establish his veracity as a credible witness, let us consider the following quotes: *"Eusebius of Caesarea, to whom we are indebted for the preservation of so many contemporary works of antiquity, many of which would have perished had he not collected and edited them."* Robert Roberts, in Good Company, vol. III, pg. 10

Eusebius, the greatest Greek teacher of the Church and most learned theologian of his time... worked untiringly for the acceptance of the pure Word of the New Testament as it came from the Apostles... Eusebius... relies throughout only upon ancient manuscripts, and always openly confesses the truth when he cannot find sufficient testimony. E.K. in the Christadelphian Monatshefte, Aug, 1923 from Mosheim, in an editorial footnote.

Eusebius Pamphili, Bishop of Caesurae in Palestine, a man of vast reading and erudition, one who has acquired immortal fame by his labors in ecclesiastical history, and in other branches of theological learning. Until about 40 years of age he lived in great intimacy with the martyr Pamphilus, a learned and devout man of Caesurae, and founder of an extensive library there, from which Eusebius derived his vast store of learning Dr. Wescott in the "General Survey", page 108

The most important writer in the first quarter of the fourth century was Eusebius of

Caesurae... Eusebius was a man of little originality or independent judgment. But he was widely read in the Greek Christian literature of the second and third centuries, the bulk of which has now irretrievably perished, and subsequent ages owe a deep debt to his honest, if some-what confused, and at times not a little prejudiced, erudition. Dictionary of Christian Biography and Literature

Of the witnesses to the text of the New Testament as it stood in the Greek Manuscripts from about AD300-340, none is so important as Eusebius, for he lived in the greatest Christian Library of that age, that namely which Origen and Pamphilus had collected. It is no exaggeration to say from this single collection of manuscripts at Caesurae derives the larger part of the surviving pre-Nicene literature. In his Library, Eusebius must have habitually handled codices of the gospels older by two hundred years than the earliest of the great uncials that we have now in our libraries. F.C. Conybeare, in the Hibbert Journal, October 1902.

20.38 Considering the honesty, ability and opportunity of Eusebius as a witness to the original New Testament texts, let us now look at his evidence concerning Matthew 28. According to Ludwig Knupfer, the editor of the Christadelphian Monatshefte, Eusebius, among his many other writings, compiled a file of corrupted variations of the Holy Scriptures, and concluded that *the most serious of all the falsifications denounced by him, is without doubt the now traditional reading of Matthew 28:19.*

20.39 His source material has been lost, as he later wrote: *through events of war I have lost all of my files and other materials connected with the magazine.* But various authorities mention a work entitled Discrepancies in the Gospels, and another work entitled The Concluding Sections of the Gospels.

20.40 According to Conybeare: *"Eusebius cites this text (Matthew 28:19) again and again in works written between 300 and 336, namely in his long commentaries on the Psalms, on Isaiah, his Demonstratio Evangelica, his Theophany... in his famous history of the Church, and in his panegyric of the emperor Constantine. I have, after a moderate search in these works of Eusebius, found eighteen citations of Matthew 28:19, and always in the following form: 'Go ye and make disciples of all the nations in My name, teaching them to observe all things, whatsoever I commanded you."*

20.41 An article from *Zeitschrift fur die neutestamentliche Wissenschaft* in 1901, a magazine edited by Dr. Erwin Preuschen, indicates Eusebius was not content merely to cite the verse in this form. It notes that Eusebius frequently commented on it in such a way as to show how much he confirmed the wording "in my name". Thus, in his Demonstratio Evangelica he wrote the following: *"For he did not enjoin them "to make disciples of all the nations" simply and without qualification, but with the essential addition "in his name". For so great was the virtue attaching to his appellation that the Apostle says, "God bestowed on him the name above every name, that in the name of Yehushua every knee shall bow of things in heaven and on earth and under the earth." It was right therefore that he should emphasize the virtue of the power residing in his name but hidden from the many, and therefore say to his Apostles, "Go ye, and make disciples of all the nations in my name."*

20.42 Conybeare wrote in the Hibbert Journal, 1902: *"It is evident that this was the text found by Eusebius in the very ancient codices collected 50 to 150 years before his birth by his great predecessors. Of any other form of text he had never heard and knew nothing until he had visited Constantinople and attended the Council of Nicaea. Then in two controversial works written in his extreme old age, and entitled, the one 'Against Marcellus of Ancyra,' and the other 'About the Theology of the Church,' he used the common reading. One other writing of his also contains it, namely a letter written after the Council of Nicaea was over, to his seer of Caesarea."*

20.43 In his Textual Criticism of the New Testament Conybeare wrote: *"It is clear therefore, that of the manuscripts which Eusebius inherited from his predecessor, Pamphilus, at Caesurae in Palestine, some at least preserved the original reading, in which there was no mention either of baptism or of Father, Son and Holy Ghost. It has been conjectured by Dr. Davidson, Dr. Martineau, by the Dean of Westminster, and by Prof. Harnack that here the received text could not contain the very words of Yehushua – this long before anyone except Dr. Burgon, who kept the discovery to himself, had noticed the Eusebian form of the reading. It is sufficient answer to point out that Eusebius' argument, when he cites the text, involves the text 'in my name'. He asks, 'in whose name?' and answers that it was the name spoken of by Paul in his Epistle to the Philippians 2:10."*

20.44 Finally, the Encyclopedia of Religion and Ethics states: *"The facts are, in summary, that Eusebius quotes Matthew 28:19 twenty-one times, either omitting everything between 'nations' and 'teaching,' or in the form 'make disciples of all the nations in my name,' the latter form being the more frequent."*

20.45 Having considered the evidence of Eusebius, let us also consider some other early writers.

20.46 *The anonymous author of De Rebaptismate in the third century so understood them, and dwells at length on 'the power of the name of Jesus invoked upon a man by Baptism'.* (The Author of De Rebaptismate, from *Smith's Dictionary of the Bible*,

Vol. I, page 352.)

20.47 *In Origen's works, as preserved in the Greek, the first part of the verse is cited three times, but his citation always stops short at the words 'the nations'; and that in itself suggests that his text has been censored, and the words which followed, 'in my name', struck out.* – Conybeare

20.48 *In the pages of Clement of Alexandria a text somewhat similar to Matthew 28:19 is once cited, but from a Gnostic heretic named Theodotus, and not as from the canonical text, but as follows: "And to the Apostles he gives the command: Going around preach ye and baptise those who believe in the name of the Father and Son and Holy Spirit."* – Excerta cap. 76, ed. Sylb. page 287, quote from Conybeare.

20.49 *Justin Martyr… quotes a saying of the Messiah as a proof of the necessity or regeneration, but falls back upon the use of Isaiah and apostolic tradition to justify the practice of baptism and the use of the triune formula. This certainly suggests that Justin did not know the traditional text of Matthew 28:19.* – Encyclopedia of Religion and Ethics

20.50 Conybeare, writing in the Hibbert Journal, quotes a passage written by Justin Martyr between AD130 and 140, which is regarded as a citation or echo of Matthew 28:19 by various scholars. The passage is in Justin's dialogue with Trypho, page 258: *"YHWH hath not afflicted nor inflicts the judgment, as knowing of some that still even today are being made disciples in the name of his Messiah, and are abandoning the path of error, who also do receive gifts each as they be worthy, being illuminated by the name of this Messiah. The objection hitherto to these words being recognized as a citation our of text was that they ignored the formula 'baptising them in the name of the Father and Son and Holy Spirit.' But the discovery of the Eusebian form of text removes the difficulty: and Justin is seen to have had the same text as early as the year 140, which Eusebius regularly found in his manuscripts from 300 to 340."*

20.51 We may infer that the text was not quite fixed when Tertullian was writing, early in the third century. In the middle of that century Cyprian could insist on the use of the triple formula as essential in the baptism even of the orthodox. Pope Stephen answered him that the baptisms even of the heretics were valid, if the name of Jesus alone was invoked. Four centuries later, this did not prevent the popes of the seventh century from excommunicating the entire Celtic Church, which had inherited the Nazarene creed, for its remaining faithful to the old use of invoking in Jesus name alone.

20.52 In the last half of the fourth century, the text 'in the name of the Father, and of the Son, and of the Holy Ghost' was used as a battle cry by the orthodox against the adherents of Macedonius, who were called 'pneumato-machi' or 'fighters against the Holy Spirit', because they declined to include the Spirit in a Trinity of persons as co-equal, consubstantial and co-eternal with the Father and Son. They also stoutly denied that any text in the New Testament authorized such a coordination of the Spirit with the Father and Son.

20.53 The *Encyclopedia Biblia* in an article on Baptism refers to the original formula as "*an old practice dying out. Cyprian (Ep. 73) and the 'Apostolic Canons' (no. 50) combat the shorter formula, thereby attesting to its use in certain quarters. The ordinance of the Apostolic Canon therefore runs: 'If any bishop or presbyter fulfill not three baptisms of one initiation, but one baptism which is given (as) into the death of the Master, let him be deposed.' This was the formula of the followers of Eunomius (Socr.5:24), 'for they baptised not into the Trinity, but into the death of Messiah.' They accordingly used single immersion only.*

20.54 Finally, we have Aphraates who wrote between 337 and 345. He cites 28:19 in the following manner: '*Make disciples of all the nations, and they shall believe in me*'. The last words appear to be a gloss on the Eusebian reading 'in my name'. But in any case, they preclude the textus receptus with its injunction to baptise in the triune name. According to Conybeare, if the Aphraates quote was an isolated case, we might regard it as a loose citation, but in the presence of the Eusebian and Justinian texts this is impossible.

20.55 How were the Manuscripts changed? Let us consider the following quotations which demonstrate how freely the scribes altered manuscripts of the New Testament, in stark contrast to the scribes of the Old Testament scriptures who copied the holy writings with reverence and strict accuracy. These quotations also show the early heretical beginning of Triune immersion at a time when the doctrine of the Trinity was being formulated, and how the texts of the New Testament were changed to conform to the syncretized practice.

20.56 In examining the text of Matthew 28:19 we face the challenge that not a single manuscript or ancient version has preserved to us the true reading. But that is not surprising, for as Dr. C.R. Gregory, one of the greatest of our textual critics, reminds us: '*The Greek Manuscripts of the text of the New*

Testament were often altered by scribes, who put into them the readings which were familiar to them, and which they held to be the right readings.' (Canon and Text of the N.T. 1907, pg. 424). *"These facts speak for themselves. Our Greek texts, not only of the Gospels, but of the Epistles as well, have been revised and interpolated by orthodox copyists. We can trace their perversions of the text in a few cases, with the aid of patristic citations and ancient versions. But there must remain many passages which have been so altered, but where we cannot today expose the fraud. It was necessary to emphasize this point, because Dr. Wescott and Hort used to aver that there is no evidence of merely doctrinal changes having been made in the text of the New Testament. This is just the opposite of the truth, and such distinguished scholars as Alfred Loisy, J. Wellhausen, Eberhard Nestle, Adolf Harnack, to mention only four names, recognize the fact."* Peter Watkins, in an excellent article 'Bridging the Gap' in The Christadelphian, January, 1962, pp. 4-8.

20.57 *Codex B (Vaticanus) would be the best of all existing manuscripts... if it were completely preserved, less damaged, less corrected, more easily legible, and not altered by a later hand in more than two thousand places. Eusebius therefore, is not without grounds for accusing the adherents of Athanasius and of the newly arisen doctrine of the Trinity of falsifying the Bible more than once.* – Fraternal Visitor 1924, page 148, translation from Christadelphian Monatshefte.

20.58 *We certainly know of a greater number of interpolations and corruptions brought into the Scriptures... by the Athanasians, and relating to the Doctrine of the Trinity, than in any other case whatsoever. While we have not, that I know of, any such interpolation or corruption, made in any one of them by either the Eusebians or Arians.* Whiston – in Second Letter to the Bishop of London, 1719, p.15.

20.59 *While triune immersion was thus an all but universal practice, Eunomius (circa AD360) appears to have been the first to introduce (again) simple immersion unto the death of Messiah. Under church law, an officiating priest would be defrocked* - Canon Apostolic 46.

20.60 *In the 'Two Ways' of the Didache, the principal duties of the candidates for baptism and the method of administering it by triple immersion or infusion on the head are outlined. This triple immersion is also attested to by Tertullian (Adverses Prax 26). The most elaborate form of the rite in modern Western usage is in the Roman Catholic Church.* Oxford Dictionary of the Christian Church – pp.125-126

20.61 *Athanasius... met Flavian, the author of the Doxology, which has since been universal in Christendom: 'Glory be to the Father, and to the Son, etc.' This was composed in opposition to the Arian Doxology: 'Glory to the Father,* **by** *the Son,* **in** *the Holy*

Spirit'. Robert Roberts, in "Good Company" (Vol. iii, page 49)

20.62 Whiston, in his 2nd Letter concerning the Primitive Doxologies, published in 1719, page 17, wrote: *The Eusebians... sometimes named the very time when, the place where, and the person by whom they (the forms of doxology) were first introduced ... Thus Philoflorgius, a writer of that very age, assures us in 'Photius' Extracts' that in AD348 or thereabouts, Flavianus, Patriarch of Antioch, got a multitude of monks together, and did there first use this public doxology, 'Glory be to the Father, and to the Son, and to the Holy Spirit'.*

20.63 Considering the evidence of the manuscripts, the versions and now the early writings, you should by now have come to conclusion that in the early centuries most if not all copies of Matthew did not contain the modern Triune wording.

20.64 In legal practice where copies of an original lost document vary, the "Internal Evidence" is used to resolve the discrepancy. That is, a comparison of the undisputed text with text in question, in order to determine which of the variant wordings is more likely to be the original. With both variants in mind, we will now turn to the scriptures themselves for our internal evidence.

20.65 Internal Evidence. In our efforts to determine which reading of Matthew 28:19 is original, lets assess both versions to ten tests of textual criticism. Doing so will reveal the genuine text and expose the spurious.

20.66 **First Test of textual criticism – Context**
When examining the context, we find that today's Trinitarian wording lacks logical syntax, that is, the true understanding of the verse is obscured by a failure of the varying concepts to harmonize. If, however, we read as follows, the whole context fits together and the progression of the instructions is comprehensible: *All power is given unto **me**... go therefore... make disciples **in my name**, teaching them... whatsoever **I** have commanded... **I** am with you...* (Matthew 28:18-20).

20.67 **Second Test of textual criticism – Frequency**
Is the phrase *"in the name of the Father, and of the Son, and of the Holy Spirit"* used elsewhere in the scripture? Not once. Did Jesus use the phrase *"in my name"* on other occasions? Yes, 17 times to be exact, examples are found in Matthew 18:20; Mark 9:37, 39, 41; 16:17; John 14:14, 26; 15:16 and 16:23.

20.68 **Third Test of textual criticism – Doctrine**
Is any scriptural doctrine based upon a threefold name, or of baptism in the threefold name? None. Is any statement in scripture based on the fact of baptism in the name of Jesus? Yes! This is clarified in 1 Corinthians 1:13: *"Is **Messiah** divided? Was Paul crucified for you? Or were ye baptised in the name of Paul?"* These words, when carefully analysed, suggest that believers should to be baptised in the name of the One who was crucified for them. Christian doctrine holds that God gave us His Son to die in our stead. Clearly, it is Jesus who was crucified, no one else, and therefore it is in Jesus name believers must be baptised in water.

20.69 According to Dr. Thomas, in Revealed Mystery, Article XLIV: *There is but one way for a believer of 'the things concerning the Kingdom of YHWH, and the name of Jesus Messiah' to put Him on, or to be invested with His name, and that is, by immersion into His name. Baptism is for this specific purpose. As for its significance, baptism is linked inseparably with the death of Messiah. It is the means of the believer's identification with the Master's death.* – YHWH's Way, page 190. The Father did not die, nor did the Holy Spirit. As Paul wrote: *"buried with **Him** (Jesus) in baptism,"* not with the Father, the Son, and the Holy Spirit. (Romans 6:3-5)

20.70 R. Roberts used this explanation in "The Nature of Baptism", page 13): *"According to triune immersion, it is not sufficient to be baptised into the Son. Thus, Messiah is displaced from His position as the connecting link, the door of entrance, the 'new and living way'. And thus, there are three names under heaven whereby we must be saved, in opposition to the apostolic declaration, that 'there is no other name (than the name of Jesus of Nazareth) under heaven given among men whereby we must be saved."* (Acts 4:12).

20.71 This, of course, is the same reasoning offered by Paul when he asks: W*ere you baptised in the name of Paul?* Jesus was the 'sacrificial lamb', not the Father nor the Holy Spirit.

20.72 Based on the above understanding alone, we can ascertain the genuine text of Matthew 28:19 used the phrase *"in my name"*.

20.73 **Fourth Test of textual criticism – Analogy**
Does any other scripture make reference to baptism in the Triune name? No. Does any other scripture reference baptism in the name of Jesus? Yes! The disciples received a gift from the Holy Spirit, a promise that came according to Jesus *"in His name"* (John 14:26). Jesus is the "common

denominator", literally the name, in both water baptism and baptism of the Holy Spirit, as made apparent by the following scriptures:

- John 16:7: *Nevertheless, I tell you the truth; it is expedient for you that I go away: for if I go not away, the Comforter will not come unto you; but if I depart, I will send him unto you.*

- John 14:26: *But the Comforter, which is the Holy Spirit, whom the Father will send in my name, shall teach you all things, and bring all things to your remembrance, whatsoever I have said unto you.* (See also John 7:39).

- Acts 8:12: *But when they believed Philip preaching the things concerning the kingdom of God, and the name of Jesus, they were baptised, both men and women.*

20.74 Notice that they were baptised as a result of the preaching of the name of Jesus, not the titles "Father, Son and Holy Ghost." By analogy, we should therefore be baptised in Jesus name, because the invoking of Jesus name is the catalyst of that prepares us for the baptism of the Spirit, which is also given in Jesus name. (Acts 2:38-39, 19:1-5, John 3:3-5)

20.75 **Fifth Test of textual criticism – Consequence**
When we are baptised, do we "put on" the name of the Father, Son and Holy Ghost? No. Do we put on the name of Jesus? Yes. When we are baptised in the name of Jesus, according to all baptismal accounts recorded in scripture, we are quite literally being baptised "into" the name of Jesus.

Galatians 3:27: *For as many of you as have been baptised into the Messiah have put on the Messiah.*

20.76 No mention is made in scripture of any baptism being related to the titles of Father, Son and Holy Ghost. Every actual account mentions a clear connection with the person of Jesus, and his atoning sacrifice.

20.77 **Sixth Test of textual criticism – Practice**
Did the disciples, as they were implementing the "Great Commission" ever once baptise into the Trinity? Never! Did they baptise in the name of Jesus? Always! (Acts 2:38; 8:16; 10:48 (inferred); 19:5, etc.) The argument has been made when defending Triune immersion; "I would rather obey God, than to imitate the Apostles." This kind of reasoning though,

places the Apostles in rebellion, and makes all Apostolic baptisms contrary to the word of God. Surely, even those who consider God's Word to be inspired should not try to pit one verse against another but rather seek to reconcile all of God's Word in proper context, and rightly apply it to our lives. It is easier to believe that the disciples followed the final instructions of Jesus, than to believe that they immediately disobeyed His command.

20.78 **Seventh Test of textual criticism – Significance**
What significance is mentioned in scripture for baptising believers in the name of the Father, Son and Holy Spirit? None. What significance is conveyed toward being baptised in the name of Jesus? First, scripture teaches that baptism in the name of Jesus is an act of repentance leading to the forgiveness of sins (Acts 2:38). Second, baptism in His name **alone** is associated with the promise of the Holy Spirit (Acts 2:38, 19:1-5). Third, baptism in the name of Jesus is compared to our personal willingness to be living sacrifices or even die for the Messiah. (Romans 6:1-4 and Colossians 2:12). Fourth, being baptised into Messiah is how we 'put on' Messiah (Galatians 3:27). Fifth, baptism in His name is called the "circumcision of Messiah," and reflects our "putting off" of the man of sin, therefore becoming a *"new creature **in Jesus**."* (Colossians 2:11-12, 2 Corinthians 5:17).

20.79 Baptism in the name of Jesus expresses faith in the physical life of Jesus, his crucifixion for our sins, and the remission of sins through His name. One might argue that Trinitarian baptism can only express faith in Catholic theology itself.

20.80 **Eighth Test of textual criticism – Parallel Accounts**
Matthew 28 is not the sole record in the gospels of the "Great Commission" of the Church. Luke also recorded this event in great detail. In Luke 24:46-47, he wrote of Jesus speaking in the third person: *"And that repentance and remission of sins should be preached **in His name** among all nations."* This passage alone, in contradiction to the falsified text, establishes the correct wording of Matthew 28:19, where Jesus spoke in the first person, *"in my name."* Further, the Gospel of Mark also records another version of the "Great Commission," using some of the same patterns of speech: *"Go ye... all the world... preach the gospel... every creature... baptised... in my name..."* (Mark 16:15-18). Of course, it is not baptism that "in my name" refers to here, but rather the works that the disciples would do. Yet compared to Matthew, the similarity is striking, although baptism is

PART THREE: JESUS, THE NAZARENE

not explicitly mentioned, the disciples should act, *"in my name."*

20.81 **Ninth Test of textual criticism – Complimentary Citation**
While there is no text that offers a complimentary citation of Trinitarian baptism, there is a striking resemblance between the actual wording of Matthew 28:18-20 and Romans 1:4-5. Matthew contains the Commission by Jesus of his apostles, while the Romans account is Paul's acceptance of his own commission as an apostle.

Consider the following similarities:

Matthew 28:18-20	Romans 1:4-5
"all power is given unto Me"	*"the Son of God with power"*
"Go ye"	*"received... apostleship"*
"teaching them to observe"	*"for obedience to the faith"*
"all nations"	*"all nations"*
"in My name"	*"for His name"*

20.82 **Tenth Test of textual criticism – Principle**
It is written: *"whatsoever ye do in word or deed, do all in the name of the Master Jesus... "* (Colossians 3:17). In this principle laid down by Paul, the implication is clear. The word *"whatsoever"* would of certain necessity include baptism, which is a command involving both word and deed. The traditional wording of Matthew, containing the Trinitarian wording, is clearly not in accordance with the above principle. The shorter wording, without the falsified insertion, follows this principle. This establishes which of the two wordings is the contradictory one. Paul not only expressed this principle, but he applied it specifically to the topic of baptism. In Acts 19:1-6 there is an account concerning the disciples of John who had been baptised under his ministry. Like baptism in Jesus' name, John's baptism was one of repentance for the remission of sins (Mark 1:4, Acts 2:38). John's message, which accompanied his baptism, was that One would come after him, who would *"take away the sins of the world"* and *"baptise with the Holy Spirit."* Paul introduced these disciples to that One, and applying the above principle re-baptised them. *"When they heard this, they were baptised into the name of the Master Jesus. And when Paul laid his hands upon them, the Holy Spirit came upon them... "* And so, applying the test of principle to our two readings in Matthew 28:19, we find very strong support for the phrase *"in My name."*

20.83 I deduce that the evidence reviewed so far is overwhelmingly conclusive that the traditional wording of Matthew 28:19 is not the original. Numerous other authors have also expressed doubts and a number of these are reproduced below.

20.84 Hastings Encyclopedia of Religion and Ethics, Article: Baptism: Early Christian. *The cumulative evidence of these three lines of criticism (Textual Criticism, Literary Criticism and Historical Criticism) is thus distinctly against the view that Matthew 28:19 (in the traditional form) represents the exact words of Messiah.*

20.85 Dr. Peake – Bible Commentary, page 723
The command to baptise into the threefold name is a late doctrinal expansion. Instead of the words 'baptising them in the name of the Father, and of the Son, and of the Holy Ghost' we should probably read simply, 'into my name'.

20.86 F. Whiteley in The Testimony (Oct. 1959, page 351. "Back to Babylon")
There is the "triune" baptismal formula, which may prove a very broken reed when thoroughly investigated, but... we leave it for separate treatment. The thoughtful may well ponder, meantime, why one cannot find one single instance, in Acts or Epistles, of the words ever being used at any of the main baptisms recorded, notwithstanding Messiah's (seemingly) explicit command at the end of Matthew's Gospel.

20.87 Williams R.R. – Theological Workbook of the Bible, page 29
The command to baptise in Matthew 28:19 is thought to show the influence of a developed doctrine of YHWH verging on Trinitarianism. Early baptism was in the name of Messiah. The association of this Trinitarian conception with baptism suggests that baptism itself was felt to be an experience with a Trinitarian reference.

20.88 Dean Stanley – "Christian Institutions": *Doubtless the more comprehensive form in which baptism is now everywhere administered in the threefold name... soon superseded the simpler form of that in the name of the Master Yehushua only.*

20.89 E.K. in the Fraternal Visitor – Article: "The Question of the Trinity and Matt. 28:19." 1924, pg. 147-151, from Christadelphian Monatshefte.
The striking contrast and the illogical internal incoherence of the passage... lead to a presumption of an intentional corruption in the interests of the Trinity. In ancient Christian times a tendency of certain parties to corrupt the text of the New Testament was certainly often imputed. This increases our doubt almost to a decisive certainty concerning the genuineness of the passage.

20.90 In his Literal Translation of the Bible, Dr. Robert Young placed the Trinitarian "names" of Matthew 28:19 in parentheses, thus indicating the words to be of doubtful authenticity. *"The very account which tells us that at last, after His resurrection, He commissioned His disciples to go and baptise among all nations, betrays itself by speaking in the Trinitarian language of the next century, and compels us to see in it the ecclesiastical editor, and not the evangelist, much less the Founder Himself."*

20.91   James Martineau – Black's Bible Dictionary, article "Seat of Authority": *The Trinitarian formula (Matthew 28:19) was a late addition by some reverent Christian mind.*

20.92   Encyclopedia of Religion and Ethics: *The obvious explanation of the silence of the New Testament on the triune name, and the use of another formula in Acts and Paul, is that this other formula was the earlier, and that the triune formula is a later addition.*

20.93   F. Whiteley in The Testimony footnotes to Article: Baptism, 1958: *Clerical conscience is much troubled that the apostles and epistles never once employ the triune name of Matthew 28:19. Even Trinitarians, knowing the idea of the Trinity was being resisted by the Church in the fourth century, admit 'the command to baptise with the threefold name is a late doctrinal expansion', but still prior to our oldest yet known manuscripts (4th Century). It's sole counterpart, 1 John 5:7 is a proven interpolation. Eusebius (A.D. 264-340) denounces the triune form as spurious, Matthew's actual writing having been baptising them 'in my name'.*

20.94   Should the text of Matthew 28:19 be restated to what seems its original text? Certainly, it is difficult to identify a more serious divinely appointed symbolism in the entire Bible. The symbolic value of baptism in Matthew 28:19 is unlikely to be of less concern to Jesus than that of the Ark of the Covenant was in ancient Israel. Uzziah died when he touched it, and few would conclude that his motives were anything but commendable!

20.95   Believers were taught to anoint the sick *"with oil in the name of the Master"* (James 5:14). The result would be *"that you may be healed"*. When two or three gather together *"in His name"*, the result is that He is there in the midst of them. As our evidence reveals, Jesus commanded us to go and make disciples *"in His name"*. As a result, He would be with them "always, even to the end of the age." Anything we do "in His name" directly involves Him. It is no wonder that Paul so clearly charged those believers in Colosse: "Whatever you do in word or deed, do all in the name of Jesus, giving thanks to God."

20.96 In 1960, The British and Foreign Bible Society published a Greek Testament, and the alternative rendering for Matthew 28:19 was phrased "en to onomati mou" ("in my name"). Eusebius was cited as the authority. The Jerusalem Bible, of 1966, a Roman Catholic production, has this footnote for Matthew 28:19: *"It may be that this formula... is a reflection of the liturgical usage established later in the primitive community. It will be remembered that Acts speaks of baptising in the name of Jesus."*

20.97 But you may ask, Matthew 28:19 and Luke 24:47 say nothing of baptism? They refer only of *"making disciples of all nations"* and *"repentance and remission of sins."* Having established that the original text of Matthew 28:19 simply says "in my name," **all** support for **baptising** "in the name of the Father, and of the Son, and of the Holy Ghost" is eliminated. Finally, let's check the internal evidence regarding baptism, in order to find any other possible support for the traditional reading, because the Trinitarian doctrinal concept that **was added** to Matthew 28:19 **is** connected with baptism. Though baptism is not specifically mentioned in Matthew 28:19 or Luke 24:47, it is inferred by the following two points:

(i) In Matthew, the command is to *"make disciples in my name"*. To "make a disciple" of necessity includes baptism in the conversion process (Mark 16:15-16, John 3:3-5), and the entire process is under the umbrella of the specification to do so "in His name".

(ii) In Luke, *"repentance and remission of sins"* would be preached "in His name". By the testimony of other scriptures (Luke 3:3, Acts 2:38), it is clear that *remission of sins* comes through baptism, preceded by repentance. Both of these are to be preached "in His name".

20.98 The Evidence of Eusebius

Jerome was born cAD342 and died in AD420. He wrote many exegetical treatises and letters, as well as the renowned Latin Vulgate translation of the Scriptures. He made an interesting statement: (from the Catalogue of Ecclesiastical Writers): *Matthew, who is also Levi... composed a gospel... in the Hebrew language and characters... Furthermore, the Hebrew itself is preserved to this day in the library at Caesurae which the martyr Pamphilus so diligently collected.*

Eusebius (AD260-340) inherited that library from Pamphilus (who died in AD309), a library that was commenced by Origen (AD185-254). The wording of that statement by Jerome apparently meant that the ***original*** manuscript of Matthew was still to be seen in the Library at Caesarea. It could have meant that an early copy of Matthew's Hebrew writing was there, but the phraseology of Jerome appeared to indicate that it was the actual manuscript written by Matthew himself.

20.99 The Mental Reservations of Eusebius

In paragraph 20.42 mention is made of the fact that, after the Council of Nicaea, Eusebius three times used the triune name-phrase in writing. The following three extracts shed light on this strange affair:

(i) *At the Council of Nicaea (AD325) Eusebius took a leading part... He occupied the first seat to the emperor's right, and delivered the opening address to Constantine when he took his seat in the council chamber... Eusebius himself has left us an account of his doings with regard to the main object of the council in a letter of explanation to his church at Caesurae... This letter... is written to the Caesareans to explain that he would resist to the last any vital change in the traditional creed of his church, but had subscribed to these alterations, when assured of their innocence, to avoid appearing contentious.* Dictionary of Christian Biography and Literature; Eusebius

(ii) *Our concern here is only with Nicaea as it affected Eusebius... his own account of the matter is transmitted to us... in the letter he addressed to his diocese an explanation of his actions at the Council, for with some misgiving he had signed the document bearing the revised text of the creed he had presented... But being satisfied that the creed did not imply the opposite Sabellian pitfall... he signed the document.* Wallace Hadrill, 'Eusebius of Caesurae', 1960.

(iii) *Eusebius occupied a distinguished position in the Council of Nicaea and was profoundly impressed by the sight of that majestic gathering. He was its spokesman in welcoming the Emperor. Moved by the express opinion of Constantine, he signed the Creed, and even accepted the anathematism appended to it — but did so, as we gather from his own statement, by dint of evasive glosses which he certainly could not have announced at that time. While then he verbally capitulated in the doctrinal decisions of the Nicene Council... he did so reluctantly, under pressure. He knew that he would be thought to have compromised his convictions, and therefore wrote his account to the people of his diocese, and, as Athanasius expresses it 'excluded himself in his own way'.* William Bright in his Preface to Burton's 'Text of Eusebius Ecclesiastical History'

20.100 Second Century mutilations of the original text

The SPCK commenting on Matthew 28:19 stated: *"One would expect this name to be that of Jesus and it is surprising to find the text continuing with 'the Father, and the Son, and the Holy Ghost,' which are not names at all. The suspicion that this is not what Matthew originally wrote naturally arises. In 'Father, Son and Holy Ghost' we have the Trinitarian formula... which was associated with Christian Baptism in the second century, as evidenced in the Didache, chapter 7."* Volume One, of the Clarified New Testament, SPCK, 1964.

F.C. Kenyon, in The Text of the Greek Bible, pages 241-242 said: *"At the first, each book had its single original text, which is now the object of criticism to recover, but in the first two centuries this original Greek text disappeared under a mass of variants, created by errors, by conscious alterations, and by attempts to remedy the uncertainties thus created."*

20.101 The final clincher

Joseph Ratzinger (who became Pope Benedict XVI 2005 – 2013) made this confession as to the origin of the Trinitarian text of Matthew 28:19 saying: "The basic form of our (Matthew 28:19 Trinitarian) profession of faith took shape during the course of the second and third centuries in connection with the ceremony of baptism. So far as its place of origin is concerned, the text (Matthew 28:19) came from the city of Rome." Introduction to Christianity, 1968 edition, pp82-83.

20.102 The Source of the Error

The earliest reference to the Trinitarian doctrinal insertion is found in the Didache. The Didache is a collection of fragments of writings from five or more documents. It is thought were written between AD80 and 160. Although we now have only 99 verses, those verses contain the seeds of many false teachings that developed into the Papal Superstitions. Some regard the Didache as containing the seeds of Indulgences, the Mass, the Confessional and the substitution of sprinkling for immersion. In the Didache, amongst all the other apostate beliefs, is found the Trinitarian phrase that later wormed its way into the text of Matthew 28:19, displacing the authentic words of Messiah.

20.103 The Inspiration for the Error

Having read all of this chapter, you may be wondering where the idea of a Trinity came from. After all, given the many statements attributed

PART THREE: JESUS, THE NAZARENE

to Jesus in the Gospels, that God is Spirit – how could Christian dogma conclude that God comprises both God and a Holy Spirit? The answer can be traced directly to the Council of Nicaea, 325, where the minority view led by Athanasius (Bishop of Alexandria) promoted the ancient Egyptian idea of a trinity based upon our old friends Osiris, resurrected by his son, Horus and his wife Isis.

20.104 Some Christian theologians, unhappy with the concept of a Trinity, link it to Semiramis and point to it having been derived from Babylon – itself a general term of theological abuse! Maybe they detect the link to Marduk, known as the pagan god of that city. I speculate that such thinking correctly spots the 'Ra' incorporated in the Semiramis name (and its original form, Sammuramat) and we know that the Egyptian Ra was also Marduk. However, this parallels the popular theological misconception that the Enuma Elish was also Babylonian – it is similarly mistaken.

20.105 Detailed records recovered from Nimrud, Assyria, explain the historic origin of the deification of Sammuramat as 'queen of heaven'. Ashurbanipal II's grandson, King Shamshi-Adad V, married Sammuramat, who upon his death in 811BC, ruled successfully in her own right for 12 years – combining beauty and success as a military commander such that her reputation became immortalised and her husband and son became seen as reincarnations of olden gods. Her husband became seen as the god Nimrod, as she ruled from the city of Nimrud (30 km south of Mosul) commemorated to Nimrod. Sammuramat became known as the embodiment of Ishtar (Sumerian: Inanna) and then became widely known in her Hellenised name of Semiramis. Her son and successor, Adad-Nirari III, became known as Tammuz – also Hellenised as Adonis.

20.106 However, this Assyrian Trinity, often mistaken by Christian writers as a Babylonian trinity, was inspired by a much older Egyptian Trinity from which the original gods were copied. In Egyptian belief there had been a longstanding idea of a Trinity based upon Osiris, his wife Isis and their son Horus – which has been traced back as far as 2400BC. The same individuals forming the Egyptian trinity were supposedly reincarnated to form the Assyrian trinity some 1500 years later. Such was the power of this tradition, that the Alexandrian school of bishops imported the concept into the Council of Nicaea in AD325 and found it enthusiastically adopted by Emperor Constantine.

20.107 Why was Emperor Constantine so enthusiastic? Constantine seized upon two opportunities that the Trinity provided. Like most Romans, Constantine hated the Jews – they were troublesome and had traditionally been persistently rebellious – so the idea that under Christianity the senior God was Jewish was an anathema. With a Trinity, Jesus got promoted into being co-equal with God – much better. Even more compelling was that Constantine saw himself as a latter-day Jesus – he was a more effective King Messiah, he won battles and controlled a huge empire. Given the Emperor must be divine, upon his death he could aspire to replace Jesus in the new Godhead.

20.108 A footnote on Baptism – after having read this chapter, do you conclude that you be re-baptised in the manner urged by Paul? Interestingly, the answer is clearly set out in Acts – arguably the single most reliable book in the Bible:

Acts 19:1-6: *And it happened, while Apollos was at Corinth, that Paul, having passed through the upper regions, came to Ephesus. And finding some disciples he said to them, "Did you receive the Holy Spirit when you believed?" So they said to him, "We have not so much as heard whether there is a Holy Spirit." And he said to them, "Into what then were you baptised?" So they said, "Into John's baptism." Then Paul said, "John indeed baptised with a baptism of repentance, saying to the people that they should believe on Him who would come after him, that is, on Jesus."* **When they heard this, they were baptised in the name of the Master Jesus.** *And when Paul had laid hands on them, the Holy Spirit came upon them, and they spoke with tongues and prophesied.*

The answer is very clear: Paul, who only spent a few minutes with Jesus, found disciples who had heard the message of the John the Baptist and responded to that message by being baptised following repentance. However, these 'disciples' had yet to hear the full gospel message. Because of this, their baptism, under the ministry and authority of John the Baptist did not reflect an association with the death and burial of Jesus that made baptism in His name effective. For Paul, the next step was obvious. Knowing that the promise of the Holy Spirit was given to those who through the obedience of faith had repented of their sins, and been baptised in the name of Jesus, he instructed them to be re-baptised.

20.109 But what of Apostles who travelled with Jesus for 3 years? Peter was also clear: In Acts 2:38, Peter says *"be baptised in the name of Jesus Christ"* and a little later *"for there is **no other name** under heaven, given among men by which we must be saved"* Acts 4:12

20.110 My conclusion on the Trinity. If you are exhausted by having carefully read through all of this section on 1 John 5:6-8 and Matthew 28:19, then by now you may be convinced that the concept of the Trinity is fundamentally a man-made invention. Understanding that the concept of the Trinity is not a genuine or relevant part of Christian belief and freedom from the dogma allows one to move closer to understanding Jesus original teaching – which is explored in Part Four of this series.

20.111 Finally, a few notes on the origin of baptism as a practise and why first century Jews may have been confused. According to Tertullian, a very important early Church father, (cAD155 to 240) in chapter 5 of his text 'On Baptism', states that the practise of baptism originated in the Egyptian worship of Osiris and Isis (grandchildren of Ra, aka Marduk). Bingo – more identification of the early influences on Christianity! According to the 1906 Jewish Encyclopedia, baptism became widespread Jewish practise during the captivity in Babylon, copying from a local practise. Jewish baptism was always self-immersion, ***three times***, as expiration of sins. Jews would not have understood baptism as being born again, but as purification before going to the Temple. The triple immersion survived to take over from the single immersion proscribed by Jesus.

20.112 This detailed inspection of Matthew 28:19 has touched upon widespread references claiming that many texts of the New Testament have been subject to numerous textual variations. I trust this has awakened your interest in understanding just what other key elements of Christian belief have been forged by, often well intentioned, tweaking of NT texts that most Christians believe are treasured originals which have been carefully preserved. Part Four examines other key elements of dogma that have been successfully suppressed or amended.

21

Prophesies in the Old Testament considered fulfilled by Jesus

21.1 If you read Part One of this series you may recall that my conclusions concerning the Old Testament were qualified by the need to examine the dozens of prophesies which many claim foretell the life of Jesus. However, under examination, the strength of prophesy crumbles, indeed some Christian academics have stunned me by saying:- 'place no faith in biblical prophesies'.

21.2 Doubts about OT prophesies fall under five main categories:

- As commented upon in earlier chapters, the gospels record numerous incidences where it seems Jesus actions are deliberately designed to fulfil prophesy – and no doubt enthusiastic gospel writers were keen to record as many fulfilments of prophesy as they could to convince their readers.

- In Part Two, we found strong evidence that some books were written so long after the events that they claim to record that the historical facts had become extremely confused in the minds of the authors – writing about historical events is hardly prophetic.

- Further, extensive editing and redaction continued for centuries – enabling prophesies to be written in to the text long after events had taken place.

- Whilst some of the most prominent references that are held to be

PART THREE: JESUS, THE NAZARENE

prophetic initially appear quite compelling, upon closer examination the claims seem highly dubious – some have been manufactured by tweaking the wording of English translations to make them appear to say things that are simply not in the Hebrew text.

- Many references claimed as prophesies are very general and could apply to many situations.

21.3 Of key OT texts most frequently quoted as prophesying events in Jesus life, the following prophesies are examined here in detail:

- Psalm 22 concerning Jesus crucifixion

- Psalm 110 with David purported to be addressing Jesus as his Lord

- Isaiah 7:14 prophesy of a virgin birth

- Isaiah 9:6-7 prophesy of a Messiah, reflecting Christians complete lack of knowledge about the meaning of the term 'Messiah'

- Isaiah 53 prophesy of Jesus crucifixion

- Micah 5:2 prophesy of Jesus as King of Israel

- Zechariah 11:12-13 prophesy of Judas blood money

Psalm 22 concerning Jesus crucifixion

21.4 Psalm 22 is one of the most popular places to look for the supposed Old Testament prophecies fulfilled by the life of Jesus. Apologists claim that it closely parallels the crucifixion story but was written roughly 1000 years earlier. Rabbinical sources relate this psalm to David's fears after Nathan chastised him for his behavior towards Bathsheba and Uriah. The analysis below is partly sourced from Bob Siedensticker, a self-proclaimed atheist from Seattle.

21.5 What does Psalm 22 state that is seen as prophetic:

- Verse 1: *"My God, my God, why have you forsaken me?"* which are the last words of Jesus according to Matthew and Mark.

- Verse 7: *"All who see me mock me; they hurl insults, shaking their heads. 'He trusts in the Lord,' they say, 'Let the Lord rescue him.'"* Sure enough, Mark records the onlookers insulting Jesus and mocking his inability to free himself.

- Verse 16: *"they have pierced my hands and my feet"* sounds like the crucifixion. This form of execution was practiced by Persians, Carthaginians and Romans from the 6th century BC until abolished by Emperor Constantine in AD337. Therefore, references to crucifixion would be prophetic.

- Verse 18: *"They divide my garments among them and cast lots for my clothing,"* as noted in Mark.

21.6 These are some clear parallels, but what best explains this — that this ancient psalm really did predict the crucifixion or that the gospel story was deliberately written to mimic a prophecy? The author of Mark was surely familiar with this psalm and could have added the distribution of the clothes, the mocking from the crowd, and the last words.

21.7 But what about the piercing of the hands and feet? It may not say that. A better translation may be, "like a lion they pin my hands and feet." The New English Translation Bible comments: *"The psalmist may envision a lion pinning the hands and feet of its victim to the ground with its paws (a scene depicted in ancient Near Eastern art), or a lion biting the hands and feet."*

21.8 Make that change and see what verse 16 says:

wild dogs surround me –
a gang of evil men crowd around me;
like a lion they pin my hands and feet.

No longer do we have a good parallel to the crucifixion story. To be fair, there are arguments for both interpretations of the verse. But, as we shall review in Part Four, the use of iron nails to pierce Jesus hands and feet is itself highly dubious.

21.9 Consider those last words: "My God, why have you forsaken me?" Does forsaking Jesus sound like part of God's plan? This doesn't sound like the cool-headed, in-control Jesus written about in Luke and John. It could be interpreted as supporting the 'separationist' belief as in the Gospel of

Philip: *"My God, My God, why, Lord, have you forsaken me?" [Jesus] spoke these words on the cross, for the Lord had left that place.* Some believed a divine spirit had entered Jesus the man at baptism (remember the dove?) but then abandoned Jesus at the crucifixion.

21.10 What about the skipped verses? Now consider the entire chapter. The apologetic claim rests on picking intriguing little fragments out of context, but taken as a whole this looks even less like the crucifixion story:

- Verse 9: *"Yet you brought me out of the womb; you made me trust in you"* – again, this sounds like an ordinary man. Surely, the first person of the Trinity wouldn't need to make the second person of the Trinity trust him?

- Verse 12: *"Many bulls surround me; strong bulls of Bashan [a place known for its cattle] encircle me. Roaring lions tearing their prey open their mouths wide against me."* Bulls and lions? That sounds like martyrdom in an arena, not crucifixion.

- Verse 17: *"I can count all my bones."* This unfortunate guy is clearly mistreated, but (again) this isn't the gospel story.

- Verse 20: *"Deliver my life from the sword, my precious life from the power of the dogs. Rescue me from the mouth of the lions; save me from the horns of the wild oxen."* Ditto.

21.11 And the biggest problem with shoehorning of Psalm 22 into the gospel story is that there's no reference to the resurrection! How can this be the story of the sacrifice of Jesus but forget the resurrection?

Psalm 110 – David purported addressing Jesus as his Lord

21.12 Rabbi Tovia Singer provides the following illumination of a mistranslated text:

21.13 Psalm 110 represents one of the New Testament's most stunning, yet clever, mistranslations of the Jewish Scriptures. Moreover, the confusion created by the Christianization of this verse was further perpetuated and promulgated by numerous Christian translators of the Bible. Tampering with Psalm 110 began when the Book of Matthew was written, introduced in the framework of an anecdotal question in Matthew 22:41-44:

PROPHESIES IN THE OLD TESTAMENT CONSIDERED FULFILLED BY JESUS

21.14   *Jesus turns to the Pharisees and asks them, "What do you think about the Christ? Whose son is he? (In laymen's terms, the question is, 'From whom is the messiah descended?') They said to him, "The son of David." He said to them, "How then does David in the spirit call him 'Lord,' saying, 'The Lord said to my Lord, "Sit at My right hand, till I make your enemies your footstool?"' If David then called him Lord, how is he his son?" No one was able to answer him a word, neither did any man from that day forth ask him any more questions.*

21.15   In Christian tradition, this is a terrific triumphant story. Jesus really showed those arrogant Pharisees how little they knew about their own Bible! Yet this story could never have occurred. No Jew with a superficial knowledge of this text would have accepted Jesus' argument as compelling.

21.16   Let us examine the original verse from which Matthew's Jesus quoted in order to grasp the way in which the original Hebrew text was manipulated to create the above storyline. The King James Version translates this passage in the following manner: *The LORD said unto my Lord, "Sit thou on my right hand, till I put thine enemies underneath thy feet."* It appears from the KJV translation that the 'Lord', which is God, said unto to 'my Lord' – who some would have you believe is Jesus (David's 'Lord') – *"Sit thou on my right hand, till I put thine enemies underneath thy feet."*

21.17   Is the above verse speaking about the Messiah? Not at all. Yet look at the first and second word "Lord" in the verse. In the "translation" they appear identical because the Christian translator cleverly masked the text of the original Hebrew.

Psalm 110:1

מִזְמוֹר לְדָוִד נְאֻם **יהוה לַאדֹנִי** שֵׁב לִימִינִי עַד אָשִׁית אֹיְבֶיךָ הֲדֹם לְרַגְלֶיךָ׃

Translation	A Psalm of David. The Lord said unto my lord: 'Sit thou at My right hand, until I make thine enemies thy footstool.'
King James Version	The LORD said unto my Lord, Sit thou at my right hand, until I make thine enemies thy footstool.
New Living Bible	The Lord said to my Lord, "Sit in the place of honor at my right hand until I humble your enemies, making them a footstool under your feet."

21.18   Although the two English words in the KJV translation were deliberately made to appear virtually identical, in the original Hebrew text they are entirely different. Whereas the first word "Lord" in the Hebrew is a correct translation of הוהי, which is the Tetragrammaton (YHWH), the name of God, the second word "Lord" is a complete and deliberate mistranslation of the text. The second word "Lord" in the verse is a mistranslation of the Hebrew word יְנֹדאַל; *(ladonee)*. The correct translation of *ladonee* is "to my master" or "to my lord." The Hebrew word *ladonee* never refers to God anywhere in the Bible. It is used only to address a person, never God. God is never called *ladonee* in Hebrew. There are many words describing God but *ladonee* is not one of them.

21.19   Look at other places where same Hebrew word, יְנֹדאַל; *(ladonee)* occurs and how it is translated:
Genesis 24:54: *"And they did eat and drink, he and the men that were with him, and tarried all night; and they rose up in the morning, and he said, Send me away unto my master. (ladonee: יְנֹדאַל;)* [Abraham]."
Genesis 32:4: *"Jacob instructed the angels to bring the following message to his wicked brother Esau: And he commanded them, saying, Thus shall ye speak unto my lord Esau; יְנֹדאַל; (ladonee) 'Thy servant Jacob saith thus, I have sojourned with Laban, and stayed there until now."*

21.20   The Hebrew word יְנֹדאַל; *(ladonee)* used in the above two verses is referring to Abraham and Esau, respectively. Notice that the Hebrew word used in both verses is identical to the Hebrew word in Psalm 110:1. Why did the King James Version translate יְנֹדאַל; correctly in Genesis 24:54 as "to my master," or in Genesis 32:4 as "to my lord," yet deliberately mistranslate Psalm 110:1 as "Lord"? Why do most Bibles make no distinction between those two words, as they do in each and every other place that they appear in the Torah? The answer is obvious. Both Genesis 24:54 and Genesis 32:4 are not texts used by the Church to "prove" Jesus from the Jewish Scriptures and therefore they had no incentive to tamper with them. Psalm 110:1, on the other hand, is a passage used by Christians as a verse that they argue "unquestionably points only to Jesus".

21.21   It should be noted that while many Christian translators indulge in this manipulation of Psalm 110:1, some do refrain from this practice. Numerous modern Bibles have corrected Matthew's mistranslation. For example, the Revised Standard Version and the New English Bible correctly render the Hebrew word *ladonee* as "to my lord," in Psalm 110:1, clearly indicating that this word is not speaking of Jesus.

21.22 As mentioned above, this tampering with Psalm 110:1 began at the time the New Testament texts were written. The Christian translators, who would later also mistranslate this verse, simply followed in the footsteps of the author of the first Gospel. If we look at the original Greek of Matthew 22:44 we find the same doctoring of the text in later Christian translations of the Book of Psalms. When Matthew has Jesus quote Psalm 110:1 to the Pharisees, the identical Greek word κύριος is used both times the word "Lord" appears in Matthew 22:44.

21.23 Finally, it is helpful to explore the meaning of Psalm 110:1. Of whom is this Psalm speaking? To whom are the words "my master" or "my lord" referring? The Psalm begins with the opening Hebrew words מִזְמוֹר לְדָוִד (Mizmor l'David). The word "Mizmor" means "a song," and thus the opening phrase of this Psalm is, "A Song of David". In fact, the word Psalms comes from the Greek word ψαλμός (psalmos), which means "a song." Why would King David be writing these songs? For whom was he writing them? Who did King David intend would sing these songs? The answers to these questions reveal the true meaning of Psalm 110.

21.24 One of King David's greatest disappointments was God's refusal to allow him to build the first Temple in Jerusalem. Although David's son Solomon undertook that task, and eventually constructed the first Temple, David's connection to Solomon's Temple was significant. Both the city and the Temple were dedicated to him, the City and Temple of David. Moreover, he made preparations for the building of the Temple, and even arranged for the Temple service (2 Samuel 7; 1 Chronicles 14-17, 22-26). According to rabbinical sources, this is where the Book of Psalms played a key role. King David is credited with was great skills as a teacher, musician and poet. Most of the Psalms are attributed to David. The main purpose of the Psalms was for the Levites to sing them in the Temple. The Levites would stand on a platform and chant the Psalms to an inspired audience. The Levites would sing:- The Lord [God] said to my master [King David] "Sit thou at my right hand..." (Psalm 110:1)

21.25 Psalm 110 contains another, probably innocent, translation error. Christians Bibles have translated Aramaic 'bar' as 'son' and jumped to a conclusion by capitalising it. However, the psalms were all written in Hebrew, as Aramaic did not exist in David's time. So 'bar' should be translated

Isaiah 7:14 – a prophesy of a virgin birth

21.26 Isaiah 7 records (probably with hindsight) the birth and reign of a King Messiah. The author of Matthew perceived parallels with Jesus and decided to improve the prophesy by claiming reference to a virgin birth when referring to Isaiah. Later theologians seeing the problems caused by the context of Isaiah 7:14, frequently argue that it is a 'dual prophecy'.

21.27 In order to fully grasp the massive theological problem which claims of a 'dual prophesy' tries to avoid, one needs to explore the traumatic circumstances that unfold in Isaiah 7. This event is completely inconsistent with Matthew's application of these passages to his virgin-birth story.

21.28 Firstly, the word "virgin" does not appear in the seventh chapter of Isaiah. The author of the first Gospel deliberately mistranslated the Hebrew word הָעַלְמָה (ha'almah) as 'a virgin'. This Hebrew word, however, does not mean 'a virgin'. It simply means "young woman" with no implication of sexual experience. Most modern Bibles have corrected this erroneous translation, and now correctly translate this Hebrew word as 'the young woman'.

21.29 However, Matthew not only changed the meaning of the word הָעַלְמָה to apply this verse from the Jewish Scriptures to the virgin birth, he also completely ripped Isaiah 7:14 out of context and used it to support his infancy narrative of Jesus. The seventh chapter of the Book of Isaiah begins by describing the Syro-Ephraimite War, a military crisis that threatened Ahaz, king of the southern Kingdom of Judah.

21.30 In the year 732BC, the House of David was facing imminent destruction at the hands of two warring kingdoms in temporary alliance: Assyria and the northern Kingdom of Israel. These two armies had laid siege to Jerusalem. The Bible relates that King Ahaz were gripped with fear. Accordingly, God sent the prophet Isaiah to reassure King Ahaz that divine protection was at hand – the Almighty would protect him, the deliverance of his citizens was assured, and the formidable armies of Assyria and Israel would fail in their attempt to subjugate Jerusalem.

21.31 In Isaiah 7:1-16 we read,

> "And it came to pass in the days of Ahaz son of Jotham, son of Uzziah, king of Judah, that Rezin, king of Aram, and Pekah son of Remaliah, king of Israel, marched on Jerusalem to wage war against it, and he could not wage war against it. It was told to the House of David, saying, "Aram has allied itself with Ephraim," and his heart and the heart of his people trembled as the trees of the forest tremble because of the wind. The Lord said to Isaiah, "Now go out toward Ahaz, you and Shear-Yashuv your son to the edge of the conduit of the upper pool, to the road of the washer's field, and you shall say to him, 'Feel secure and calm yourself, do not fear, and let your heart not be faint because of these two smoking stubs of firebrands, because of the raging anger of Rezin and Aram and the son of Remaliah. Since Aram planned harm to you, Ephraim and the son of Remaliah, saying: "Let us go up against Judah and provoke it, and annex it to us; and let us crown a king in its midst, one who is good for us." So said the Lord God, "Neither shall it succeed, nor shall it come to pass...."
> The Lord continued to speak to Ahaz, saying, "Ask for yourself a sign from the Lord, your God; ask it either in the depths, or in the heights above." Ahaz said, "I will not ask, and I will not test the Lord." Then he said, "Listen now, O House of David, is it little for you to weary men, that you weary my God as well? Therefore, the Lord, of His own, shall give you a sign: Behold the young woman is with child, and she shall bear a son, and she shall call his name Immanuel. Cream and honey he shall eat when he knows to reject bad and choose good; for, when the lad does not yet know to reject bad and choose good, the land whose two kings you dread, shall be abandoned."

21.32   It is clear from this chapter that Isaiah's declaration was a prophecy of the unsuccessful siege of Jerusalem by the two hostile armies of Assyria and Israel, not a virgin birth more than seven centuries later. If we interpret this chapter as referring to Jesus' birth, what possible comfort and assurance would Ahaz, who was surrounded by overwhelming military enemies, have found in the birth of a child seven centuries in the future? Both he and his people would have been long dead and buried. Such a sign would make no sense.

21.33   Isaiah 7:15-16 states that by the time this child reaches the age of maturity ("he knows to reject bad and choose good"), the two threatening kings, Pekah and Rezin, will have been removed. In 2 Kings 15-16, it becomes clear that this prophecy was fulfilled contemporaneously, when both kings, Pekah and Retsin, were assassinated. It is clear from the context of Isaiah's seventh chapter that the child born in Isaiah 7:14 is not Jesus or any future virgin birth. Rather, it is referring to the divine protection that King Ahaz and his people would enjoy during the Syro-Ephraimite War.

PART THREE: JESUS, THE NAZARENE

21.34   This is where the Christian apologists response of a dual prophecy comes in. Some attempt to explain away Matthew's complete indifference to the biblical context of Isaiah 7:14 by claiming that Isaiah's words to Ahaz had two different applications. They concede that the first application of Isaiah's prophecy must have been addressed to Ahaz and his immediate crisis. That child that was born contemporaneously, and the first leg of this dual prophesy was fulfilled at the time of Ahaz, 2700 years ago.

21.35   Those promoting a dual prophesy insist that the second leg applied to Jesus' virgin birth 700 years later. Using this elaborate explanation, these apologists maintain that Matthew's use of Isaiah 7:14 is entirely appropriate. In short, it is claimed that Isaiah's prophecy was fulfilled twice: in 732BC and again in the year 4BC. Problem solved? Not quite.

21.36   The self-inflicted problems spawned by this adventurous dual-fulfillment explanation are staggering. The notion of a dual prophecy was fashioned without any Biblical foundation. Nowhere in the seventh chapter of Isaiah does the text indicate or even hint of a second fulfillment. This notion of a dual prophecy was contrived in order to conceal a stunning theological problem – the seventh chapter of Isaiah does not support Matthew's virgin birth story. Matthew's claim that Mary was untouched by a man when she conceived Jesus is unsupported by the Book of Isaiah.

21.37   The seventh chapter of Isaiah describes, in great detail, a contemporaneous, traumatic civil war which occurred 2700 years ago, not the birth of a Messiah seven centuries later. Simply put, Matthew ripped Isaiah 7:14 completely out of context. Moreover, if as some theologians argue, the Hebrew word "almah" can only mean a "virgin," and, as they insist, Isaiah 7:14 was fulfilled twice, who was the first virgin to conceive during Ahaz's lifetime? Were there two virgin births?

21.38   As explained earlier, the virgin birth of Jesus was in any case a fabrication to be competitive with 'pagan' gods – the virgin birth idea was not recognized by Jesus contemporaries, conflicts with other beliefs and is in any case illogical and unnecessary.

21.39   Furthermore, if it is claimed that Isaiah 7 contains a dual prophecy, how do the verses that follow, Isaiah 7:15-16, apply to Jesus where the prophet continues to discuss this lad? The following passages state, "Cream and honey he shall eat when he knows to reject bad and choose good; for, when the lad does not yet know to reject bad and choose good, the land

21.40 If Isaiah 7 contains a dual prophecy, at what age did the baby Jesus mature? Which were the two kingdoms identified by the prophet Isaiah that were abandoned during Jesus' lifetime? Who, during the first century AD, 'dreaded' the Kingdom of Israel when there had not been a Northern Kingdom of Israel in existence for 700 years? When did Jesus eat cream and honey? Does this biblical somersault make any sense? This argument is devoid of reason because this wild assertion of a dual prophecy was born out of a hopeless attempt to explain Matthew's transparent mistranslation of Jewish Scripture.

21.41 In a similar way, Jesus seeming endorsement of Daniel as a prophet (Matthew 24:15) is taken as indicating Jesus belief in the historicity of Daniel – whom Judaism has always regarded as a mythical actor in a series of theological stories. The only way to 'protect' Jesus integrity is to excise the 'fake' sections of Matthew and treat The Writings (including the Book of Daniel) as Judaism does – as morality tales not revelations.

Isaiah 9:6-7 – prophecy of a Messiah

21.42 Many Christians understand Isaiah 9:6-7: *"For unto us a Child is born, unto us a Son is given; and the Government shall be upon his shoulder. And his name shall be called Wonderful Counsellor, Mighty God, Everlasting Father, Prince of Peace. Of the increase of his government and peace there will be no end; upon the throne of David and over his Kingdom, to order it and establish it with judgment and justice, from that time forward, even forever"* as a prophesy of Jesus.

21.43 Isaiah 9 continues against the backdrop of Isaiah 7's description of Ahaz and a child born to restore the glory of Judah. Accordingly, other Christian scholars treat the prophecy in Isaiah 9 as referring to the birth of Hezekiah. There are several issues to be considered in interpretation of the passage.

21.44 With respect to the child

The issue is whether the passage is referring to literal birth or royal succession. R.E. Clements, writing in *New Century Bible Commentary* translates verse 6 as "For to us a child is born, to us a son is given", and proposes that it should be understood as a reference to a royal succession and not to a literal birth. Thus, he concludes that the passage is referring to the accession of Hezekiah after the death of Ahaz. George Gray writing in *The International Critical Commentary* also takes the child in verse 6 as referring to Hezekiah:- "shortly after the birth of the prince, after he has been recognized as prince of Israel but before the wide extension of his kingdom has begun." Hans Wildberger's *Continental Commentary* points to usage of the imperfect consecutive tense and suggests that this birth is not in the distant future but it has possibly already taken place. In the same light, Wildberger takes the phrase "the sovereign authority came upon (cf. the imperfect consecutive) his shoulder" as that will make most sense in the context of a royal enthronement: "This sentence does not assert something about enthronement but must be interpreted as an act of investiture, by means of which the child is officially elevated to the status of crown prince and is proclaimed the future ruler" i.e. anointed a King Messiah.

21.45   With respect to the names

Wonderful Counsellor, Mighty God, Eternal Father, Prince of Peace – Clement claims that these titles portray various functions of the king, using the imagery and ideology of Egyptian origin: 'The series of four names which follow, built up in word couplets, almost certainly derives from the Egyptian practice of giving throne names to the Pharaoh. The Egyptian practice was for a series of five names to be given, suggesting that this was originally the case here, and that one name has been lost in the transmission'.

Clement explains the titles as follows:

- Wonderful Counsellor describes the king's role as political guide;

- Mighty God emphasizes the extraordinary skill and strength of the king as a warrior. Wildberger explains this should understood in the context of the contemporary meaning of kingship, in which the king was portrayed as the divinity whom he represented;

- Everlasting Father should be understood as "father for ever" and expresses the king's fatherly concern for the well-being of his people. Gray also understands the third title as 'Father forever' rather than as 'Eternal Father', and takes its meaning as "the benevolent guardian of his people so long as he and they endure". He supports his view by giving other instances in which the word 'forever' is used in the Old

Testament which do not necessitate understanding the title as equivalent to 'Eternal Father', which implies the eternity of God: Isaiah 47:7: *"You said, 'I will continue forever – the eternal queen... ";* Deuteronomy 15:17 *"Then you shall take an awl and pierce it through his ear into the door, and he shall be your servant forever... "* Gray also directs attention to Job 29:16 and Isaiah 22:21 where 'father' was used figuratively of a protector and benefactor;

- Prince of Peace underscores the king's role as the promoter of peace and prosperity.

21.46 With respect to the nature of the promise in verse 7

Clement takes the proclamation in verse 7, *"There will be no end to the increase of His government or of peace... "* as a promise of a solid and independent kingdom under a Davidic ruler rather than a promise of a great universal kingdom ruling over many nations – which was fulfilled in the accession of Hezekiah who provided a reprieve for the dynasty. Gray also takes the similar approach to the promise in verse 7 and understands the main thought of the promise to be that Yahweh will establish and secure a righteous and just government under the new Davidic dynasty. Wildberger finds several motifs in verse 7: the stable order, the possibility of flourishing development, the steadfastness and permanence of the rule, and the quality of the rule as that of justice and righteousness. Wildberger also notes: "This section, 9:1-6, is targeted for a time which addresses a situation full of distress brought on by foreign domination."

The message is thus not about an absolute, unalterable, eternal plan of salvation by God but with events surrounding the loss of the territory of Israel to the Assyrians. Isaiah is talking about the birth of a crown prince, from the house of David. It has either already taken place or will happen in the very near future. Wildberger also notes that there is no place in the OT which speaks of a Messiah as a saviour figure who comes from heaven and brings world history to an end. The child, about whose birth Isaiah speaks in this passage, will sit upon the throne of David in Jerusalem. Yet his birth is a salvation event; the future ahead of him will be more than just a drawn-out continuation of the present; it is indeed still history in the normal, human realm, but it is at the same time fulfilled history.

21.47 The prophetic viewpoint

Scholars such as John Oswalt and J. A. Alexander take the birth of the child in verse 6 as referring to the birth of Jesus. Both reject the view that Isaiah 9:6 is simply referring to the birth of the crown prince Hezekiah because the description of the child seems beyond a human king and the nature of the rule promised in verse 7 transcends a normal earthly rule.

According to Oswalt, the titles in verse 6 are above normal and highlight the ultimate deity of the child. Oswalt argues this is a birth announcement and not an enthronement hymn, whilst Egyptian throne-names were expression of their belief that the kings were gods – asserting that this goes against the grain of Hebrew monotheism. However, archaeological evidence clearly shows the Hebrews were polytheistic in Isaiah's time.

Conclusions on interpretation of Isaiah 9

21.48 Two factors need to be considered interpreting OT prophecy: (i) the original meanings in light of their historical backgrounds and (ii) the covenant theology that undergirds prophetic writings. Scholars such as Oswalt and Alexander overlook the fact that messiahs were never thought of as divine, but as those eligible descendants of either Aaron or David and anointed for office as respectively Priest Messiah or King Messiah.

21.49 Theses verses are part of Isaiah's response to the Assyrian crisis in the days of Ahaz, in which Ahaz fails to trust God and makes Judah an Assyrian vassal state. In the oracles of judgment and hope surrounding the event, Isaiah pronounces the royal hope of David in 9:6-7. The original audience of Isaiah was Ahaz and Judah facing the Assyrian threat. These were the words of hope held out to the people living in a stressful situation caused by threats of Assyrian conquest.

21.50 The relationship between messianism and the Davidic dynasty is crucial to understanding this passage:

(i) The messianic thinking of the prophets is frequently linked to specific historical events with the following themes: that the family of anointed kings would be subject to judgment; that however, their line would be restored after exile; and that they would take a leading role in rebuilding the temple. The prophets often show how the Davidic covenant was to be interpreted in particular, historical circumstances.

(ii) The messianic aspect is inherent in the Davidic covenant. And the messianic concepts attached to David's dynasty bring focus to the hopes offered by the prophets in relation to both the present and future.

(iii) Thus, much of the messianism found in the prophets is a form of dynastic messianism – expressions of hope that all descendants of David will be the king par excellence.

(iv) However, the ruler on the throne at the time often fell far short of the ideal, and thus needed to be replaced. In the end, there will be a seed of David who will not fail but bring to full realization the hopes for eternal peace and world dominion of righteousness under the Davidic dynasty.

21.51 The application of dynastic messianism to the text reveals the undergirding covenant theology of the prophets. Isaiah 9:1-7 seems to be a restatement of the Davidic covenant in 2 Samuel 7 – where the Lord promises that David's dynasty will never be utterly rejected, although individual Davidic kings may be chastised. Judaism relies upon God to raise up Davidic offspring and guarantee the continuity of the kingdom forever.

21.52 Thus from all the above it appears that the royal hope pronounced in Isaiah 9:6-7 had its immediate reference to the Davidic king born in the prophet's own days i.e. Hezekiah. However, it has been adopted as a prophesy of another king that is to come in fulfilment of the pronounced hope – the one who is the antitype that completely and truly satisfies all the criteria of the king par excellence.

21.53 The scholarly consensus with respect to Isaiah 9:6-7 is split between those who do see it as messianic and those as purely a reference to Hezekiah. Conventional Christian views have been formed from misunderstanding what messiah meant and assuming any reference to a messiah must be a reference to Jesus. Hezekiah certainly plays a key role in Isaiah, he is the king par excellence that replaces Ahaz. Hezekiah was the most righteous king after several 'failures'. For Isaiah and the people of Judah living in the 8th century, Hezekiah signified God's presence with them in most precarious circumstances. Hezekiah may also be seen as a type, a king in whose reign some of the promises remained unfulfilled, and who thus points beyond himself to another Davidic monarch to come. One can certainly see how reading these verses today, some see them as prophetic

Isaiah 53 – prophesy of Jesus crucifixion

21.54 Isaiah 53. Apologists point to several phrases in Isaiah 53 (and the last few verses of the preceding chapter) that parallel the crucifixion:

- Verse 52:14: *"there were many who were appalled at him; his appearance was so disfigured beyond that of any human being."* Some say that this refers to the beatings Jesus received, though his ugly appearance is never mentioned in the New Testament.

- Verse 53:3: *"He was despised and rejected by mankind, a man of suffering, and familiar with pain."* Jesus was recognized as a King Messiah, although the gospels say he was rejected after his arrest – but this may be just the gloss written to shift blame from the Roman authorities for marketing purposes. Certainly, *"he was despised"* doesn't sound like the charismatic rabbi who preached to thousands of attentive listeners and had a triumphal entry into Jerusalem on Palm Sunday. And *"a man of suffering... familiar with pain"* might have reflected the life of an ascetic like John the Baptist, but this doesn't describe Jesus.

- Verse 53:7: "he did not open his mouth; he was led like a lamb to the slaughter, and as a sheep before its shearers is silent." The synoptic gospels agree that Jesus was silent before his accusers – though John 18:34–19:11 does not.

- Verse 53:8: in response to the trial and sentencing of Jesus, "who of his generation protested?" Jesus was on his own, and none of his disciples tried to intervene.

- Verse 53:9: "He was assigned a grave with the wicked, and with the rich in his death." This is often interpreted to mean that Jesus ought to have been buried with criminals but was actually buried with the rich. This ties in with the burial of Jesus in the tomb of Joseph of Arimathea.

- Finally, from 53:5 to the end of the chapter, almost every verse gives some version of the idea of the suffering servant taking on the burdens of his people—"he was pierced for our transgressions ... by his wounds we are healed" (v5), "for the transgression of my people he was punished" (v8), "he bore the sin of many, and made intercession for the transgressors" (v12), and so on.

21.55   Taken as this collection of verse fragments, the case looks intriguing, but taken as a whole the chapter is clearly not a prophesy at all.

21.56   Apologists claiming this chapter is a prophesy overlook many verses which are contradictory:

21.57   Verse 52:15: *"so will many nations be amazed at him and kings will shut their mouths because of him."* The nations will be amazed and the kings speechless? No, not only was Jesus not internationally famous during his lifetime, history records nothing of his life outside the gospels. True, we have evidence *of his followers* from historians such as Josephus, Tacitus, and Suetonius, but it is curious that we have nothing about the works of Jesus himself from prolific contemporary authors such as Philo of Alexandria, Seneca, and Pliny the Elder. Apparently, he wasn't as famous as imagined prophecy describes Jesus to be.

21.58   Verse 53:10: *"he will see his offspring and prolong his days, and the will of the Lord will prosper in his hand."* Those who argue Jesus did have offspring are derided as heretics and fantasists. If Isaiah is prophesy then it resembles Job – Jesus endures great trials and then he is rewarded with children, prosperity, and long life. As Proverbs 17:6 says, *"Grandchildren are the crown of old men."* But, this is not how the gospel story plays out.

21.59   Verse 53:11: *"my righteous servant will justify many, and he will bear their iniquities."* Let's revisit 'suffering servant': Jesus, a person of the Trinity and equal to God the Father, is now God's servant? As explored in chapter 6, "messiah" simply means "anointed one" and the Old Testament is fairly liberal with the title messiah. Kings and high priests were anointed as messiahs. Famously, Cyrus the Great of Persia was even a messiah (Isaiah 45:1). But surely no Christian can accept the logic, "Well, David was a messiah, and he was a servant of God; why not Jesus as well?" Jesus is hardly comparable with David.

21.60   Verse 53:12 is particularly jarring: "Therefore I will give him a portion among the great [or *many*] and he will divide the spoils with the strong [or *numerous*]". Like a warrior who gets a share of the spoils of the battle, the servant will be richly rewarded. This servant is just one among many who gets a portion. This describes Jesus as one among equals, just "one of the great"? This cannot be a prophesy of Jesus as described in the gospels.

21.61 The reason this group of extracts from Isaiah fails as prophesy is that throughout (as in its preceding chapters) the reference to the first person singular, the servant, is the nation of Israel. Accepting this, the whole chapter makes perfect sense. Again, as with the analysis of Psalm 22 – the whole point of the crucifixion story is the resurrection – which is missing.

21.62 It is also very noteworthy that Paul, who clearly knew the texts by heart and quotes Deutro-Isaiah a few times in Romans chapter 10, in verses 15, 16 and 21 – never tries to equate descriptions of the Suffering Servant with Jesus – clearly Paul understood one does not relate to the other. Whilst Paul quotes from Isaiah 52.7 (how beautiful the feet of those who bring good news) and 53.1 (who has believed the message), Paul does not quote from 53.5, 53.8 or 53.12 – the 3 key verses quoted by many as prophetic – because Paul knows these verses are not about Jesus.

Micah 5:2 prophecy of Jesus as King of Israel

21.63 Micah 5:2 is widely accepted as prophesy of a coming Messiah by both Judaism and Christians. Reading this verse in isolation sounds convincing but closer examination raises some doubts.

21.64 Micah 5:2 states, "But you, O Bethlehem Ephrathah, who are too little to be among the clans of Judah, from you shall come forth for me one who is to be ruler in Israel, whose coming forth is from of old, from ancient days."

21.65 The verse clearly speaks of a coming king in Israel, but does it predict the coming of the Jesus? Most commentators, indeed most Christians, misunderstand the meaning of 'messiah' – linking the term exclusively to Jesus. However, the meaning understood in biblical times was simply a legal descendent of David, eligible to be King of Judah, or a descendant of Aaron, eligible to be High Priest.

21.66 At the time spoken it made immediate sense: Micah, who was active in Jerusalem from 737BC to 696BC was telling of King Ahaz's son, King Hezekiah, who ruled Judah from 715BC to 686BC. Hezekiah is widely

PROPHESIES IN THE OLD TESTAMENT CONSIDERED FULFILLED BY JESUS

remembered as a righteous and devout king. So, it would have natural for Micah to praise Hezekiah, and the verse is suggesting Hezekiah might regain rule over Israel (recently lost to the Assyrians), as well as Judah. Therefore, originally this may have been endorsement of a promising young prince who might already have become king and a prophecy that he would deliver Judah and push back the Assyrians. "Coming forth from ancient days" is probably a reference to the Line of David – although some claim to equate this with 'eternity' and thereby claim it is prophesying Jesus.

21.67 In verse 5:6, Micah identifies the ruler as confronting the widely expected invasion of Judah (following on after the fall of Israel) by the Assyrians – and that this righteous ruler would rise up and destroy the Assyrians – "they will rule the land of Assyria by the sword". However, as a prophecy, Micah gets a bit carried away – Israel never ruled any part of Assyria. There was high expectation of invasion by Sennacherib, particularly when Hezekiah decided to stop paying the annual tribute to the Assyrians. The invasion started in 701BC, laying waste to most of Judah and soon Jerusalem was under siege. Jerusalem survived the siege as either Sennacherib's army succumbed to a plague or to the wrath of Yahweh. However, Hezekiah never even attacked the Assyrians and agreed to restart paying tribute.

21.68 Whatever Micah meant, when Matthew wrote his eponymous gospel, Matthew quoted Micah as a prophesy of Jesus born in Bethlehem from the line of David. To emphasize the connection, Matthew tweaked the words quoted, adding "in the land of Judah" to make it clearer that the reference was to the town of Bethlehem rather than the clan, the descendants of a man named Bethlehem, whose mother was named Ephrathah. (In the Bible there is such a man who is named Bethlehem, and whose mother was named Ephrathah). But this is a 'non-point' – the clan gave rise to the settlement and Micah is using it only to emphasize the person of whom he speaks is from the line of David – pointing to Jesus eligibility to be a messiah.

21.69 Matthew's description of the events surrounding Jesus birth, as already assessed in chapter 4, is somewhat unreliable. Remember, when writing Matthew sometime after the destruction of the Temple with all its family records in AD70, the author was trying to 'prove' Jesus royal descent from the House of David. The quote from Micah would have looked very helpful, the quote is focused around the birthplace of the future 'ruler of Israel' and not as many writers focus on, that person being the messiah. Matthew writes that Jewish advisers told King Herod that it was prophesied that a messiah would come from Bethlehem based on Micah – Herod, as a foreign usurper, would have been nervous. Indeed, given Herod's paranoid personality it is highly plausible that he ordered the massacre of the innocents.

21.70 It may also be noted that no contemporaries saw Jesus as King of Israel – in those days Israel had become Samaria, Jesus was acclaimed as King of the Jews (Judah). And of course, Jesus came far too late to destroy Assyria and rule their lands by the sword.

Zechariah 11:12-13 prophecy of Judas blood money

21.71 Zechariah 11:12-13 offers an intriguing account regarding 30 silver coins, bringing to mind the betrayal of Jesus by Judas Iscariot. The New Testament identifies this as a Messianic prophecy, which found its fulfillment in Jesus Christ.

21.72 The verses read, *"I told them, 'If you think it best, give me my pay; but if not, keep it.' So, they paid me thirty pieces of silver. And the Lord said to me, 'Throw it to the potter' – the handsome price at which they priced me! So, I took the thirty pieces of silver and threw them into the house of the Lord to the potter."*

21.73 Earlier, Zechariah had been commanded to watch a flock of sheep doomed to slaughter (Zechariah 11:4). He obeyed, using two shepherd's staffs that he named Favor and Union (verse 7). Within a month, Zechariah fired the three shepherds working under him (verse 8). Then Zechariah abandoned the flock and broke his staff named Favor. Observers realized these actions were "the word of the LORD" (verse 11). The Lord would remove His favor from His people, allowing them to be harried by their enemies (verse 6).

21.74 In verses 12-13 Zechariah tells his employers to pay him his wages if they saw fit to do so. They pay him 30 pieces of silver, the price of a slave (Exodus 21:32), as an insult to Zechariah. The prophet sarcastically calls it a "handsome price." God then commands Zechariah to give the coins to the potter in the house (or temple) of the Lord.

21.75 The corresponding passage in the New Testament is in Matthew 27.

Judas is filled with remorse for betraying the Lord, and he tries to return the thirty pieces of silver to the chief priests (verse 3). When the elders refuse to accept the money, Judas throws the coins into the temple then leaves and hangs himself (verses 4-5). Not wanting to put "blood money" into the treasury, the priests use it to buy a potter's field (verses 6-7). "Then what was spoken by Jeremiah the prophet was fulfilled: 'They took the thirty silver coins, the price set on him by the people of Israel, and they used them to buy the potter's field, as the Lord commanded'" (verses 9-10). The text of Zechariah 11 is identified as a prophecy by Matthew – but surprisingly Matthew attributes the prophecy to *Jeremiah*. The explanation provided is that Jeremiah also bought a field at the Lord's command (Jeremiah 32:6-9).

21.76 Zechariah's prophecy had a dual fulfillment: one in the prophet's contemporary context, and one in the more distant future. The Jewish people of Zechariah's day would be judged, as seen in the breaking of Favor, and the specific details regarding 30 pieces of silver and a potter's field found a future fulfillment in the betrayal of Jesus by Judas Iscariot. Non biblical sources indicate that Judas was indeed a potter, or more specifically, owned a pottery, which may have prompted the author of Matthew to refer to the stories from Zechariah/Jeremiah.

21.77 Matthew's reference to the 30 pieces of silver looks like a deliberate attempt to create a prophetic fulfillment – shame he got the name of the prophet wrong!

22

Conclusions on the two questions left from Part One

22.1 So let's return to the two questions that I left outstanding from Part One: How to explain the prophesies in the Old Testament that are believed to point to Jesus, and, Jesus' views as recorded in the New Testament concerning Yahweh's Laws.

22.2 Looking at Gospel accounts of Jesus reported sayings and actions, it appears that on many occasions Jesus made arrangements specifically "so that scriptural prophesies would be fulfilled". These were therefore not accidentally fulfilled but deliberately acted out, presumably to help buttress claims to be the anointed Messiah. Later, as the Gospels went through drafting, the authors appear to have added, as commentary about Jesus, a number of prophetic fulfilments to further bolster the case. However, given that probably none of the authors were first hand witnesses to the events weakens their credibility. In some instances, their enthusiasm went too far – as with Matthew 2:23, where he quotes a non-existent prophesy about Jesus dwelling in Nazareth. This may be a case of mistranslation – later translators being confused about Jesus being a Nazarite (devout Jew) or a Nazarene (which may have been named after an Essene settlement near Galilee) and assuming references were to what archaeological evidence indicates may have only been an isolated farmstead in Jesus time. Nazareth appears to have grown to a village following an influx of priestly refugees following the destruction of the Temple in AD70 and had by the 3rd century AD become a recognised town. This might point to either gospels being written much later than claimed, or of significant edits during the early centuries.

22.3   If Jesus was a Nazarite, he followed a tradition that included both historical (Samson) and contemporary heroes (John the Baptist).

22.4   Early church theologians were creative in inventing prophesies from blatant twisting of meanings – as in Isaiah's 7:14 prophesy of a 'virgin' birth and Psalm 110:1 *'the Lord said to my Lord'* – as analysed in the previous chapter.

22.5   It is also possible that the authors of the gospels simply used older extant sources to write up events that they were not present at nor knew first hand observers of. The gospel descriptions of Jesus suffering prior to his crucifixion may have been inspired by the 'Suffering Servant' verses in Isaiah 53:4-12 and also by Plato's Republic (II v361/2) the latter being quoted thus by Pope Benedict XVI *"according to Plato the truly just man must be misunderstood and persecuted in this world; indeed, Plato goes so far as to write: 'They will say that our just man will be scourged, racked, fettered, will have his eyes burned out, and at last, after all manner of suffering will be crucified'. This passage, written 400 years before Christ, is always bound to move a Christian deeply"*.

22.6   Over time Biblical enthusiasts have identified dozens of other statements in the OT which they maintain are prophesies fulfilled by Jesus – some are incredibly weak, such as "and I shall raise up a prophet from amongst you".

22.7   When considering prophesy, it is also worth considering the claim that Jesus was descended from King David. Whilst Jesus descent from David is an integral part of Christian theology, I suggest that there is really no evidence at all, nor is it relevant. In Judaism there are many references to Yahweh's promises of an everlasting Davidic dynasty. However, as covered in Part Two, there is no direct evidence that King David ever existed. Assuming there was a House of David, there is no evidence of any line surviving Zedekiah and the destruction of Jerusalem. In 586BC, Nebuchadnezzar captured Jerusalem and killed all King Zedekiah's descendants in front of him before plucking out Zedekiah's eyes so that it was the last thing he would see. Matthew and Luke invite us to believe that Joseph and/or Mary are descended from David but both genealogies are manifestly fake. After 80 years exile from which only c4% returned to a Jerusalem lying in ruins – what dynastic records were maintained? How reliable were records during centuries of Persian control followed by Greek and then Hasmonaean control. It is true that the people of

CONCLUSIONS ON THE TWO QUESTIONS LEFT FROM PART ONE

Judah had high expectations of a righteous king messiah would arise to take political control, throw off the yoke of foreign domination and rule as Yahweh's appointed – but that was not the role Jesus assumed.

22.8 Christian dogma claims Jesus descent from David to support claims of messiahship, ideas of prophesy and cement links to the Old Testament – none of which is remotely relevant to Jesus teaching, as his message is completely independent of his parents.

22.9 Moreover, as noted earlier, the term 'messiah' is fundamentally misunderstood nowadays. In OT times it meant one of two officials (i) the senior being the rightful and anointed descendant of Aaron eligible to be the High Priest and (ii) the junior being the rightful and anointed descendant of the House of David eligible to be the earthly King of Israel. Even Cyrus, the Persian Emperor, clearly not a descendant of David was made an honorary messiah by Yahweh – according to Isaiah. Accordingly, for those believing in prophesies, it must be right to consider that they could relate to other messiah's over the history of Israel.

22.10 The frequently used liturgical term "Jesus Christ, the Son of God" is for biblical inerrantists an oxymoron – one cannot be a Christ (messiah) unless your father is a descendant of Aaron or King David – but Jesus is held to be fathered by the Holy Spirit. Moreover a messiah had to be anointed with a very specific salad oil mixture by the high priest – a vital step not mentioned in any gospel.

22.11 As for Jesus views concerning Yahweh's laws, we have found considerable evidence pointing at Jesus frequenting the Temple but (as examined in Chapter 10) Jesus is recorded as dismissing virtually every tenet of Judaism. Matthew stresses Jesus as a living exemplar of compliance with the Law, whilst Jesus original followers in the Nazarene Church seem to have 'added' Jesus to Judaism. However, Mark, Luke and particularly Paul, all focused primarily on Gentile audiences, portraying Jesus as dismissing the Law (as in food laws, circumcision, etc) or positioning the Law as fulfilled or superseded, or as being only for Jews.

22.12 Jesus frequently referred and prayed to his 'father', much as we would do representing a term of endearment and submission rather than meant literally. My personal view is that Jesus references to doing his father's commands might be interpreted as references to doing what is commanded by Love. Jesus guiding principle was Love, he did what Love indicated should be done.

22.13 Jesus never referred to God as the 'El Elyon' of Hebrew scripture. Equally, Jesus is never quoted referring to Yahweh – notwithstanding the attributed quote in John 8:58 "before Abraham was born, I am", which as analysed in Chapter 19, appears to be misunderstood. Jesus never claimed to be God, or even the Son of God. His Nazarene followers did not believe he was divine and even the Catholic Church views his divinity as something that only begun to be believed some centuries after the crucifixion.

22.14 My conclusion is that there is no biblical evidence that Jesus endorsed belief in Yahweh or Yahweh's extensive rule book (the Mosaic Law). When Jesus taught his followers to love God and one another He was clearly referring to God (Designer of the universe) rather than the jealous tribal entity named Yahweh.

22.15 Actually, I feel sorry for El Elyon (Sumerian 'Enlil'), the god of Abraham and throughout Genesis, whom we also know from tablets found at Ugarit was the chief god of Canaan and (from Genesis 14:18) of Jerusalem (Melchizedek was King of Jerusalem and High Priest to El Elyon). Later, after Yahweh succeeded as the Israelite tribal god, El Elyon continued to be worshipped intermittently – his symbol was the zodiacal sign for then concluding Age of Taurus which ran from around 4200BC to circa 2100BC (hence the golden calf symbolising his son, Nannar/Sin).

22.16 When David captured Jerusalem c1000BC, El Elyon was rediscovered as the city god – in 2 Samuel 22:14 in David's final song to YHWH he sings (in Hebrew): "YHWH thundered from heaven and El Elyon uttered his voice". Modern Christians assume these references are to a single God with multiple names, but in Hebrew, David is noting El Elyon's paternal support for the tribal Israelite god, Yahweh. Indeed, it appears that niches in the Temple provided for worship of many gods, El Elyon clearly continued to be worshipped until such practise was scorned by Ezekiel. Ezekiel also objected to the worship of Tammuz. Tammuz (aka Dumuzid in Sumerian) being the husband of Inanna, a granddaughter of El Elyon. The Levite priests seem to have decided to focus exclusively on one of the 70 sons of El Elyon (the versions of Deuteronomy 32:8 found amongst the Dead Sea scrolls make clear the original text was "sons of El Elyon") as their tribal god and, under the reforms of Hezekiah, spurn the

CONCLUSIONS ON THE TWO QUESTIONS LEFT FROM PART ONE

rest.

22.17 Interestingly, on tablets unearthed in Ugarit has been found a 'story' named as the 'Ba'al Cycle'. In the episode of the 'Palace of Ba'al' the god Ba'al Hadad (Sumerian 'Ishkur', aka 'Adad', another son of El Elyon) invites the '*seventy sons*' of Athirat' to a feast in his new palace. Note: 'sons' is better understood as 'descendants'.

23

Puzzling aspects of Jesus strategy

23.1   From time to time, I have mused about Jesus strategy. Firstly, we must consider whether he was briefed prior to his arrival – either by a more senior deity or by God himself. Or, maybe Jesus was selected after birth and briefed during his early life, which would fit with the early belief that Jesus was born purely human and the Spirit only descended upon him at his baptism by John. Jesus is frequently quoted as explaining he was carrying out his Father's instructions and undertaking his Father's work. Most people would conclude Jesus main task was to teach mankind to love one another and thereby achieve a harmonious and meaningful life preparatory for the next phase following their short incarnate lives on Earth.

23.2   So, from the records we have, what can we conclude about Jesus mission to carry out his Father's work – what was his plan? Some aspects are puzzling – why restrict the mission to such a tight geographical area? Why leave the wider theological thesis to others after he departed? Why depart after only a few years? Given he must have appreciated the power of sacred writings – why not write a text, something that really would be the Word of God? Given the extraordinary legacy that, despite Jesus being literate and being on Earth for c33 years, he appears to have left no written record – or did the Church decide that it was heretical and successfully destroy every copy? Would Jesus judge his mission a lasting success? Let's explore these issues.

The role of Paul

23.3   When we search for the theological guidance given by Jesus, we only have the canonised biblical texts and a few surviving copies of the numerous texts deemed heretical by the church. Our reliance upon these raises puzzling questions over the strategy. The Gospel record provides much in terms of how to live, how to build a relationship with God and how to attain eternal existence. However, most of the complex theology appears to have been left to Paul to espouse – a very great and devoted person – but someone Jesus only contacted after his Ascension – seemingly almost an afterthought? Objectively, from a biblical perspective, the role of Paul in spreading the gospel message to later generations seems very critical – second only to Jesus himself. However, outside the biblical texts, we know his brother James played the key role spreading the gospel across the Fertile Crescent, North Africa and up the Atlantic coast whilst Thomas, quite probably Jesus twin brother, spread the gospel across Iran and the Indian sub-continent. Whilst conventional Christians will arguably claim the strategy clearly worked, it seems odd that Jesus did not "call" Saul to teach and inform him directly during the three years of his ministry. Whilst Paul's theology, as amended by Constantine, became the dominant surviving denomination, the more extensive geographical missionary work by two of Jesus brothers (James and Thomas) was doomed to ultimately fail – through absorption and suppression – hardly omniscient.

Jesus focus on the Jews

23.4   The biblical message is that Jesus came to bring the Word to all humanity and many of the Apostles deliberately sought to spread the Gospel as widely as possible. Jesus himself appears to have sought out any ethnicities – Romans, Samaritans, etc, that he came across – but his ministry is recorded as restricted to just Israel and a few Phoenician cities. Given the political reality of the period that Jesus came to Earth and our conviction that his message was for all mankind, it seems very odd that he never ventured far out of Israel – teaching in Rome, Alexandria in Egypt and other centres of Greek civilisation would seem (to a human) to be obvious places to prioritize spreading the Word.

Jesus impact during his Ministry

23.5   Some theologians, including the senior pastor of my evangelical church in Hong Kong, estimate the number of Jesus committed followers before the crucifixion numbered only a hundred or so. This seems extremely odd. We understand that the earthly ministry of Jesus lasted for around 3 years. If Jesus preached for around 1,000 days such estimates suggest he converted only one person every 10 days. I find this difficult to accept.

23.6 My own work, after full time employment, has included mentoring a business owner and junior professionals – ranging from providing guidance on strategy to formulating details of negotiating tactics.

23.7 Applying, similar logic to Jesus ministry yields some interesting observations: – below are brief notes that I would have made if Jesus has approached me for ideas on how to develop his ministry during his period on Earth:

1. Jesus was very effective ministering one on one – in particular, I note his recorded discussions with the senior Pharisee Nicodemus, the Samaritan woman and the disabled beggar at the Pool of Bethesda. Yet, as far as we know, Jesus never spoke with or 'called' Saul. Saul was supposedly the brightest Pharisee of his age and therefore one might assume Jesus would at a minimum have known of him and of his hostility towards Jesus followers. Therefore, an early one-on-one with Saul might have been a good idea. Investing time on Saul during his ministry on Earth could have led to a far more accurate transmission of Jesus teaching than leaving it up to Paul to theorise by himself later. But, Jesus only 'called' Saul after his departure from Earth;

2. With larger groups, for example when teaching in the Temple grounds, Jesus rhetoric often generated hostility and he had to fade away into the crowd. Given his mission and intellect, managing the crowd should have been second nature;

3. The Jews had experienced many false messiahs over the previous few centuries, some gained traction with tens of thousands of followers but the multiple attempted rebellions led only to massacres – hence the crowds were often sceptical – there was a missing ingredient;

4. The Jews looked to their religious leaders for guidance – so publicly attacking these religious leaders, however justified, may not have helped achieve Jesus objectives;

5. If his first objective was to reveal himself as a special messiah, albeit

a very different kind of messiah than the prophets had led Israel to expect, then a more effective approach might have been to target individual Pharisees and Sadducees – convincing them in the same way as Jesus did with other individuals – and, after revealing himself, discreetly pointing out their deficiencies in private. This would have brought out support from the religious leadership, the missing ingredient referred to above – with dramatic effects on temple crowds.

6. Gaining recognition from the Pharisees and Sadducees as both a King Messiah and the incarnation of the Logos (the intermediary created by God to speak to humanity) would have been transformational. Jesus second objective would be easy to achieve – acceptance by the Jews would have been rapid.

7. Being part of a state recognised religion, the Roman authorities would have been very relaxed about Jesus message, "respect authority, pay your taxes" was helpful, particularly against the backdrop of the campaign of agitation and terror pursued by the Zealots.

8. Indeed, Jesus promotion of love towards all and respect for Roman authority would have been seen by the Roman authorities as a disavowal of the Zealots tactics and objectives – bringing possible Roman support and certainly more Roman converts likely to spread the message across the empire.

9. Having redeemed Israel, Jesus and his disciples could have used the next three decades to convert the Gentiles.

10. One might consider whether basing his strategy on a make-over of a well-known existing brand, Judaism, would have provided a ready platform and immediate brand recognition without having to start from scratch with a new brand.

11. Moreover, working with an established brand, Judaism, would have meant working with a brand recognised across the Roman Empire as a legal religion. This would have probably avoided most of the persecutions and martyrdoms by Rome.

12. Accepting the conventional belief that his third objective was to die for our redemption, Jesus might have seen that such a dramatic ending would have more impact if performed in the imperial capi-

tal than in a relative backwater province of Judea. Jesus could have worked his Ministry for another 30 years – relying on a confrontation with Nero cAD66 to trigger his death and, if part of the plan, his resurrection.

13. In the much longer duration of his ministry, say 35 years instead of 3 years, Jesus could have written his own Gospel – dispelling all the confusing, overlapping and sometimes contradictory messages that failed to be accurately preserved from the 1st Century. Jesus could have provided clarity about whether the Torah was fulfilled or abolished; the role of women; the afterlife; judgment; resurrection; whether there is a Trinity; etc.

14. Whether one believes that Jesus was a man granted divine power (maybe at baptism), a junior God (as in the Logos) or even God himself in human form – surely it was wholly predictable that humans would distort and mangle the message brought by Jesus if reliance for its presentation to the Gentiles across the planet and its preservation for future generations was left to relative amateurs and chancers.

15. By the time of a crucifixion and resurrection delayed by say three decades until say, AD66, much of the Roman Empire could have been converted to Christianity.

23.8 A strategy combining at least some of the elements set out above, would have led to a huge improvement in outturns over the past two millennia. I admit, I am claiming this with all the benefits of hindsight. But, unlike me, most Christians endow God with 100% foresight, hence it is entirely valid to question the strategy employed to convey the vital message to humanity. I see several weaknesses in the actual strategy followed which led to untold suffering, dissention and confusion – much of which could have been avoided. Probable benefits from a strategy incorporating the ideas outlined under 23.7 above include:

1. During a ministry lasting c35 years, a Gospel written by Jesus would surely have provided enormous clarity for humanity. Jesus would presumably have written in Greek, and issued his own Latin translation. I think most agree that Jesus was an excellent communicator and would have produced a stunning text to convey his message to humanity.

2. Such an authoritative document, backed by 30 odd years of ministry across the Empire would likely have ensured a single unified belief system backed by a single authoritative text. Christianity, possibly continuing to be known as the Nazarene faith, having absorbed Judaism, would have probably remained a single denomination. All other NT texts would have been treated as secondary tracts of lesser importance and never have formed part of canon. Indeed, many texts sought out and destroyed by the church as 'heretical' would have probably become more revered than some of the NT canon we have today. The original embellishments made to the synoptic gospels would have pointless and subsequent redactions and editing would have served no purpose.

3. With 30+ years to write the articles of faith himself, Jesus would have left a very clear and unambiguous description of faith, works and beliefs – and Jesus' teaching would easily predominate across the world. With Articles of Faith written by Jesus, no one would have retained the ancient and often misleading Jewish scripture. Under this scenario, most Jews would have realised Jesus was their long-awaited special Messiah. Jews might have understood Jesus 'triumph' over 'foreign occupiers' and Gentiles generally, was achieved by those Gentiles accepting Jesus was the Logos and converting to follow the Nazarene faith.

4. If Jesus had personally led his Church for another 30 odd years, Paul, under Jesus direct guidance, would have had less scope or reason to develop his own version of Christian theology.

5. It would seem unlikely that the revolt and destruction of the Temple in AD66 would have happened, as the Nazarene faith would likely have been head-quartered in Jerusalem, with mass pilgrimages from all across the Roman Empire by then. The biggest saving would have been avoiding the many millions of Christian martyrs.

6. Nero attempting to execute someone that half the Empire believed to be sent by God (John 6.28-29), someone who had clearly shown he was empowered by God, would likely have led to a coup – saving millions more lives. Possibly, Jesus might even have been appointed Emperor by the Roman Senate.

7. More importantly, it would have been very unlikely that Christian-

PUZZLING ASPECTS OF JESUS STRATEGY

ity would have subsequently been changed by the overlay of pagan dogma inserted by Emperor Constantine. Clarity from Jesus direct writing would also have avoided the invention of the Trinity.

8. With what would have become an Empire wide Nazarene faith, probably head-quartered in Jerusalem, the Jewish revolts would have petered out, the Temple likely have become a Church and the genocides of AD132 to 135 avoided. Moreover, the separateness created by old Jewish practises would have been abolished (along with concept of kosher and avoiding foods offered to other gods) and the entire subsequent history of the Jews would have been very different – probably no diaspora, no persecution from Christians in the Middle Ages, no pogroms, no ghettos, no holocaust.

9. The incredibly valuable libraries at Alexandria and Caesarea might have survived – certainly the Serapeum would not have been destroyed, it is argued, upon the instructions of Pope Theophilus in AD391. The terrible loss of ancient learning and information in these repositories was a very sad blow for humanity.

10. Instead of separate and increasingly antagonistic traditions of Judaism and Christianity, a strong, unified and vibrant monotheistic faith would have become established right across the Roman empire and (led by James and Thomas) throughout its adjacent territories. One might speculate that the existence of such a strong unified monotheistic faith might have seen Mohammed (PbuH) develop as a prophet acting to reinforce and further spread that combined faith rather than his followers develop Islam separately. Retaining unity of the three Abrahamic faiths would have had profound implications for humanity over the following millennia.

11. In many ways, Islam reflects a more original Nazarene view of Jesus than Christianity itself does. If Jesus had spread his teaching across the Roman Empire, Jesus new Nazarene version of Judaism could have become widespread in its original pure form. The Prophet Mohammed is thought by many academics to have grown up in an Arab tribe holding Nazarene beliefs – which laid the foundations for his strong monotheistic convictions. In an alternative outcome, Mohammed might be remembered for leading a rebirth of Jesus teaching about God and the renaissance brought from Islamic arts, science

PART THREE: JESUS, THE NAZARENE

and mathematics might have had an even greater geographic impact.

12. Even if Mohammed had responded to the revelations he received by leading a new monotheism, the closeness to Nazarene beliefs may have led to an accommodation rather than multiple bouts of hostility between nation states adhering to the two traditions.

23.9 That Jesus bequeathed no written scripture himself and departed after a brief period of ministry does convey a certain lack of preparation and perhaps indicates that God does not know the future? It might have helped if, after the crucifixion, Jesus had simply walked into the Temple and given a sermon to the presumably dumbstruck Pharisees. Indeed, Jesus post resurrection strategy seems distinctly low key, and, I suggest has led to his message being widely distorted; unparalleled suffering as belief fractured into a myriad of denominations; and, a confusing patchwork of beliefs.

The Prophets did not prepare the Jews for a Messiah anything like Jesus

23.10 Prior to Jesus arrival, the Jews had high expectations of a coming King Messiah who would remove the imposter Herod and restore the Davidic monarchy. But if Yahweh is believed to have spoken to his people through the prophets, the message was very misleading. The Jewish belief was that a King Messiah was coming to restore them, to lead them politically and militarily, to free them from the yoke of foreign oppression. No wonder they questioned claims that Jesus was that Messiah. There had been a long succession of people claiming to be the coming Messiah. The Jews had a collective experience of past Messiahs – Ezekiel had told them Cyrus, the Persian Emperor who defeated the Babylonians, freed the Jews from the Exile, sponsored their return to Jerusalem and encouraged the rebuilding of the Temple had been recorded as being specifically described as Messiah by Yahweh himself. This Cyrus was a good role model – how could Jesus measure up. Jesus may have been an eloquent and apparently extremely learned speaker and of regal appearance but where was his army and how could he ask them to kow-tow to the beastly Romans??

Jesus teaching of how to live is at odds with human psychology

23.11 Jesus own message, as recorded in the Gospels, teaches a very demanding way of life, selfless love for all others and a communal attitude to wealth. Yet this seems to directly contradict the way humans are genetically wired – primarily to protect and provide for our own close family, to accumulate resources for a narrow purpose and to compete vigorously for the preservation of our immediate bloodline. Prioritising our actions this way fits naturally with most other mammalian species on our planet. Nor does this basic instinctive drive seem to have any relation to sin. So, why did a Creator God wire us up this way? Having given us a spark of his own freewill, it is clear the Creator does not want a puppet species.

23.12 Some Christians read Genesis literally, understanding that God the Creator made humans "in his own image". If so, then God would seem to bear a direct responsibility for the way we are wired. Personally, as written in Part 1, the creation stories in Genesis appear to be derived from much older original written evidence and, moreover, Genesis appears to be a garbled version of the creation of our planet rather than of creation of the universe.

How reliable are the four Gospels?

23.13 Harry Boer comments that "all we know of the words of Jesus in which he expressed his teaching, we know of through reports of the four evangelists – the same kind of human medium through which the rest of the Bible comes to us". Inerrancy buffs recoil in horror at this analysis, but it is worthy of consideration. Firstly, only one of the Gospels was even partly authored by an eyewitness of Jesus – this fact alone puts in question the accuracy of the numerous quotations purporting to be and generally taken to be the exact words spoken by Jesus. When reading an account of any event, how much credibility would you give to "direct quotes" included by the author who claims that the exact words were spoken 40 years previously by someone that the author had never met? Can you remember the exact words used in a lesson by your favourite school teacher 40 years ago? Yet most theologians carefully weigh every word used in a Biblical passage for inner meaning. One sincerely hopes Eusebius was correct when attributing early Gospel texts to a document he described as "The Sayings of Jesus" written in Aramaic by the apostle Matthew – which may indeed be the missing common source document "Q" for the three synoptic Gospels.

23.14 Of course, in making his statement above, Henry Boer is completely

PART THREE: JESUS, THE NAZARENE

ignoring all texts declared heretical by Rome. The final work in this series examines the heretical texts to reveal the authentic teaching that the Roman church strove so hard and very effectively to suppress.

23.15 The early chapters of this book have challenged many aspects of the gospel story but it is one thing to identify details that defy credibility and another to back such claims with facts identifying the source of such misinformation. The gospels tell of events before Jesus ministry, his teaching and parables and the events at the end of his ministry. The problems with the story canonised in the bible arise primarily with the events.

23.16 When the authors of the gospels wrote about Mary and Jesus, did they use details of the story of Isis and her son Horus, fathered miraculously by the god Osiris, as a model? Astonishing as this might seem, there are many details from the stories of Isis and Horus which do seem to have been woven into the birth of Jesus, the role and personality of Mary and even the descriptions of numerous miracles performed by Jesus.

23.17 Consideration of the prevailing religious scene at the time Christianity spread across the Roman Empire is very revealing. Worship of Egyptian goddess Isis had spread around the Mediterranean long before Egypt was subsumed into the Roman Empire – historians indicate the process occurred around the 4th century BC. A temple dedicated to Isis existed in the Greek port of Piraeus when Alexander the Great (356BC-323BC) first attacked the Persians, 330BC. Indeed, Alexander was convinced he was the semi divine son of the god Amen Ra, grandfather of Isis.

23.18 By the time of Jesus, Isis was one of the most popular divinities across the Empire. Isis, known as the virgin mother of Horus was acclaimed as the *Isis Mery*, the *beloved Isis*. The birth of Horus was described as a virgin birth because Horus father, Osiris, had been murdered and his body parts scattered. The virgin birth was not exceptional as most pagan gods were believed to be born from virgins. Isis was usually depicted as a mother presenting the new born Horus in a crib or holding the baby in her arms, widely known as the Black Madonna. Isis goes on to resurrect Osiris. Despite always being the partner of Osiris, both before his murder by his brother Set and after his resurrection, it was always maintained that Isis remained a virgin, the *perpetual* virgin. Again, given the popularity of Isis across the Empire, it seems statues of Isis holding the baby Horus inspired the Roman church to copy the idea for Mary – often by simply relabelling the statute!

23.19 Thus, when Christian missionaries arrived telling of a god born from a virgin named Mary and telling of a miraculous resurrection – it all sounded very familiar. The obvious question is: did the cultural understanding of Osiris, Isis and Horus influence the development of Roman dogma? It certainly feels that lots of dogma was appropriated from pre-existing beliefs to 'package' Jesus message – maybe to make it more familiar, absorbing existing beliefs and rituals rather than trying to abolish them.

23.20 Egyptian craftsmen manufactured vast quantities of 'Black Madonna & child' statutes which were exported all over the Empire and huge numbers can still be seen in churches, repurposed as Mary holding Jesus. Using the Latin names, Serapis, Isis and Harpocrates, Isis plus husband and child naturally formed a tight knit trinity and arguably became the model for the Alexandrian bishops led by Athanasius and Hosius at the Council of Nicaea in 325 to promote this element of Egyptian belief.

23.21 Serious students of Judaism reading the NT can identify Jesus' birth being described as occurring around the middle of September. Murdoch in her erudite work *Christ in Egypt* explains why the precise identification of December 25th was regarded as highly auspicious **millennia** before Jesus birth and the reasoning behind Jesus birthday being moved to that date. Surviving texts from church fathers Epiphanius and Plutarch draw attention to the older celebrations held on December 25th to commemorate the virgin Isis giving birth to the baby Horus.

23.22 The choice of December 25th links directly to the winter solstice on December 21st. At this time the period of daylight is at its shortest and the sun reaches its furthest point in its annual cycle, daily movement of the sunrise slows to become stationary and the first morning which shows a clear movement in its return being the morning of the 25th. Thus the 25th was celebrated as the annual rebirth of the god associated with the Sun. In ancient times, say 2000 years before Jesus birth, this was already the well-established celebration in Mesopotamia of the birth of Shamash (the Sumerian name for the grandson of El Elyon, the Lord Most High) and in Egyptian culture of the birth of Horus by the virgin Isis. The Roman incarnation of the sun god, Sol Invictus, naturally also enjoyed its annual feast day on December 25th. Thus, as this date was already the most important celebration of the miraculous birth of a very important god by Isis, the *Virgin Mery*, it was logical for the early church to adopt December 25th to rededicate an existing festival than try to launch a new celebration and have to try to ban the old one. The definition of Christmas in the Catholic Encyclopedia even acknowledges this: *The well known solar feast of Natalis Invicti, celebrated on December 25th, has a strong claim on the responsibility for our December date for Jesus birth* – part III p727.

23.23　Egyptian inscriptions associate the insemination of Isis with the arrival of Sirius, the brightest star in the sky, representing Osiris. As well as a bright star foretelling of the birth of Horus, the Three Kings also appear on the horizon soon after Horus birth – the three bright stars forming the belt of the Orion constellation were known as the Three Kings for thousands of years before Jesus arrived. These three stars form a straight line pointing directly to Sirius, known as the *Dog Star*. This naming reflects the tradition that Osiris annual cyclical rising occurred just before the Nile flooded – Osiris '*barked*' to warn people to move away from low lying ground ahead of the rising waters. These traditions formed a central role in the life of Egypt for millennia. Thus, popular motifs appear to be added into the gospel story. As examined earlier, the gospel story of the bright star beckoning the 3 kings to visit the baby Jesus has no credibility as a 'star' occupying a geostationary orbit could only be a spacecraft. Indeed, whilst popular understanding is that there were 3 kings, the gospel of Matthew only refers to three gifts.

23.24　The bible is silent concerning most of Jesus life – the only reference to his life between the ages of 12 and 30 is that he was a 'carpenter'. Even this seems to be a mistranslation, the Greek term, *tekton*, is more associated with a skilled metal worker. Murdoch also points out that Jesus teaching makes no reference to woodworking but often to masonry. Jesus references to the 'cornerstone' have likely been mistranslated as the Greek term *akrogoniaios* means the chief stone or a high stone – probably the capstone of a pyramid rather than one of many cornerstones used to mark out the base of a building. The link to Egyptology is reinforced by the modern Greek usage of *tekton* as denoting a freemason.

23.25　In addition to Osiris and Horus, Anubis (aka Anup the Baptiser) was another god frequently worshipped at temples dedicated to Isis. Anubis was associated with purification referred to as the Preparer of the Way for the eternal life of Horus. Anubis was always shown holding an ankh, a cross with a handle. Ancient Egyptian baptism was a purification ritual, submersion in water to purify the soul, celebrating renewal and 'rebirth' by the addition of a new name. Horus was baptised by Anubis.

23.26 Representations of Anubis in Egypt date back some 6000 years. Anubis was born of a union between Osiris and his sister Nephthys (see the Appendix). A direct translation of Nephthys is 'god of seven' which we found in Part Two chapter 16 is the exactly the same as the translation of the Hebrew 'Elisheba'. So, both John the Baptist and Anup the Baptiser had a mother named Elisabeth – a coincidence? Hence, the eerie similarity with Jesus baptism by John, also a close relation.

23.27 The connections go on…the Feast of the Assumption, the Roman celebration of when Mary ascended to heaven, occurs on August 15th. This is the same date as the Romans celebrated the assumption of Astraea, the beloved virgin mother and a daughter of Zeus in the Greek pantheon. Of course, Zeus was the Greek name for Ra (aka Amun Ra) and Astraea was another name for Isis, granddaughter of Ra. Isis was naturally associated with the sign Virgo and the morning sun rises in that constellation from August 15th – hence the celebration of the assumption of Isis on that date. Thus, we find yet another example of the Roman church taking over a 'pagan' ritual and relabelling it. Indeed, the festival was ready made – the Assumption of the *Mery Virgin*, the beloved Virgin Mother.

23.28 Isis was closely associated with healing – resuscitating both Ra and Horus from poisoning. Codicils to the Book of the Dead (chapter 156) written during the 18th Dynasty (1550BC to 1292BC) detail the magical healing powers of Isis blood and her abilities to endow fertility to other women. Thus, may have grown the ideas of healing attributed to her successor Mary and the growth of pilgrimages to sites such as Lourdes where prayers are offered to Mary to restore health. The idea of blood washing away sin may also have been influenced by stories of Isis.

23.29 All Christians are familiar with the story of Jesus miraculously feeding the 5000 from seven loaves of bread. But, how many know that during the preceding millennia, Horus was also closely associated with multiplying seven loaves of bread into thousands he distributed to the people – as described in chapters 52, 53 and 189 of the Book of the Dead? It seems a number of popular stories of 'miracles' performed by older gods were directly incorporated into the gospel accounts. References to Jesus

PART THREE: JESUS, THE NAZARENE

being the 'bread of life' echo numerous Pyramid Texts and Coffin Texts describing Horus the same way. There are also references to Horus using his spittle and saliva to heal wounds and restore sight – again also attributed to Jesus in the gospels.

23.30 The story of Jesus calling out an evil spirit from a possessed individual and casting it into a herd of pigs, who then run off and cast themselves over a cliff to drown in a lake has always seemed rather odd to me. Why would Jesus direct an evil spirit to depart a person only to result in the death of a large herd of pigs – which would hardly kill an evil spirit (if one believes in such things)? This story appears in all three synoptic gospels (Matthew 8:32, Mark 5:13 and Luke 8:33) indicating it was present in the 'Q' document. But, for me at least, it does not smell right – *unlike* the highly authentic sounding story of the woman caught in adultery, which was added to John some centuries later. The inspiration for the story of the pigs drowning in a lake might have been a very similar Spell set out in the Egyptian Coffin Texts.

23.31 Jesus is often referred to as the Lamb of God. The astrological sign of Ra, the greatest Egyptian god, was Aries (Latin for 'Ram'). The constellation of Ares is narrower than 1/12th of the sky (being 2150 years for complete precession through a sign), so the Age of Aries in the Middle Eastern cultures was seen starting around 1900BC, just around the time Ra is recorded as returning to DingurRa and renaming it Babylon followed quickly by the rise of the first Babylonian Empire. Amen Ra was the grandfather of Horus, so the new born Horus was referred to as the 'son of a sheep' and literally called a lamb of god – at least a millennia before Jesus arrived. Jesus birth coincided with the start of the Age of Pieces, so Christians naturally adopted the sign of the fish.

23.32 There are many depictions of Horus being accompanied by 12 helpers – their exploits described in the Book of Amduat (copies dating back to 1070BC) and the Book of Gates (copies dating before 1200BC).

23.33 Even the reference in Revelations (20:2-7) of a divine rule of Earth in a second coming lasting for 1000 years seems a direct addition of a story describing Horus return to rule from the House of a Thousand Years – as denoted on a stela built by a Nubian king, Harsiyotef (404-369BC). The same 'prophesy' also found its way into the Koran.

23.34 From the Egyptian records we know that for many centuries prior to the birth of Jesus there was a widely performed annual ceremony celebrating the birth of Horus, son of a god, born on December 25th by a virgin mother, Isis Mery.

23.35   We have identified the date chosen to celebrate Jesus birth as being astrologically determined. The same applies to Easter. The church formula to determine Easter is the first weekly day dedicated to the Sun god after the first full Moon occurring on or after the spring equinox. This is an ancient formula to fix the date that day finally triumphs over night, as days get longer and nights get shorter, the spring equinox is the date that the two are equal and then days win the greater part of each 24-hour cycle. In Egyptian theology this represents the triumph of good over evil. What better time to celebrate the resurrection of the Sun god? So, do we think Jesus resurrection was a historical fact or written up adopting a well-known existing motif.

23.36   The ascension into 'heaven' of both Osiris and of Horus is covered extensively in numerous Pyramid Texts (29 identified) and is extensively written about by a number of tenured Egyptologists. The ascension of Jesus merits only brief coverage in Luke 24:50-53 and a throwaway line in Mark 16:19 where it is claimed to be witnessed by the 11 remaining disciples. Imagine you had witnessed this extraordinary event, having travelled with Jesus for three years of his ministry, sometimes doubting whether he was what he was claimed to be. Then he was crucified but he resurrected himself and now you watch him walk into the light and is beamed up alive by Scotty. Neither Mark nor Luke were present but they claim John was – yet John never mentions this extraordinary event!! Again, was part of the popular Horus myth used to embellish the Jesus story?

23.37   Sadly, for those whom they are important, the reliability of the gospels is undermined by:

- The improbable immaculate conception and birth narrative in Matthew and Luke which seems to be drawing heavily upon the story of Isis and Horus;

- The clearly fake genealogies in Matthew and Luke;

- The raising of Lazarus (exclusive to John) which copies the story of Osiris in many details;

PART THREE: JESUS, THE NAZARENE

- A number of miracles performed seemed to be copying stories associated with pagan gods;

- The dubious details of the crucifixion, the bodily resurrection and the ascension;

- Deliberate edits to support new dogma – e.g. Matthew 28:19;

- Stories added centuries later – e.g. the woman caught in adultery and the blind man in the Pool of Bethesda – a building constructed in 135 with a foundation dedicated to Hadrian (Emperor 117 – 138).

23.38 For me to discover that the gospels are unreliable, in so many aspects, is disappointing but on the other hand I do feel liberated and enlightened by engaging with the so-called heretical texts – and none more so than the Gospel of Thomas. (Examined in detail in Part Four)

23.39 For those interested in how early Christianity emerged around the Mediterranean, I highly recommend Murdoch's excellent work *Christ in Egypt*. Murdoch identifies the importance of Alexandria as a trading and religious centre, estimated contemporaneously to be 40% or 50% Jewish. These Hellenised Jews adopted elements of Egyptian religion, particularly the worship of Serapis (Osiris) the resurrected god who reincarnated as Horus through a union with his sister Isis. Numerous religious societies sprung up all around the Mediterranean during the two centuries *before* Jesus birth, many referred to as Therapeuts. The communities of Therapeuts bonded closely, were initiated into 'mysteries', committed to help each other as brothers, settle disputes amongst themselves to avoid court and arrange burials for members. These groups employed hierarchical terms adopted by later Christian organisations – ekklesia (assembly or church); diakonos (deacon); presbyteroi (elected elders) and ephemereut (bishop).

23.40 Many cities where Paul later preached already had such religious societies embodying these beliefs and operating these structures in their community – including Antioch, Ephesus and Philippi – which were all major centres of Isis (aka Artemis) worship. The magnificent temple to Isis at Ephesus is one of the seven ancient 'wonders of the world'. In the 4th century, Eusebius commented upon Philo's references to the Therapeuts and asserted that the Therapeut members in Alexandria were a community of the first converts by the apostle Mark in Egypt. Philo of

Alexandria lived c20BC to cAD50 and whilst it is generally agreed that it was Mark who took the gospel to Egypt, the exact years that Mark was in Egypt are disputed. A number of church fathers (including Dionysius the Areopagite, a 1st century Athenian judge; John Cassien; Eusebius and Jerome) conflated the decidedly pre-Christian Threapeut societies as being Christian churches and monasteries. Certainly, the early churches clearly adopted the Therapeut hierarchy of bishops, presbyters and deacons!! Perhaps the network of 'churches' that Paul addressed his epistles to were societies originally formed as Therapeut groups, dedicated to the Alexandrian trinity whose beliefs Paul easily morphed into his modified Nazarene faith.

23.41 George Mead (1863-1933) an English historian, recognised as authoritative on Hermetic and Gnostic religions, identified the dilemma presented by the recognition of Therapeut societies as Christian. Having been recognised as the earliest church in Egypt, Philo was describing them in the year 25 – and their existence dates back maybe 200 years before that. Given the dating, the Therapeuts could not have been followers of Jesus yet the early church fathers regarded them as the model of a Christian Church. Either Christianity existed centuries before Jesus or the canonical dates are significantly wrong?

John & Paul link salvation to belief

23.42 According to Jesus himself (John 6.28-29), "the only work God requires of us is to believe in the One that He sent". From this comes the denial that 'works' are required for salvation – only that we believe. But what exactly are we to believe – note the request is not to believe Jesus is the Son of God, or even that Jesus is divine – just that Jesus was **sent** by God. 'Sent' is also odd, we know the original Church did not believe in a virgin birth nor that Jesus was divine, nowadays we know that if (as we believe) Jesus was fully human he must genetically have had a human father as well as a human mother. So, 'sent' may be better expressed as 'energised' or 'directed' – by the Spirit of God?

23.43 Standing back, this request must seem even odder to Jewish believers. According to their scripture (our OT), Jews understood that they were already covenanted with God. Then the rules changed – now they were only saved if they believed that Jesus was sent by God. It seems very strange if that is the **only work** to be done. Indeed, it begins to sounds more like a management succession plan – with Jesus trying to convince the Jews that now God has delegated all authority to him.

23.44   The rest of us were not covenanted BUT, according to theologians, what we identify as our 'conscience', our sense of right and wrong, reflects scriptural references to God having written his laws upon our hearts – Jeremiah 31:33, Romans 2:14 and Hebrews 10:16. But if having God's laws written on our hearts is sufficient for most of humanity why bother with a Chosen People at all? On the other hand, no one suggests that Jewish people do not have a conscience to guide their moral compass? However, the laws of evolution and survival, hardcoded into our inherited DNA, create tension. Freewill allows our natural instinct for self-preservation to qualify and often overcome our conscience that is prodding us to be just. Our survival instinct triggers seizure of resources; prudence and fear of scarcity makes us hoard resources and to overindulge when resources are plentiful. Our conscience may hold us back, suggesting we share – firstly, with those who carry our own genes and secondly, with those who do not. This unceasing internal battle has nothing to do with any third party such as Satan but is a direct result of the way we have been designed to evolve.

23.45   And, what of people that already believe in a Creator God but do not believe that God sent Jesus, nor that God resurrected Jesus from death?

God's foreknowledge of the future

23.46   Conventionally it is argued that God has perfect knowledge of the future, along with other attributes of an all-powerful, all knowing omnipresent divinity. But, although by definition God existed before the creation of our universe, and we presume has continued to exist throughout its evolution – it is not obvious that our Creator does know the future. Such knowledge may be assumed from intellect and an understanding of causality and the momentum of evolution but maybe God does not have detailed foreknowledge.

23.47   Certainly, there is plenty of evidence both in the Bible and from real life that suggests God does not know the future events that befall us – or, one would have to assume, God does not care. For me, the evidence suggests God designed the rules governing our universe to naturally evolve immeasurable bounty – everything we see in nature is vastly oversupplied, thereby generating a high probability that a remnant will survive. Think of the billions of seeds produced by most life-forms that seem designed to guarantee at least some will survive. Look at the number of stars created – presumably so that a few will lead to intelligent life developing on any hospitable planets. This over-abundance should certainly make us feel expendable – and maybe worry more about our sinning!!

23.48　If God knows the future – what were the dinosaurs about? The dinosaurs had effective control of Earth for around 300 million years – maybe whilst God pondered what to do next? The intervention which caused the prototype Adam (of homo sapiens sapiens) is dated by analysis of female mitochondria to have occurred only c172,000 years ago. It would seem little foresight was involved in the selection of the Chosen People – as Yahweh was frequently frustrated by their behaviour. Freewill might predict they would not only sin but do so frequently – surely an all-knowing Yahweh should have already known this? If so, why the frustration expressed, as in Isaiah 65:2 – "All day long I have stretched out my hands to a disobedient and obstinate people." Surely, this is further evidence that Yahweh had little knowledge of the future and is not God.

23.49　The, self-declared, Chosen People seem to have suffered terribly for their selection – not only the exile in Babylon for 70 years but the genocide attempted by the Nazi regime and the lesser known but even more severe genocides during the Roman occupation both between AD66 to AD70 and from AD132 to AD135. Together with regular pogroms, expulsions and persecutions throughout the last 2,000 years – it is hard to identify another racial group who has endured anything like the suffering inflicted upon the Jewish people.

23.50　The Jewish people believe they were Chosen and given a divine set of Laws to follow and, whether or not all followed these laws diligently, their God made numerous promises which ring rather hollow in retrospect.

23.51　They were repeatedly told of a future messiah who would free them from oppression, provide peace and lead them to glory. They were never told that a future messiah would be divine. So, with many imposters claiming to be a messiah, they were naturally cautious in accepting Jesus – particularly when their religious leaders, whom they were trained to respect, were highly sceptical. When one claiming to be a messiah then asserted comparable authority to God (the power to forgive sins) they just heard blasphemy.

23.52   The interchange between Jesus and Judas, as recorded by John, indicates Jesus certainly had foreknowledge of Judas intentions. But the dialogue that ensued, as recorded by John, risked either Judas changing his mind or one of the other disciples attacking Judas. There is some evidence that the disciples were armed and acted as an armed guard to protect Jesus. If Jesus had clearly indicated to the one sitting next to him "that the person I next offer bread will betray me" – surely his close friends gathered around him would have reacted. But consider, Jesus was already resigned to what was about to befall him, he is recorded as stating so a number of times, to fulfil his Father's will. So, the statements recorded in John risked Judas being revealed as the traitor and being stopped – thereby causing Jesus to frustrate his Father's will. Maybe John added comments to condemn Judas as the traitor for posterity, referencing the Psalm by David "sharing bread with his enemy" to further bolster claims of prophesies fulfilled. It is also a bit odd, given Jesus established notoriety and popularity in Jerusalem, that the Temple guards even needed anyone to point Jesus out.

… PUZZLING ASPECTS OF JESUS STRATEGY

24

Conclusions

24.1 Firstly, congratulations if you have read this far – I appreciate some of the detail is heavy going. My only excuse is that the subject matter is of utmost importance, and as noted earlier, it is an issue where ignorance will feel a very feeble excuse when the time comes!

24.2 Jesus demands very careful consideration. Whilst unfortunately we have no surviving text of Jesus writing, we do have the canonised Gospels. These would provide a strong foundation if we could accept the Gospels as being accurate. However, it does not take much effort to discover that, sadly, they are unreliable in a number of respects. Firstly, they include many embellishments of dubious veracity and many that are simply not historically true and partly copied from Egyptian religious beliefs – e.g. the virgin birth, the journey to Bethlehem, the flight to Egypt, Jesus genealogy. Secondly, there are strong indications that the NT (in the form we now have it) is not consistent in accurately reflecting what Jesus taught – did he indeed come to abolish the Law or not change the tiniest element of it? Thirdly, the authors sought to show Jesus actions fulfilled dozens of prophesies recorded in Jewish scripture – and some they made up themselves – such as a messiah coming from Nazareth. Fourthly, we have clear evidence of a number of late additions – e.g. the odd story of the attempted stoning of the adulteress and the invention of the Comma Johanneum to "pop in" the idea of the Trinity.

24.3 In addition to the four types of problems noted above – which research does equip us to largely edit out – we are still left with the fundamental

PART THREE: JESUS, THE NAZARENE

issue of the time between Jesus uttering his teaching and parables and the date the Gospels were written. Given the generally accepted view by all scholars that none were written until at least 25 years and some maybe 40 years after the crucifixion – and by authors who had never met Jesus – one wonders how accurate the quotations really are. Other historians, noting the complete absence of any references to any of the 4 canonised gospels until after 170, suggest authorship may have been in the 2nd half of the 2nd century. Perhaps the text of Luke included in the first New Testament by Marcion in 144 was not a sanitised version as asserted by the Church but the original which was then progressively puffed up into the version that became canonised later. It is noteworthy that whilst the earliest Church Fathers were quoting texts later deemed heretical – none quoted the 4 canonised gospels until a century after it is claimed they were written.

24.4 This problem is compounded by theologians who deeply analyse the exact meaning of each word of the Gospel passages – without ever recognising that these same words were second-hand interpretations written mainly by persons who were not present at any of the occasions when Jesus taught.

24.5 When reading the accounts of Jesus prayers at Gethsemane, just prior to his arrest, both Matthew (26:36-56) and Mark (14:32-42) describe Jesus going to pray and upon returning (after an hour), waking them all (Peter, James and John) from sleep. And yet John 17 reads as a long verbatim prayer. One wonders how John, writing many decades after the event, could quote Jesus long and private prayer to God....*verbatim* – when he and the others had apparently fallen asleep? It seems very unlikely that Jesus gave John a transcript?

24.6 Christians have a distorted meaning of 'messiah' – most think in terms of a saviour whereas in truth it means anointment to a rightful position – either to the throne of Israel as a descendant of David or to the office of High Priest as a descendant of Aaron. For Jews, it has always been blasphemous to consider a messiah could be God or even consider the implausible concept of 'God's son'.

24.7 Jesus never claimed to be divine, he claimed to the Son of Man – if he had claimed to be God or God's son he would have been instantly stoned to death. The evidence of Jesus sayings in the gospels consistently records his deference to the Father – to whom he always prays, seeks guidance, acts on behalf of, and has received authority from. We are asked, in John, simply to believe Jesus was 'sent' by God – which is entirely consistent with John's description (v1.1) of Jesus being the Logos (the Word), an intermediary sent by God to mankind.

24.8 Jesus never mentioned a Trinity (the gospel references are proved to be much later additions), and he always referred to God as 'spirit' (John 4:24, Luke 24:39). Jesus positioned himself as an *intermediary* between God and man: Jesus is in God and God in Him – as we are in Jesus and Jesus in us. This suggests some form of spiritual implant/indwelling. It is much more credible to consider God is an all-pervasive force, with the ability to manifest itself as desired but not physically detectable by us.

24.9 Let us consider the story of Jesus being tempted by Satan whilst spending 40 days in the desert (Matthew 4). Leave aside for a moment whether Satan is real or whether you believe in the story – it seems really odd that Jesus went along on the journey with Satan. Even more peculiar is that it is recorded as though it was witnessed by the writer, or another who obtained a first-hand account. It seems rather strange behaviour for Jesus to relate this verbatim and for it to be passed on and eventually incorporated by the author of Matthew? Further, the story undermines the concept of the Trinity – if Jesus was part of God, extant since the creation – why would Satan waste his time trying to tempt the untemptable? However, if Jesus was born a man, of two human parents, and later filled with the Holy Spirit at baptism – then Satan might consider him fair game!

24.10 The gospel record shows Jesus somewhat equivocal about Judaism – indeed, as herein, it can be argued that Jesus rejected every tenet of Judaism – except loving the Creator and replaced the rest of the Law with a command to love everyone else. He seems to specifically reject circumcision as a command of God thereby destroying the key symbol marking the Jews as the Chosen People. Jesus rejected the Mosaic food laws (it is not what enters a man's mouth but what comes out from his heart) and aspects of observing the Sabbath (healing the sick and telling his disciples to gather food).

24.11 The statement attributed to Jesus that he did not come to change the Law – but fulfil it, is ingenious as a clever way to effectively abolish the Law. Paul evidently took this literally even though most early followers

PART THREE: JESUS, THE NAZARENE

tried to 'add' Jesus to Judaism.

24.12 Another puzzling aspect is that two gospels describe the Last Supper as Jesus celebrating the Passover with his disciples (Matthew 26:17-35 and Mark 14:12-21.). However, John 13:1-2 describes the Last Supper as occurring just before the Passover celebration; the events recorded as the Last Supper itself as just "the evening meal"; and, the Passover being celebrated the evening *after* the crucifixion.

24.13 Why do I find Jesus celebrating the Passover puzzling? In his recorded teaching, Jesus points out a number of key falsehoods in the Torah – that circumcision was a pagan idea not an instruction from God; that no one stated in the Torah to have seen God actually had; etc. Therefore, it seems unlikely that Jesus would have subscribed to the unbelievable concept in the story of Moses and the Exodus, that God could supposedly distinguish first born Egyptians from second and third born but was unable to distinguish Egyptians from Israelites. Furthermore, the idea that enormous numbers of lambs had to be killed to obtain blood to smear on door frames so God would know Israelite homes from Egyptian is ludicrous. Therefore, it seems to me that this is yet another example of the writers of the synoptic gospels inventing details.

24.14 Apart from visiting Tyre and Sidon, Jesus made no attempt to reach Gentiles outside Israel, but continued the Jewish practise of welcoming Gentiles who sought 'their' God or believed in him. After his ascension, Jesus original Nazarene Church led by James and Peter adhered to the Law but added belief that Jesus was sent by God. However, Paul gradually diverged from this – allowing Gentiles to become believers without circumcision or adherence to Mosaic laws – and was reprimanded by Jesus' Nazarene church a number of times. Eventually, after Jerusalem was largely destroyed in AD70 and completely cleared of Jews in AD135, the original Nazarene Church was scattered, surviving in only small pockets whilst the Roman Church founded on Pauline theology grew vigorously whilst ironically accusing those churches derived from the Nazarenes of being heretics!!

24.15 In AD325, Constantine forced the Roman Church to adopt many pagan aspects alien to Pauline theology, pushing Christianity even further from its Nazarene roots – firstly promoting Jesus to divine status and in AD381, the Council of Constantinople promoted Jesus again to cohabitation in the Godhead. Later the Roman Church started a process of elevating Jesus' Mother, Mary, to divine status and subsequently to being also born of a virgin herself and as recently as 1951 to having ascended bodily to heaven, alive.

24.16 Ignorance is never accepted as a defence for infringements of Man's Law. So, once we discover that what we are told is God's Word has serious discrepancies perhaps we are on notice to make a rational assessment of what may be fact or fiction and then to seek out the truth for ourselves rather than rely just on what other men tell us. If one day we are called upon to justify our beliefs by a supreme Creator – ignorance may not be an acceptable defence. Surely Christians are on notice to seek out the real truth and kick away the crutches and barnacle encrusted myths developed by the Church of Rome over many centuries – of which Luther only managed to scrape away a tiny fraction.

24.17 After reading this booklet, how does one feel about the importance, relevance and accuracy of the Bible to one's belief in God and in Jesus. How reliable is Paul's claim in (2 Timothy 3:16) that 'all scripture is God breathed' – one of the key pillars of the Inerrants? Pause for a moment, Paul must have spoken about 'scripture' as he knew it – he was referring only to the Torah and the Prophets, excluding the Writings which are regarded by Jews, accurately, as fairy tales containing moral themes but not as scripture. And, the NT did not exist although numerous early texts may have been in circulation.

24.18 It is surprising that official Christian dogma, as developed by men, directly contradicts what the Bible records Jesus as teaching:

- Jesus never claimed to be God but repeatedly showed his respect and subservience to God – yet man has determined Jesus is God;

- Jesus repeatedly stated that no man has seen God, yet many OT texts that directly contradict this are treated as 'inspired by God';

- when Jesus stated to others that 'no man has seen God' that also means Jesus is saying he is not God;

24.19 We should be very concerned by how man has subverted Jesus original teaching and how profoundly the truth has been twisted by those claiming to be his followers. This is addressed by the final book in this series.

Key – colours indicate name of each 'god' in principal languages:
Sumerian; *Akkadian*; *Egyptian*; Hebrew

* Until Moses met the Burning Bush, the god of Genesis was named El Elyon, the Canaanite name for Enlil. From Moses up to Saul, the Hebrew deity appears to have Nannar but by the Psalms of David the title had passed to Shamash. In all translations of Jewish scripture into Greek, Latin, English, etc., all names of 'god' are assumed to refer to a single entity.

Appendix

Selected family members of ruling elite – survivors of 'the Flood' or perhaps ET's?

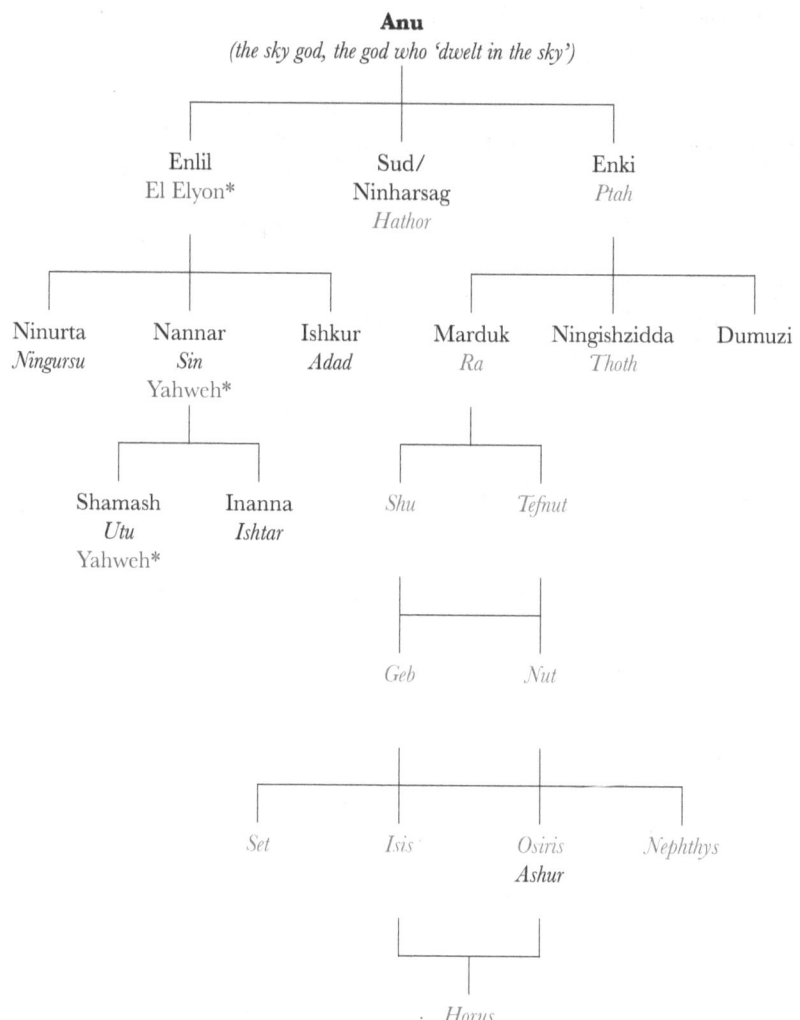

Index

Aaron, *Moses brother*	7.19, 13.6, 13.12-14, 13.32, 21.48, 21.65, 22.9, 22.10, 24.6
Abgar V, *king of Edessa, dAD50*	13.30
Abraham	2.19, 8.8, 8.15, 10.6, 10.7, 10.9, 16.25, 19.1, 19.25, 19.29-34, 21.19, 21.20, 22.15
Adad – *see Ishkur*	
Adad-Nirari III, *king 811-783BC*	20.105
Adam	16.16, 19.1
Ado, *Archbishop of Vienne AD800-874*	15.40, 15.41
Adonis	16.43
Ahaz, *king of Judah, 763-710BC*	21.29-34, 21.43, 21.44, 21.49, 21.66
Akhenaten, *pharaoh 1353-1336BC*	17.13
Alexander V, *pope 1409-10*	15.71
Alexander the Great, *356-323BC*	10.12, 23.17
Alexandria, Egypt	8.6, 12.18, 22.18, 23.4, 23.8, 23.39
Alford, Michael, *1587-1652*	15.36
Amarna Letters, *written 1360-1332BC*	9.11
Ambrose of Milan, *AD340-397*	13.25
Amen – *see Ra*	
Amenophis III, *pharaoh 1386-1349BC*	5.8
Ananius ben Nedebeus, *high priest AD46-58*	16.9
Ananus ben Ananus, *high priest AD63*	12.6
Andrew, apostle	15.48
Andromeda, galaxy	10.9
Antioch, School of	12.12, 12.13, 12.26, 16.19
Antiochus Epiphanes, *king 175-164BC*	8.4, 8.16
Anubis	23.25, 23.26
Aphraates, *writing 337-345*	20.54
Aristobulus, *1st Bishop of Britain, AD37-59*	15.35-41
Arius, *Arians*	12.25, 20.58, 20.61

Arviragus, *British king AD44-74*	15.26
Ashurbanipal II, *king 883-859BC*	20.105
Ashtoreth/Asherah	5.9, 5.11-13, 17.8, 20.105, 22.16
Assyrian church	12.7, 12.15
Athanasius, bishop of Alexandria *ADc297-373*	12.13, 15.52, 17.11, 20.15, 20.58, 20.61, 20.99, 20.103, 23.20
Augustine, *archbishop of Canterbury 597-604*	15.12, 15.21, 15.67, 15.74, 15.75
Augustus, *Caesar 27BC – AD14*	3.13, 5.17
Avalon, aka Glastonbury	5.4
Avignon, *France*	15.71
Babylon, originally Dingir-Ra	15.4, 15.42, 23.31
Bar-Daisan *AD154–223*	13.24
Baronius, *cardinal 1538-1607*	15.15, 15.16, 15.33, 15.59, 15.73, 15.75
Bartholomew, *Gospel of*	13.28
Basra, Iraq	1.8
Bathenosh, *wife of Lamech*	8.15
Bathsheba	21.4
Bede, the Venerable, *670-735*	15.45, 15.51, 15.62, 15.69
Benedict XVI, *pope 2005-2013*	2.11-15, 5.2, 6.10, 13.25, 20.101, 22.5
Beth Lehem Zoria *(aka Zebulun)*	5.23, 9.17
Bethlehem, Judea	5.16-24, 5.27, 5.33-35, 7.11, 9.17
Boer, Henry	23.13, 23.14
Burgess, *1756-1837, bishop of St David's*	15.53
Caesarea, *and Library at*	9.19, 23.8
Cana, *Galilee*	9.9, 9.20
Cassien, John *c360-c435*	23.40
Catechism, *Catholic*	20.25
Cathars	10.4, 16.19
Celtic church	12.24-29, 15 *passim*, 20.51
Chrysostom, John *AD349-407*	15.51, 15.65
Chi Rho, *aka Labarum*	17.5
Circumcision	1.8, 9.23, 10.11-21, 16.2, 16.7, 16.10, 16.14, 16.15, 24.13

Claudius, *Roman emperor AD41-54*	15.12
Clement of Alexandria *AD150-215*	12.18, 20.35, 20.48
Clement *AD35-99, 3rd Bishop of Rome*	15.52, 16.1
Cohort, *division of Roman legion*	11.5
Comma Johanneum – *1 John 5:6-8*	20 *passim*, 24.2
Community Rule document	8.1, 8.6, 8.14, 13.12
Constantine, *Roman emperor AD325-337*	12.9, 12.13, 12.19, 12.29, 13.33, 16.18, 16.27, 17 *passim*, 20.14, 20.99, 20.106, 20.107, 21.5, 23.3, 23.8, 24.15
Copernicus, *1473-1543*	18.6
Coptic church	16.45
Council of Elvira, *AD306*	15.64
Council of Arles, *AD314*	15.64
Council of Nicaea, *AD325*	8.5, 8.11, 12.12, 15.64, 16.18, 16.27, 17.3, 17.4, 20.11, 20.15, 20.99, 20.103, 20.106, 23.20, 24.15
Council of Rimini-Seleucia, *AD359*	15.64
Council of Constantinople, *AD381*	12.12, 24.15
Council of Chalcedon, *AD451*	5.3, 12.13
Council of the Lateran, *AD649*	5.3
Council of Pisa, *1409*	15.71
Council of Constance, *1414*	15.71
Council of Sienna, *1424*	15.71
Council of Basle, 1434	15.71
Cyrus I, *the Great, reign c560-530BC*	21.59, 22.8, 23.10
Damascus Document	8.1, 8.7-13
David, *king, reign c1010-970BC*	5.22, 5.38, 7.4-6, 7.11, 7.19, 9.19, 13.3, 13.32, 21.14-25, 21.48-53, 21.65, 22.6-9, 22.16, 24.6
Dead Sea Scrolls	8 *passim*, 9.20, 13.10-12, 16.42
Dei Verbum, *Vatican II 1962-5*	2.5
Desposyni	12.9, 12.10
Didache, *consensus cAD100*	2.12, 20.60, 20.100, 20.102
Dionysus *(Bacchus)*	16.43

Dionysius the Areopagite *(1stC)*	23.40
Donation of Constantine	17.2
Doomsday Book, *published 1086*	15.27, 15.29
Dorotheus *AD255-322, Bishop of Tyre*	15.32, 15.37
Drake, Sir Francis	15.8
Druidism	15.22, 15.23
Dumuzid, aka Tammuz	16.43, 20.105, 22.16
Ebionites, *inc. gospel of*	9.24, 12.10, 12.11, 13.5, 16.8-10, 16.31
Edessa, *just north of Harran*	13.30
Edward I, *king of England 1272-1307*	15.8
Edward III, *king of England 1327-1377*	15.25
Egyptians, *gospel according to*	16.31
Ein Karem, Jerusalem	5.20
El Elyon, *aka Enlil*	5.9, 6.7, 8.15, 10.7, 10.8, 10.17, 10.20, 22.11, 22.15, 22.16, 23.22
Eleca, *Bishop of Zaragoza*	15.28
Eleutherus, *Pope c174-189*	15.45
Elijah	10.7, 14.2-4, 16.25, 18.3
Encyclical Munificentissimus Deus *1950*	5.3
Enoch	8.15, 10.7, 16.25, 19.29
Enoch, *Book of*	2.22, 8.11, 8.12
Enuma Elish	20.104
Enki, *aka Ptah*	5.9, 5.11
Epiphanius, *310-403, bishop of Cyprus*	9.19, 9.23, 9.24, 10.4, 12.10, 16.8, 16.10, 16.12, 16.19, 23.21
Erasmus *1466-1536*	20.8, 20.9
Esau	21.19
Essenes	8 *passim*, 9.12, 9.13, 9.19-21, 10.2, 10.4, 12.19, 22.2
Ethiopian Church	16.45
Euphrates	13.21
Eusebius *265-340*	2.3, 2.15, 5.40, 9.24, 12.7-10, 13.21, 13.25, 15.30, 15.33, 15.35, 15.51, 15.52, 15.55, 15.64, 20.12-15, 20.23, 20.35, 20.37-46,

	20.58, 20.62, 20.93, 20.96, 20.98, 20.99, 23.13, 23.40
Ezekiel	19.21, 19.29, 22.16
Festus, *procurator*	12.1, 12.6
Flavian, *bishop of Antioch c350*	20.61, 20.62
Francis, *pope 2013 to date*	6.10
Freculphus, *bishop of Lisieux 823-850*	15.70
Galatian tribes	16.28-29
Gamaliel, *rabbi, died AD52*	16.9, 16.11
Genesis Apocryphon	8.15
Gildas *516-570*	15.66
Glastonbury	15.5, 15.15, 15.19, 15.21, 15.24-27, 15.29, 15.38, 15.70
Gobekli Tepe	13.30
Goldilocks planets	18.7
Gregory, *538-594, bishop of Tours*	15.28
Gregory of Nazianzus	13.25
Gregory I, *pope AD590-604*	15.21, 15.60, 15.67, 15.75
Habakkuk Commentary	16.42
Hadrian, *Roma Emperor, 117-138*	2.14
Hebrews, *gospel according to*	16.31
Hadrian, *emperor 117-138*	23.37
Halakhah	10.2
Haleca, *bishop of Augusta*	15.36, 15.41
Hasmonean dynasty *167BC – 31BC*	16.31, 22.7
Hathor – *see Isis*	
Harran	13.30
Harsiyotef, *Nubian king 404-369BC*	23.33
Heaven, *asteroid belt, rakia*	8 *passim*
Hebron	19.29
Hegesippus	15.16
Helena, *Constantine's mother*	17.7
Henry II, *king of England 1154-1189*	15.74, 15.75

Henry VIII, *king of England*	15.29
Herod I, *the Great, 37 to 4BC*	4.2, 4.4, 5.25, 5.34-36, 7.4, 7.7, 21.69
Herod Antipas	3.14, 9.15, 15.50
Herodotus	15.17
Hezekiah, *king of Judah 716-687BC*	21.43-47, 21.53, 21.66, 21.67, 22.16
Hippolytus, *theologian AD170-235*	15.37
Homer	15.17
Horus	5.12, 5.13, 20.106, 23.16-23, 23.25, 23.28, 23.29, 23.31-39
Hosius of Cordoba, *257-359*	23.20
Hippolytus of Thebes, *C7th, AD*	5.4, 15.34, 15.35
Inanna, Ishtar, Isis – *see Asherah*	
Ine, *King of Wessex*	15.29
Ineffabilis Deus, *Papal Edict, 1854*	5.3
Instantius, *Spanish bishop c370-385*	12.21, 12.22
Irenaeus *130-202*	2.3, 15.35, 15.52, 15.55
Isaac	19.25
Ishkur, *aka Adad, Ba'al*	22.17
Isis	20.106, 20.111, 23.16-22, 23.27, 23.34, 23.37-40
Jacob	10.7, 15.8, 19.25, 21.19
James I, *king and KJV*	15.8, 20.7, 20.16, 21.18, 21.20
James, *apostle*	10.24-28, 11.2, 12.1-4, 12.6, 12.8, 12.23, 12.28, 13.1, 14 *passim*, 16.1, 16.31, 23.3, 23.8, 24.5, 24.14
James, *Proto-Evangelium of*	5.20
Japha, *Galilee*	9.5, 9.11
Jeremiah, *prophet*	21.75
Jerome, *of Stridon (AD342-420), author of the. Vulgate*	9.23, 9.24, 10.4, 13.25, 15.30, 15.51, 16.19, 20.98, 23.40
Job	10.7
John, *apostle*	2.2, 2.11-16, 11.2, 12.4, 14 *passim*, 16.3, 23.36, 23.52, 24.5
John, *Presbyter*	2.15

PART THREE: JESUS, THE NAZARENE

John the Baptist	4.3, 5.18, 5.36, 7.10, 9.15, 13.5, 13.9, 13.11, 13.13-15, 14.3, 20.108, 21.54, 22.3, 23.1, 23.26
Joseph, *Jesus father*	4.5, 5.21, 5.26-33, 5.38, 5.40, 9.6, 13.31, 22.7
Joseph of Arimethæa	9.6, 15.5, 15.6, 15.12-32, 15.38, 15.66, 15.70, 15.71, 15.73, 21.54
Josephus, *Titus Flavius cAD37-c100*	5.17, 9.5, 9.10, 9.11, 9.21, 12.6, 15.16, 15.42, 16.9, 21.57
Jubilees, *book of*	2.19, 8.11, 8.12, 13.8
Judah, *Testament of*	13.8
Judas Iscariot	7.9, 11.2, 11.9-13, 21.71, 21.75-77, 23.52
Julius Caesar	15.12
Kefar Hananya	9.9
Lazarus	13.20, 15.15, 15.16
Lennon, John	6.6
Leonardo da Vinci	13.31
Levi, *Testament of*	13.12
Licinius, *Roman emperor 308-324*	17.6, 17.7
Linus, *pope 64-76*	15.55, 15.56
Logos	2.11, 5.10, 16.27, 23.7, 23.8
Lorber, Jakob	2.16, 11.12, 11.13
Loyer, *French Huguenot*	15.8
Lucius, *British king, 2ndC AD*	15.45
Luke, *apostle*	12.2, 13.16, 16.2, 16.8, 22.11, 23.36, 23.37
Luther	24.16
Luxor	5.8
Maccabean	16.31
Macedonius, *bishop of Constantinople 342-360*	20.35, 20.52
Maelgwyn of Llandaff	15.24
Magdalene, Mary	7.9, 15.15, 15.16
Magi	4.1, 4.3, 5.24, 7.3
Marcion, *AD85-160*	15.16, 16.12

Marduk – *see Ra*	
Martyr, Justin *cAD100-165*	2.3, 9.24, 20.35, 20.49, 20.50
Mary, *Jesus Mother*	1.9, 4.5, 5 *passim*, 15.16, 22.7, 23.16-20, 23.27, 23.28, 24.15
Masada	16.40
Matthew, *& Gospel of, in Hebrew*	13.25, 16.3, 16.8, 16.17, 20.98, 23.13, 23.23, 23.36, 23.37
Mead, George *1863-1933*	23.41
Megiddo	9.11
Melchizedek	8.15-17, 22.15
Metaphrastes, Simon *ADc900-c984*	15.47
Methuselah	8.15
Micah, *prophet 737-696BC*	21.63-69
Midrash	10.2
Milky Way, *galaxy*	10.9, 18.6
Mithras	16.43, 17.7
Mitzvot, *Mosaic Law*	1.7, 10.2, 10.28, 16 *passim*, 17.14, 17.16, 22.14, 24.2, 24.10
Mohammed *(PbuH)*	12.17, 23.8
Moses	10.7, 10.15-17, 13.6, 14.2-4, 16.16, 24.13
Muratorian Fragment	15.51
Mut-em-ua, q*ueen of Egypt*	5.8, 5.11
Nag Hammadi	16.30
Nannar, *aka Sin*	6.7, 17.8, 22.15
Nathan, *prophet C9th BC*	21.4
Nazarene, *Nasrani*	9.25, 12 *passim*, 13.21, 13.26, 15.12, 15.67, 15.75, 16 *passim*, 20.26, 20.51, 22.2, 22.3, 22.11, 22.13, 23.8, 24.14
Nazareth	4.2, 5.16, 5.19, 5.21, 9 *passim*, 22.2, 24.2
Nazirite	9.19, 22.3
Nebuchadnezzar, *king 605-562BC*	5.38, 7.19, 22.7
Nephilim	8.8
Neththys, *sister of Osiris*	23.26
Nero, *Roman emperor AD54-68*	15.51, 23.7, 23.8

PART THREE: JESUS, THE NAZARENE

Nestorians, *Nestorius*	12.11-15, 12.26, 12.29, 13.30, 16.19
Nicephorus, *Patriarch of Constantinople*	15.32, 15.33
Nicodemus, *pharisee*	23.7
Nimrud, *Assyria*	20.105
Nineveh	15.4
Ninharsag – *see also Isis*	
Nisibis	12.15, 13.30
Orange, *city of*	15.16
Origen, *AD185-254*	9.24, 15.30, 15.52, 20.35, 20.37, 20.47, 20.98
Osiris	16.43, 20.106, 20.111, 23.16-20, 23.23, 23.25, 23.26, 23.36-39
Pamphilus of Caesarea, *d309*	20.37, 20.98
Pantaenus of Alexandria	13.25
Papias, *cAD60-130*	2.3, 2.15
Paradise	15.19, 15.20
Passover, *the Last Supper*	24.12, 24.13
Patrick, *saint*	12.25
Paul *(previously, Saul)*	1.7, 4 *passim*, 8.18, 9.19, 9.21, 9.23, 10.2, 10.3, 10.6, 10.19-21, 10.24-26, 10.28, 12.1-3, 12.8, 12.10, 12.16, 13.16, 13.26, 15.35, 15.36, 15.44, 15.49-61, 16 *passim*, 17.17-19, 18.2, 20 *passim*, 21.62, 22.11, 23.3, 23.7, 23.8, 23.40, 24.14, 24.17
Pelagius I, *pope 556-561*	20.24
Pella, *aka Decapolis, in Syria*	9.23, 12.7
Peter, *apostle*	11.2, 12.1, 12.13, 13.28, 14 *passim*, 15.42-47, 15.55, 15.59, 16.31, 24.5, 24.14
Pharisees	3.5, 12.3, 16.9, 16.11, 16.25, 16.42, 17.15, 19.5-14, 21.14, 21.15, 21.22, 23.7, 23.9
Philip, *apostle*	15.6, 15.15, 15.27
Philo of Alexandria *c20BC-cAD50*	21.57, 23.40, 23.41
Pilate, Pontius	3.14, 7.2, 7.6, 15.14
Pius XI, *pope 1922-1939*	15.60, 15.75
Pius XII, *pope 1939-1958*	5.3

Plato, *Greek philosopher, c426-348BC*	22.5
Pliny the Elder, *AD23-79*	21.57
Plutarch, *c46-119*	23.21
Pole, *cardinal, archbishop of Canterbury*	15.72
Polybius, *Greek historian c200-118BC*	15.17
Polycarp, *AD69-155*	15.35
Priscillian, *bishop of Avila 380-385*	12.20, 12.23, 12.25
Prydain	15.38
Ptah – *see Enki*	
Ptolemy III, *pharaoh 246-222BC*	17.5
Pudens	15.44, 15.55-58
Q document	2.2, 2.6, 2.10, 6.8, 14.3, 16.3, 16.17, 23.13, 23.30, 24.17
Quirinius, *Governor*	5.17, 5.22, 5.34
Qumran	8 *passim*, 9.13, 9.20, 9.21, 12.19, 16.42
Qur'an	9.25
Ra/Amen/Marduk	5.11, 20.104, 20.111, 23.17, 23.27, 23.28, 23.31
Rakia – *see Heaven*	
Sabbath	17 *passim*
Sabeans	4.3
Sadducees	12.5, 12.19, 16.9, 16.11, 23.7
Samasata, Paul, *bishop*	12.12
Samson	22.3
Samuel, *prophet*	7.10, 13.6
Sanhedrin	16.9, 16.11
Santiago de Compostela	12.23
Sarai/Sarah	8.15
Satan	24.9
Sauniére, Bernard, *1852-1917*	13.31
Schumacher, E. F.	11.12
Scillonia Insula, *Scilly Isles*	12.22
Semiramis *(aka Sammuramat)*	20.104, 20.105

PART THREE: JESUS, THE NAZARENE

Seneca, *4BC-AD65, philosopher*	21.57
Sennacherib, *king*	21.67
Senusret I, *pharaoh (Abimelech)*	8.15
Sepphoris	9.9, 9.12, 9.15
Serdica, *Edict of, 311*	17.6
Serenus de Cressy	15.24
Sextus, *Sentences of*	16.12
Shamash	10.7, 17.8, 17.13, 23.22
Shamshi-Adad V, *king*	20.105
Sharp, Mary, *C20th historian*	15.59
Shoel	8.2, 19.29
Shofarot	9.8
Siculus, Diodorus	15.17
Sidon	15.4, 24.13
Simeon, *cousin of Jesus*	12.7
Simon Bar Jonah, *Apostle*	11.2
Simon of Cyrene, *bore Jesus cross*	3.3
Simon Zelotes *(or the Zealot)*	11.2, 15.32-34
Sin – *see Nannar*	
Sinai	17.7
Sirius *(Dog Star)*	23.23
Sol Invictus	12.29, 16.27, 17.4, 17.7, 17.8, 17.13, 23.22
Sonnini Document *(Acts 29)*	15.54, 15.61
Solomon, *king*	21.24
St Michael's Mount	15.17
Stone of Scone	15.8
Stow, John *1524-1605*	15.45
Suetonius, *historian AD69-122*	21.57
Sylvester, *pope AD314-336*	12.10
Syriac church	12.7, 13.22, 13.26, 16.45
Tacitus, *historian AD56-120*	21.57
Taliesin, *druid, 6th Century AD*	15.22
Tammuz – *see Dumuzid*	

Targum	8.15
Temple, *Solomon's*	21.24, 22.16
Temple, *AD70 destruction of Jerusalem*	2.8, 2.18, 3.5, 5.22, 5.23, 5.35, 5.37, 7.17, 10.2, 10.4, 11.5, 11.8, 13.16, 16.40, 21.69, 22.2, 23.8, 23.9
Tertullian, *author AD155-240*	12.25, 15.30, 15.52, 15.63, 16.13, 20.51, 20.60, 20.111
Thecla	16.12
Theodore of Mopsuetia	12.26
Theodoret, *bishop of Cyprus AD393-457*	15.52
Theodosius, *Roman emperor 379-395*	20.24
Theophilus, *pope of Alexandria 384-412*	23.8
Therapeuts	23.39-41
Thessalonica, *Edict of, 380*	17.12
Thomas, *apostle, aka Jude, Judas*	10.9, 10.28, 12.8, 12.21, 13 *passim*, 23.3, 23.8
Thomas, *Acts of*	13.27, 13.30, 13.33
Thomas, *Gospel of*	2.17, 10.28, 13.27, 13.33, 16.31, 23.38
Tiberius, *Galilee*	9.15
Titus, *disciple of Paul*	16.12
Timothy, *disciple*	10.19
Trajan, *Roman emperor, AD98-117*	12.9
Trinity	1.9, 1.11, 6.5, 12.12, 12.13, 12.27, 12.28, 14.5, 17.11, 19.1, 19.17, 19.19, 19.27, 19.34, 20 *passim*, 21.10, 21.59, 23.7, 23.8, 24.2, 24.8, 24.9
Twelve Patriarchs, *Testament of*	13.8
Tyre	15.4, 15.17, 15.31, 24.13
Ugarit, *Canaan*	22.15, 22.17
Ur, *Sumeria*	10.7
Uriah	21.4
Virgin birth	5 *passim*, 6.5, 12.12
Vitalian, *pope AD657-672*	15.62
Vulgate	9.4, 20.2, 20.8, 20.35
Watchers	8.8

Whitby, *synod of, AD664* — 12.25, 12.27, 15.68
William of Malmesbury, *c1095-1143* — 15.27
Wisdom, *Book of* — 8.6
Yahweh, *YHWH, YWH* — *passim*
Zacharias, *father of John the Baptist* — 5.34
Zealots *(aka Lestai, Sicarii)* — 5.22, 7.18, 9.14, 9.15, 10.13, 10.14, 11 *passim*, 12.4, 12.5, 23.7
Zedekiah, *king of Judah, 597-586BC* — 7.19, 22.7
Ziusudra – *aka Utnapištim, Noah* — 8.8, 8.15, 16.25, 19.1
Zoroastrianism — 8.3, 16.26, 16.31, 17.9

Biblical References

Acts 1:1	12.2
Acts 2:22	9.2
Acts 2:36	13.15
Acts 2:38	20.18, 20.22, 20.25, 20.74, 20.77, 20.78, 20.82, 20.97, 20.109
Acts 4:12	20.22, 20.70, 20.109
Acts 8:12	20.18
Acts 8:16	20.18, 20.25, 20.77
Acts 9:15	15.49
Acts 10:48	20.18, 20.25, 20.77
Acts 11:26	9.3
Acts 12:1-2	12.4
Acts 12:12-17	3.2, 15.42
Acts 13:13	3.2
Acts 13:14	17.17
Acts 13:42-44	17.17
Acts 16:3	10.19
Acts 16:21-26	10.23
Acts 17:2	17.18
Acts 17:24-28	10.3
Acts 18:1-8	17.18
Acts 18:2	15.43
Acts 19:1-6	20.74, 20.78, 20.82, 20.108
Acts 19:5	20.18, 20.25, 20.77
Acts 21	12.2
Acts 22:16	20.18, 20.22
Acts 23:6-8	16.9
Acts 24:5	9.19
Acts 24:27	12.1
Acts 29	15.61

Amos 5:26-27	8.9
1 Chronicles	5.43
1 Chronicles 5:1-2	15.9
1 Chronicles 14-17	21.24
1 Chronicles 22-26	21.24
Colossians 2:11-12	20.19, 20.78, 20.79
Colossians 3:17	20.82
Colossians 4:10	3.2
1 Corinthians 1:13	20.18, 20.21, 20.68
1 Corinthians 7:1	16.12
1 Corinthians 7:4	16.13
1 Corinthians 8:6	16.21
1 Corinthians 9:5	12.8
2 Corinthians 5:17	20.78
2 Corinthians 11:3-4	16.2
2 Corinthians 12:7-8	16.14, 16.21
Daniel	8.4, 8.5, 8.16, 21.41
Daniel 7:13-14	19.21
Daniel 9:25	7.20
Deuteronomy 15:17	21.45
Deuteronomy 19:15	19.8
Deuteronomy 19:18-21	19.9, 19.12
Deuteronomy 23:18	10.21
Deuteronomy 30:11-16	16.16
Deuteronomy 32:7-9	22.16
Exodus 3:14	19.19
Exodus 21:32	21.74
Exodus 29:7	13.6
Exodus 30:22-32	7.20
Exodus 33:17-23	10.7
Ezekiel 8:14-15	16.43
Galatians 1:1	16.31, 16.35
Galatians 1:6-9	16.31

Galatians 1:14	16.33
Galatians 1:17	16.31
Galatians 2:6	16.34
Galatians 2:11-16	16.34
Galatians 2:20	16.35
Galatians 3:11-13	16.15
Galatians 3:16-25	10.2
Galatians 3:27	20.18, 20.75, 20.78
Galatians 5:2-4	16.15
Genesis 1 – 3	8 *passim*
Genesis 3:8-10	10.7
Genesis 4:6-7	16.16
Genesis 5:23	10.7
Genesis 14:18	22.15
Genesis 17:9-14	10.17, 10.20
Genesis 24:54	21.19, 21.20
Genesis 32:4	21.19, 21.20
Genesis 32:30	10.7
Genesis 49:22-26	15.9
Hebrews 1:9	7.20
Hebrews 4	17.19
Hebrews 10:16	23.44
Isaiah	17.15
Isaiah 7:14	21.3, 21.26-41, 22.4
Isaiah 9:6-7	21.3, 21.42-53
Isaiah 11	13.4
Isaiah 22:21	21.45
Isaiah 38:18	8.2
Isaiah 45:1	21.59
Isaiah 47:7	21.45
Isaiah 52:7	21.62
Isaiah 52:14	21.54
Isaiah 53	21.3, 21.54-62, 22.5

Isaiah 61	13.5
Isaiah 65:2	23.48
James 2:26	16.32
James 5:14	20.95
Jeremiah 22:30	5.38
Jeremiah 23:5-6	13.4
Jeremiah 31:15	5.28
Jeremiah 31:33	23.44
Jeremiah 32:6-9	21.75
Job 29:16	21.45
Job 42	10.7
John 1:14	14.3
John 1:18	10.7, 14.1
John 1:49	7.6
John 2:6	9.9
John 3:3-5	20.74, 20.97
John 3:13	10.7
John 3:16	18.1
John 4:25-26	7.12, 24.8
John 4:44	9.16
John 5, 6 & 7	2.14
John 6:15	7.2
John 6:28-29	23.8, 23.42
John 6:46	14.1
John 7:22-25	10.15, 10.17
John 7:31	7.11
John 7:39	20.73
John 7:53 – 8:11	2.11
John 8	19 *passim*
John 8:1-11	19.4-8
John 8:12-18	19.10-14, 20.73
John 8:19	19.16, 19.17
John 8:20-24	19.18, 19.19, 19.21

John 8:25-27	19.20
John 8:28-30	19.21
John 8:31-41	19.23-25
John 8:41-44	19.26-27
John 8:48-53	19.23, 19.28-30
John 8:54-56	19.31
John 8:57	19.32
John 8:58	10.9, 19.1, 19.15, 19.21, 19.23, 19.25, 19.32-34, 22.13
John 9:16	17.15
John 9:22	2.5
John 10:30	10.9
John 11:16	13.20
John 12	7.9
John 12:34	7.11
John 13:1-2	24.12
John 14:6	19.17
John 14:9	19.17
John 14:14	20.67
John 14:26	20.67, 20.73
John 14:28	10.9
John 15:16	20.67
John 16:7	20.73
John 16:23	20.67
John 17:3	16.21
John 17:5	9.2
John 18:3	11.5
John 18:5	9.2
John 18:34-19:11	21.54
John 19:19	9.2
John 19:21	7.2
John 20 & 21	2.11, 2.12
John 20:24	13.19

John 20:28	10.9
John 21:20	2.4
1 John 4:12	10.7, 14.1
1 John 5:6-8	20.1-10, 20.34, 20.93, 20.110
Judges 13:5	9.19
2 Kings 2:11	10.7
2 Kings 15-16	21.33
Leviticus 12	10.17
Luke	2.3, 3.10-15, 4 *passim*, 5 *passim*
Luke 1:5	5.34
Luke 1:8-13	5.34
Luke 1:23-36	5.34
Luke 1:35	5.44
Luke 2:10-14	3.13
Luke 2:22-24	5.35
Luke 2:32	3.12
Luke 3:3	20.97
Luke 4:16-30	9.5, 9.16, 17.11
Luke 4:34	9.2
Luke 6:6	17.14
Luke 6:6-11	17.15
Luke 7:26-30	13.13, 18.3
Luke 8:33	23.30
Luke 9:28-36	14.2
Luke 10:10	15.35
Luke 12:10	18.10
Luke 13:10	17.14
Luke 13:11-17	17.15
Luke 22:36	11.3
Luke 22:51	3.14
Luke 23	7.6
Luke 23:4	3.11
Luke 23:12	3.14

Luke 23:14, 22	3.11
Luke 23:34	3.14
Luke 23:39-43	3.14
Luke 23:47	3.11
Luke 23:50	15.14
Luke 24:39	24.8
Luke 24:46-47	20.80, 20.97
Luke 24:50-53	23.36
Maccabees	8.4
1 Maccabees 1:11, 15	10.14
1 Maccabees 1:29-38	10.13
1 Maccabees 1:48	10.13
1 Maccabees 1:60-61	10.13
1 Maccabees 2:44-46	10.13, 10.14
1 Maccabees 5:22, 28, 35, 49-51	10.13
2 Maccabees 6:8-11	10.13
Malachi	20.30
Malachi 3:1-2	13.9-11
Mark	3.2, 3.3
Mark 1:4	20.82
Mark 1:24	9.2
Mark 2:28	17.15
Mark 3:2-3	17.15
Mark 5:13	23.30
Mark 6:1-6	9.16
Mark 7:6-8	17.15
Mark 7:24	15.4, 15.31
Mark 9:2-8	14.2
Mark 9:37, 39, 41	20.67
Mark 10:47	9.2
Mark 12:14	3.3
Mark 12:15	3.3
Mark 14:3-9	7.9

Mark 14:12-21	24.12
Mark 14:32-42	24.5
Mark 14:67	9.2
Mark 15:39, 44, 45	3.3
Mark 16:9-20	2.12
Mark 16:15-18	20.80, 20.97
Mark 16:16	20.22
Mark 16:17	20.67
Mark 16:19	23.36
Matthew	3.4-3.9, 4 *passim*, 5 *passim*
Matthew 2:23	9.4, 22.2
Matthew 3:16	7.20
Matthew 4	24.9
Matthew 5:17	3.6
Matthew 5:23-24	3.8
Matthew 7:19	3.6
Matthew 8:32	23.30
Matthew 10:6	15.4
Matthew 10:34	11.3
Matthew 11:11	18.3
Matthew 13:52	3.4
Matthew 13:54-57	9.16
Matthew 15:21	15.4, 15.31
Matthew 16:16-18	7.14
Matthew 17:1-8	14.2
Matthew 18:15-17	3.8
Matthew 18:20	20.67
Matthew 21:4	7.8
Matthew 21:9	7.6
Matthew 21:43	15.22
Matthew 22:11-14	3.5
Matthew 22:41-44	21.13, 21.22
Matthew 24:15	21.41

PART THREE: JESUS, THE NAZARENE

Matthew 26	7.9
Matthew 26:17-35	24.12
Matthew 26:36-56	24.5
Matthew 26:62-64	7.13
Matthew 26:71	9.2
Matthew 27:3-10	21.75
Matthew 28:9-10	3.8
Matthew 28:18-20	20.66, 20.81
Matthew 28:19	6.10, 20.1, 20.11-110, 23.37
Micah 5:2	13.4, 21.3, 21.63-70
Numbers 6:13	9.19
Numbers 23:19	19.21
1 Peter 5:13	15.42
Philippians 3:2	10.21
Proverbs 17:6	21.58
Psalm 2:2	7.20
Psalm 6:5	8.2
Psalm 22	21.3-11, 21.61
Psalm 78:10-12	8.2
Psalm 82	8.16
Psalm 84	17.13
Psalm 104	17.13
Psalm 110	21.3, 21.12-25, 22.4
Revelation	20.30
Revelations 20:2-7	23.33
Romans 1:4-5	20.81
Romans 2:14	23.44
Romans 3:20	16.15
Romans 6:1-4	20.78
Romans 6:3-5	20.18, 20.69
Romans 7:1-4	16.15
Romans 8:14	18.4
Romans 10:4	16.15

Romans 10:8	16.16
Romans 10:15-16, 21	21.62
Romans 15:28	15.49
Romans 16:10	15.35, 15.37
1 Samuel 10:1	13.6
1 Samuel 16:13	13.6
2 Samuel 2:4	13.6
2 Samuel 7	21.24, 21.51
2 Samuel 22:14	22.16
1 Timothy 1:4	5.39, 16.7
1 Timothy 6:14-16	16.24
2 Timothy 3:16	16.25, 24.17
2 Timothy 4:21	15.44, 15.55
Titus 3:9	5.39
Zechariah	11.10
Zechariah 4	13.7
Zechariah 6:13	13.7
Zechariah 9:9	7.8
Zechariah 11:4-11	21.73
Zechariah 11:12-13	21.3, 21.71-77

Bibliography

Bacchiocchi, Samuele. *Rome and Christianity until AD62, Andrews University Seminary Studies, Volume 21.* Andrews University Press, 1983

Boer, Harry. *A Short History of the Early Church.* Wm. B. Eerdmans, 1984

Bray, Dr Gerald. *Biblical Interpretation: Past and Present.* Intervarsity Press, 1996

Broderick, Robert C, ed. *The Catholic Encyclopedia.* New York: Nelson, 1987

Brown, Raymond. *An Adult Christ at Christmas.* Liturgical Press, Minnesota, 1978

Clements, R E. *New Century Bible Commentary.* Grand Rapids: Eerdmans Publishing, 1980

Conybeare, F. C. *History of New Testament Criticism.* Knickerbocker Press, 1910

Dark, Dr Ken. *Roman-Period and Byzantine Nazareth and its Hinterland.* Routledge, 2020

Dobson, Rev C.C. *Did our Lord visit Britain? As they say in Cornwall and Somerset.* Covenant Publishing, 2008

Ehrman, Bart D. *Lost Scriptures.* Oxford University Press, 2003

Glass, Michael. *The New Testament and Circumcision.* Circumcision Information, 2001

Gonzalez, Justo L. *Church History: An Essential Guide.* Abingdon Press, 1996

Gray, George B. *The International Critical Commentary.* Edinburgh: T & T Clark, 1980

Kee, Alastair. *Constantine v Christ.* Trinity Press International, 1982

Kitchen, K. A. *Ancient Orient and Old Testament.* Chicago, InterVarsity 1966.

McBirnie, William Steuart. *The Search for the Twelve Apostles.* Tyndale Momentum, 1973

Murdock, D.M. *Christ in Egypt, the Horus-Jesus Connection.* Stellar House Publishing LLC, 2009

Nickelsburg, George W. E. *Resurrection, Immortality and Eternal Life in Intertestamental Judaism and Early Christianity.* Harvard Theological Studies, 2007

Pines, Shlomo. *The Jewish Christians of the Early Centuries of Christianity*, 1996

Pinnock, Clark H. *Biblical Revelation.* Moody Press, 1971

Ratzinger, Joseph (Pope Benedict XVI). *Jesus of Nazareth.* Ignatius Press, San Francisco, 2007

Roberts, Rev L.G.A. ComRN. *The Early British Church − Originally Hebrew Not Papal.* 1927

Talmage, Dr. *Lost Books of the Bible.* Chartwell Books, 2016

Various. The 28:19 *Forgery.* Church of the Living EL, Jerusalem

Vermes, Geza. *The Complete Dead Sea Scrolls in English.* Penguin, 2004

Westcott, Brooke Foss. *A General Survey of the History of the Canon of the New Testament.* Macmillan & Co., London, 1896

Wildberger, Hans. *Isaiah 1-12 (Continental Commentary).* Augsburg Fortress, 1991

Wood, Fr Michael. *The Liturgy of St John the Divine.* Saint Bride Hermitage

The Truth Will Set You Free – Series

Prequel: Younger Dryas meteor impacts, The Flood & Atlantis

We now have compelling evidence of the devastating event which spawned hundreds of tribal memories of a terrible and rapid change in the Earth's climate. In the aftermath of the Flood, 'men of renown' appeared and the leading family literally became immortalized, forming the pantheon of 'pagan gods' worshipped across the ancient Middle East. Second Edition published December 2023.

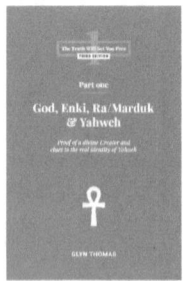

Part One: God, Enki, Ra/Marduk & Yahweh

Proof of a divine Creator is not to be found in the Bible. However, the real identity of Yahweh may be discerned from biblical texts. The most memorable figures from the Old Testament include Noah, Abraham, Moses and kings David & Solomon – one might expect these find international recognition, with references to their exceptional feats in the historical record of surrounding affected cultures. But only one of these hero's has been verified, one appears to be adopted from another culture, one surprises by his total invisibility and the kings are acknowledged only by an isolated and obscure fragment. Third Edition published September 2023.

Part Two: The Promised Land, 2000 BC to 1000 BC

The Old Testament books covering the time of Abraham to David (c2000 BC to c1000 BC) tell of the Israelites led from slavery to conquer the Promised Land. However, clear evidence reveals these books were largely written during the Babylonian captivity, after 596BC, by priests with only hazy notions of geography and history. The biblical story overlooks the fact that the entire area of the Promised Land formed part of the Egyptian Empire for the greater part of the entire millennia. Third Edition published November 2023.

Part Three: Jesus, the Nazarene

Arguably, Jesus has had the most formative impact on humankind. Today, the New Testament stands as the only authoritative source of his life and teaching – but almost all of the books written about him in the first century have been destroyed. How authentic and reliable are those texts selected for the New Testament? The Old Testament is reputed to contain hundreds of prophesies concerning Jesus – are they credible? We name him Christ, meaning Messiah, a term the church has allowed to be widely misunderstood. Is Jesus part of a Trinity? Second Edition published in July 2022.

Part Four: Truth Revealed – What Jesus Really Taught

This final work identifies many significant changes made to the Gospels to mould Christian beliefs in line with Church dogma. The majority of early Christian texts were ruthlessly destroyed by the Roman Church – why? What did they say? Aided by the earliest uncorrupted manuscripts and the few surviving examples of texts declared heretical, we can piece together Jesus original teaching. What is revealed dovetails well with ancient belief systems, explaining why Nazarene teaching spread like wildfire in the first century. Many of the difficult to grasp elements of conventional Christianity are exposed as being man-made. Many clues have survived, even in the New Testament, which support these findings. First Edition published August 2022.

Documents available for download from the Series website:
www.truthpublications.co.uk

Texts ruled heretical by the Roman Church

Truth Series Master Index of Issues

Thomasine Creed - a radical update of the Nicaean Creed

www.ingramcontent.com/pod-product-compliance
Lightning Source LLC
LaVergne TN
LVHW030318070526
838199LV00069B/6495